Northwestern University
STUDIES IN *Phenomenology &*
Existential Philosophy

GENERAL EDITOR
John Wild

ASSOCIATE EDITOR
James M. Edie

CONSULTING EDITORS
Herbert Spiegelberg
William Earle
George A. Schrader
Maurice Natanson
Paul Ricoeur
Aron Gurwitsch
Calvin O. Schrag

A Study of Husserl's
FORMAL AND
TRANSCENDENTAL LOGIC

Suzanne Bachelard

Translated by Lester E. Embree

A Study of Husserl's

FORMAL AND

TRANSCENDENTAL LOGIC

NORTHWESTERN UNIVERSITY PRESS

1 9 6 8   EVANSTON

Originally published in French under the title *La Logique de Husserl: Étude sur* LOGIQUE FORMELLE ET LOGIQUE TRANSCENDENTALE, by Presses Universitaires de France. Copyright © 1957 by Presses Universitaires de France.

Passages from Quentin Lauer's translation of Edmund Husserl's "Philosophie als strenge Wissenschaft," which appeared as "Philosophy as a Rigorous Science" in *Phenomenology and the Crisis of Philosophy* (New York, 1965), translated and edited by Quentin Lauer, are reprinted with the permission of Harper Torchbooks, Harper & Row, Publishers, Inc., New York.

Permission to quote from the following works by Edmund Husserl has been granted by Martinus Nijhoff, The Hague:

Cartesianische Meditationen, in *Husserliana,* Vol. I, 1950. English translation by Dorion Cairns, *Cartesian Meditations,* 1960.

Formale und transzendentale Logik. First edition, 1929. English translation by Dorion Cairns, *Formal and Transcendental Logic,* forthcoming.

Ideen zu einer Phänomenologie und phänomenologischen Philosophie. Book I: *Allgemeine Einführung in die reine Phänomenologie.* New edition, enlarged on the basis of the author's handwritten additions, edited by Walter Biemel, 1950.

Logische Untersuchungen. First edition, 1900. Second edition, three volumes, 1913. Third and fourth editions, unaltered, 1922, 1928.

Contents

[ix]

Translator's Preface

LA LOGIQUE DE HUSSERL, *étude sur "Logique for-melle et logique transcendentale,"* the original of the present translation, was published by Suzanne Bachelard in 1957 as a companion to her simultaneously published French trans-lation of Husserl's *Formale und transzendentale Logik.* In advance reply to any who question the value of translating a commentary, I can only assert that the depth, lucidity, and comprehensiveness of this cornerstone of French Husserl-scholarship justify my undertaking.

For a commentary to be useful, it must conform in ter-minology to the text commented upon. In order that I might meet this requirement, Professor Dorion Cairns made page proofs of his English translation of *Formale und transzen-dentale Logik* available to me. The ease that I experienced while attempting to express Miss Bachelard's thought in the English terminology developed for Husserl by Dr. Cairns indi-cates the value of the work of both these scholars vis-à-vis Husserl.

It goes without saying, however, that failures to establish the required terminological conformity are my responsibility. Professor Cairns's aid implies responsibility neither for this commentary nor for my translation of it. Miss Bachelard has sent changes for Part I, Chapter 3, has answered questions, and has read and accepted this translation of her book.

[I] REMARKS CONCERNING TERMINOLOGY USED IN THIS TRANSLATION

1. Since the original title of this work is difficult to render in English with the proper connotations, I have based the English title upon the original subtitle.

2. The ubiquitous expression "judgment" (*Urteil, jugement*) elicited the following translator's note from Professor Cairns:

> . . . in numerous . . . passages *Urteil* must signify *judging* and not *what is judged,* and in numerous others it probably signifies *judging* but may signify *what is judged.* In almost every case it has been translated here as judgment – with a corresponding ambiguity in many contexts. In the few cases where it has been translated as *judging,* the original word is given in brackets. Unless the original word *Urteil* is given, the substantive *judging* represents the gerundial infinitive *Urteilen.*[1]

In neither her commentary nor her translation does Miss Bachelard draw explicit attention to this verbal problem. In many places she does use *juger* in a manner which I take as corresponding to Husserl's *Urteilen* and which, following Dr. Cairns, I render as *judging.* Nevertheless, in many other places her *jugement* must mean or probably means the mental process of judging rather than what is judged. This is traditional in French. With rare exceptions (where the original word is given in brackets), I render Miss Bachelard's *jugement* as *judgment.*

3. Cairns's translator's note, quoted above in part, is attached to the following sentence in Husserl's text:

> A sharp distinction must be made between the mental process of meaning and the intended meaning, the sense [*zwischen Meinen und Meinung*]: between judging and judgment [*Urteilen und Urteil*], wishing and wish, and so forth.[2]

An ambiguity quite similar to that pertaining to *Urteil* exists for *Meinung* and *Meinen.* Cairns uses *meaning* and sometimes *opinion* to translate both of these terms; Bachelard uses

1. *FTL*, p. 25, n. 1.
2. *Ibid.*

opinion and conjugations of *opiner*. I follow Cairns in using *meaning,* as in the quotation above, to express the concept of a mental process in which something is meant, as well as the concept of what is meant therein, i.e., the sense, though I occasionally substitute or add the English word *opinion.* At times this is somewhat at variance with ordinary usages of *meaning,* but the term is technical, English and German are not isomorphic, and consistency between commentary and text commented upon is mandatory. The French word *sens* (German: *Sinn*), whose "sense" is more like the ordinary usage of *meaning,* is rendered as *sense.*

4. In another translator's note Cairns writes:

> In this essay *Gegenstand* and *Objekt* do not usually express the same sense. Having found no acceptable alternative to translating them both as *object,* I differentiate by spelling the word with a small letter when it represents *Gegenstand* and with a capital when it represents *Objekt.* All this applies, *mutatis mutandis,* in the case of any word derived from *Gegenstand* or from *Objekt.* If object, or a word derived from it, stands first in a sentence, the German word is given in brackets.[3]

Relative to a similar problem, Bachelard writes, in a note to her French translation of *Formale und transzendentale Logik:*

> We translate *Gegenständlichkeit* with *objectité,* on the one hand to prevent any confusion between the notion of *Gegenständlichkeit* and that of *Objektivität* (of *objectivité* in the most usual sense), and on the other hand to respect a nuance that Husserl wanted to introduce between *Gegenständlichkeit* and *Gegenstand* [*objet*]. Cf. *Log. Unt.,* Second Edition, Vol. II, Part I, p. 38, n. 1: "I often choose the less definite expression *Gegenständlichkeit* [objectivity], because here it is always a matter not merely of objects in the narrower sense but also of syntactically formed affair-complexes, distinctive traits, non-selfsufficient real or categorial forms, and the like." In *Formal and Transcendental Logic* we have the same situation: an Objectivity can as well be a categorial form as an object of the external world. The use of this notion avoids every possibility of interpreting Husserl's thought as a naïve realism.[4]

3. *Ibid.,* p. 3, n. 2.
4. *Logique formelle et logique transcendentale* (Paris, 1957), p. 18, n. 1.

There are two intersecting distinctions and hence four terms involved in this situation. On the one hand, we have the concrete nouns *Objekt* and *Gegenstand,* and, on the other hand, we have their abstract forms *Objektivität* and *Gegenständlichkeit.* By means of his capital and small letters, Cairns renders all four terms. The French term *objet* can have the sense expressed in the German term *Gegenstand* or the sense expressed in the German term *Objekt.* Therefore, Miss Bachelard had only to distinguish the abstract nouns, which she did by using the neologism *objectité* for *Gegenständlichkeit,* as the note quoted above indicates. I translate *objectité* as *objectivity* (small letter), *objectivité* as *Objectivity,* and *objet* and its other derivatives with small letters. In quotations, however, where Husserl wrote *Objekt,* or a word formed from it, *Object* (with a capital), etc., will be found.

5. In yet another note, Cairns writes:

> Sometimes Husserl uses *Ego* and *Ich* to express different senses. Because the homophony of *I* and *eye* makes the English *I* intolerable, *Ich* has been translated as *Ego* (spelled with a capital) and *Ego* has been translated as *ego* (spelled with a small letter).[5]

In neither her commentary nor her translation does Miss Bachelard call special attention to this verbal distinction, though several passages do show that she is well aware that her French term *ego* expresses more than one sense. Frequently her italics matches Husserl's usage of the Latin term. In all cases I have translated *ego* as *ego* (spelled with a small letter), although capitalization will be seen to occur in quotations; italicization in this case as in others follows the usage in *La Logique de Husserl.*

6. Husserl's important term *etwas überhaupt* is translated by Miss Bachelard as *quelque chose en général* and is translated by Dr. Cairns as *anything whatever.* I follow Dr. Cairns's usage, but I believe that there is value in drawing attention to this matter.

7. Husserl uses two words, *Datum* and *Gegebenheit,* which Dr. Cairns renders as *Datum* (capital) and *datum,* while Miss Bachelard renders them both as *donnée.* Except in quotations, the reader will find *datum* (small letter) where the author wrote *donnée.*

5. *FTL*, p. 19, n. 1.

8. There is a basic theoretical and terminological problem with the key word *Leistung* that resembles the problems with *Urteil* and *Meinung* mentioned above. I take the following sentence from *Formal and Transcendental Logic* to indicate that this ambiguity may have been at least to some extent deliberate on Husserl's part:

> Everywhere it is a matter of rational productions [*Vernunftleistungen*], in a double sense: on one side, as productive activities and habitualities; on the other side, as *results* produced by activities and habitualities and afterwards persisting.[6]

In addition to the double sense of *Leistung*, there is the question of a translation for it. In French, Bachelard appears to use *effectuation* most of the time. Now, if one must have only *one* English term, *performance* is preferable to *achievement*. On the other hand, Cairns, in his unpublished "Guide for Translating Husserl," recommends the following possibilities for *Leistung* in English:

> production, product, producing, productivity; performance, something done, doing; effective performance, performance effected; effect, produced effect, effect produced; (result); work done, work; (*Dienstleistung:*) function; (of an expression:) what it conveys; (accomplishment); (achievement).

Leistung is an outstanding example of the technical character a philosophical word can have, particularly in Husserl. The lesson here is that a word should not be taken to have the sense one at first glance confers upon it but instead should be examined for its sense or senses in the various ways and contexts in which it is employed.

In general, it should be obvious that in a scientific endeavor participated in by an open plurality of investigators, personal inclinations about words are less important than a commonly accepted terminology. The ideal of such a collective philosophical undertaking was dear to Husserl. The French have worked out a disciplined vocabulary for phenomenology in their language. I suggest that the English-speaking phenomenological community attempt to do the same, using the translations of Dorion Cairns as a foundation.

6. *Ibid.*, p. 33.

[II] Matters Concerning Texts Used in This Work

In the present work, all translations from Husserlian texts were made by Professor Dorion Cairns, with the following exceptions. Passages quoted from *Erfahrung und Urteil* were translated by Robert Jordan, and passages from "Philosophie als strenge Wissenschaft" are from the translation by Quentin Lauer, "Philosophy as a Rigorous Science," which appeared in *Phenomenology and the Crisis of Philosophy,* translated and edited by Quentin Lauer (New York, 1965). Translations from non-Husserlian texts have been made by me.

The quotations located in the expository order of *Formal and Transcendental Logic* that *La Logique de Husserl* shares in did not originally bear citations. However, since I had to locate them in order to quote them, I have included the page numbers of these passages in parentheses. Words in square brackets are additions made by me or Dr. Cairns, while words in angle brackets are glosses. Throughout, the italicization is Miss Bachelard's, which frequently differs from Husserl's usage in the original.

With rare exceptions, only works published by Husserl in his lifetime are used in the present work. These are of two sorts:

1. Husserl's works in logic, with the exception of articles and reports, comprise:

Philosophie der Arithmetik, Psychologische und logische Untersuchungen (Halle, 1891).

Logische Untersuchungen (Halle) (referred to as *Log. Unt.*):
First edition, Part I: *Prolegomena zur reinen Logik* (1900) (referred to as *Prolegomena*); Part II (1900).
Second edition, reworked into three volumes (*Prolegomena,* Part I, Part II) (1913).
Third and fourth editions, unaltered (1922 and 1928).

Note.—Where references do not mention the edition, the fourth edition of the *Prolegomena* and Part I, and the third edition for Part II, are used.

Formale und transzendentale Logik (Halle, 1929), translated

by Dorion Cairns, forthcoming from Martinus Nijhoff, The Hague (referred to as *FTL*).

NOTE.—Numbers in parentheses following quotations in the text refer to page numbers in this translation by Cairns.

Erfahrung und Urteil, Untersuchungen zur Genealogie der Logik, edited and published by Ludwig Landgrebe (Prague, 1939). Reference is to the republication of this work (Hamburg, 1948) (referred to as *Erf. u. Urt.*).

2. The other principal Husserlian sources used in the present work are:

Cartesianische Meditationen und Pariser Vorträge, translated by Dorion Cairns, *Cartesian Meditations* (The Hague, 1960) (referred to as *CM*).

Ideen zu einer Phänomenologie und phänomenologischen Philosophie. Book I: *Allgemeine Einführung in die reine Phänomenologie.* New edition, enlarged on the basis of the author's handwritten additions. Edited by Walter Biemel (The Hague, 1950) (referred to as *Ideen* and cited according to the marginally included pagination of the German edition of 1913).

Die Krisis der europäischen Wissenschaft und die transzendentale Phänomenologie. Eine Einleitung in die phänomenologische Philosophie, edited by Walter Biemel (The Hague, 1954) (referred to as *Krisis*).

For the most complete list of Husserl's works compiled to date see *Edmund Husserl 1859–1959, Recueil commémoratif publié à l'occasion du centenaire de la naissance du philosophe* (The Hague, 1959).

For his enormous assistance, I express my deepest gratitude to Professor Dorion Cairns. I thank Professor Aron Gurwitsch and my wife Veronica for their patient encouragement. The actual labor I dedicate to my father, Lester Borden Embree.

LESTER E. EMBREE

New York, 1967

Author's Preface

IF WE DISREGARD THE *Philosophie der Arithmetik* of 1891, Husserl's works in logic can be seen to span some forty years, and, despite the undeniable evolution of thought, these works reveal a fundamental unity. This unity derives from Husserl's antipsychologism.

We disregard the *Philosophie der Arithmetik,* Husserl's first work, because we feel that this work should be taken as representing Husserl the mathematician's new interest in epistemological reflection rather than as the first appearance of his fundamental logical conceptions. Husserl offers a neat characterization of his plan in the Preface of that work: It is not a question of following the mathematician in the development of his constructions; rather it is a question of conferring a genuineness upon the already constituted mathematical science by means of a criticism. In this undertaking one could think that one already had before one the task of *Formal and Transcendental Logic* – that of approaching the technique of existing sciences with a grounding activity which alone enables these sciences to become genuine and truly consequential sciences. However, in the *Philosophie der Arithmetik* this activity of critical grounding unhesitatingly finds its source in psychology and thus participates in the psychologistic attitude against which, later, Husserl never ceased to struggle.

It will be objected against our exclusion of the *Philosophie der Arithmetik* that the opposition between psychologism and antipsychologism is not the only perspective under which to study phenomenology. Without going so far as to say that

[xix]

"the doctrine of intentionality and even the entirety of phenomenology are *germinally* contained within the *Philosophie
der Arithmetik*," [1] we can show the prefiguration of important
phenomenological themes in that work and advance the fact,
which Husserl himself recalls in *Formal and Transcendental
Logic*,[2] that, through its investigations into the original sense
of the fundamental concepts of the theories of wholes and
numbers, the *Philosophie der Arithmetik* brought a first contribution to what later came to be called constitutional phenomenological analysis. But, for the logician, the problem of
psychologism is not just one problem among other problems:
it is a *determining* problem; for either the logician welcomes
psychological justifications, or he considers such recourse to
psychology a *radical vice*. This choice is decisive for the
logician. In the book which followed the *Philosophie der
Arithmetik* — the *Prolegomena* of 1900 — Husserl decides
against psychologism and expressly denies the orientation of
the *Philosophie der Arithmetik*. We shall see that this choice
was definitive.

With the *Philosophie der Arithmetik*, therefore, Husserl
undertook a critical task before applying himself to arithmetic,
a particular mathematical domain. But a criticism of science,
no matter how restricted, when it means to be radical, of
necessity soon breaks down the limits it originally set for itself. It is the misfortune of all who undertake an activity of
radical grounding that they cannot keep it in one place. The
provinces of the sciences can indeed appear to be separate.
But in their roots the sciences intermingle; the problems encountered there lead into one another. As soon as one pene-
trates to the substructures, one can no longer "separate each
of the difficulties into as many parts as is possible and necessary
in order to solve them better"; on the other hand, one is driven
to a set of problems larger and more complex than that which
was initially proposed in a clear delimitation of problems to
be solved. Hence it is not astonishing that Husserl announced
investigations for the Appendix of Volume II of the *Philosophie
der Arithmetik* which would be "wholly outside the bounds

1. Q. Lauer, *La genèse de l'intentionnalité dans la philosophie
de Husserl* (Paris, 1954), p. 56.
2. *FTL*, p. 86.

of a philosophy of arithmetic" and would have in view "the general logic of symbolical methods," investigations by which he would "attempt to fill an essential gap in hitherto existing logic." [3] The projected appendix quickly became the center of his investigations, and Volume II of the *Philosophie der Arithmetik* was never published. Hence, Husserl was led by the very essence of his subject matter to *shift* his task, and, as he says in the Preface to the first edition of the *Prolegomena:* "They forced me to considerations of a very general sort, which rose above the narrower mathematical sphere and tended toward a general theory of formal deductive systems." [4] Beginning with the *Philosophie der Arithmetik*, Husserl recognized that traditional logic was a limited critical instrument; but, as we have just said, at that time he thought it possible to remedy the insufficiencies of traditional logic by turning to psychology: "I had started from the prevalent conviction that, like all other logic, the logic of the deductive sciences must hope to get its philosophical clarification from psychology." [5] He adhered to this psychologistic attitude with so much confidence that he formulated a slightly visionary criticism of the still quite revolutionary investigations of the symbolic logician Frege. The logician is not a little astonished when he reads from Husserl's pen: "The goal Frege sets for himself is, therefore, to be called chimerical. Hence it is no wonder if his work, despite all acuteness, loses its way in fruitless hypersubtilities and ends without positive results." [6] Meanwhile, when Husserl became involved in the problems of logic, he disavowed his own criticism of Frege: "That I no longer approve of the *radical* criticism I directed against Frege's anti-psychologistic position in my *Philosophie der Arithmetik*, Vol. I, pp. 129–32, I hardly need to say." [7] And one can suppose that he did not reread without self-directed irony the note in the *Philosophie der Arithmetik* where he cites as an example of logicistic intransigence — a note which, to be sure, can be found a bit ridiculous in its aggressiveness — such an affirmation on Frege's

3. *Philosophie der Arithmetik*, Preface, p. vi.
4. *Prolegomena*, p. v.
5. *Ibid.*, p. vi.
6. *Philosophie der Arithmetik*, p. 131.
7. *Prolegomena*, p. 169, n. 1.

part: "The number is no more an object of psychology . . . than is for example the North Sea."[8] Therefore, Husserl was poorly prepared for the logical reform, whose need he felt so keenly, by the psychologistic attitude in which the *specificity* of the logical theme is misapprehended. Soon he found himself, as he admits, before "the insoluble difficulties in which the psychologistic conception, in the philosophy of arithmetic, entangled me."[9]

His efforts to arrive at a clarification of a properly mathematical system were "stove in and finally burst" by the urgency of a new set of problems to which his efforts were necessarily turned: to grasp the essence of deductive science in general and, even more broadly, to set up the problems of a general logic and a theory of cognition. Hence he was "compelled to set entirely aside [his] investigations in the philosophy of mathematics, till [he] might succeed in pushing ahead to sure clarity in the fundamental questions of epistemology and in the critical understanding of logic as a science."[10]

Once the logical problem was set up in its universality, Husserl quickly recognized that psychologism could not provide the universal solution. Psychological analyses could be useful, for example, in questions concerning the origin of mathematical representations or the formulation of the methods practiced by the mathematician. But when it is a question of accounting for the interconnectedness and the unity of a theory, psychological explanation is revealed to be an inadequate instrument. In a word, psychology is incapable of accounting for the *Objectivity* of scientific theories. With the problem of the Objectivity of cognition theoretically set up, we are dealing with a *specific* problem of logic which we cannot hope to solve through psychological considerations, even through those of genetic psychology. This problem is therefore a center of interest for an effort at typically logical understanding. Thus the *Prolegomena zur reinen Logik*, having addressed an indictment against psychologism, undertakes to characterize that which makes up a theory as such, and hence to separate the ideal conditions for the possibility of a theory thus understood. Necessarily connected with this

8. *Philosophie der Arithmetik*, p. 130.
9. *Prolegomena*, p. 212, n. 1, footnote continued from p. 211.
10. *Ibid.*, Preface to first edition, p. vii.

resolutely logicistic attitude is the conception of truth as truth-in-itself — absolute — independent of the subjectivity which grasps it. "What is true is true absolutely, true 'in itself'; the truth is identically one, whether men or monsters, angels or gods, in judging seize upon it." [11] Psychologism, on the contrary, never ceases to relativize truth. Whatever particular form it takes, it is at base a relativism that arises through an argument as simple as this: All cognition is subjective; all cognition is a phenomenon of consciousness and as such is subject to the laws governing human consciousness; hence one cannot account for the laws of cognition without calling upon psychology. But to mix up the "province" of the psychological laws of thinking with that of the purely logical laws is a veritable μετάβασις εἰς ἄλλο γένος [change to another genus].

Hence the *Prolegomena* constitutes an attempt at the grounding of pure logic which rejects every justification that is psychological in nature. Husserl's reaction against the psychologistic attitude is the more vigorous because he set out by adopting it. And it is in thinking of the *Philosophie der Arithmetik* that, in order to explain the criticism of psychologistic logic and epistemology which he carried out in the *Prolegomena,* he refers to Goethe's words: *"Man ist gegen nichts strenger als gegen erst abgelegte Irrtümer"* ["One goes against nothing more vigorously than against just-abandoned errors"].[12] But the vigor of the reaction, as healthy as it may be, brought forth a readiness for unrestricted investigations. Husserl did not hesitate to recognize that his conception of truths-in-themselves was "imperfect." On the one hand, it was uniquely focused on *"vérités de raison."* On the other hand, it remained overly independent of the problems of the cognizing subjectivity. Husserl felt the need to complete the *Prolegomena* with more extensive investigations and to relate these to a description of the processes of consciousness in which logical ideas originate. These investigations make up the second volume of the *Logische Untersuchungen,* which appeared in 1901, one year after the *Prolegomena zur reinen Logik.*

Then Husserl developed a new interest, which was nevertheless continuous with the theme of the *Prolegomena:*

11. *Ibid.,* p. 117.
12. *Ibid.,* p. viii.

The fact, namely, that all thinking and cognizing concern objects, or affair-complexes, whose unity relative to the multiplicity of actual or possible acts of thinking is precisely "unity in multiplicity" and therefore ideal in character; the further fact that in all thinking a *form of thinking* is lodged, which comes under ideal laws and, more particularly, laws delimiting the Objectivity or ideality of cognition of every sort – these facts, I say, constantly excite afresh the *questions* of how the "in itself" of Objectivity is able to become mentally objectivated and thus become after all, in some measure, subjective again, of what it signifies to say the object is "in itself" and "given" in cognition; of how the ideality of the universal, as concept or ⟨as⟩ law, can enter the flow of real psychic life-processes and become the cognitional possession of the thinking subject; of what the cognizant *adequatio rei ac intellectus* signifies in different cases, according to whether the cognizant seizing concerns a matter of fact, or a law, and so forth. But it is clear that these and similar questions are entirely inseparable from the above-indicated questions concerning clarification of what pertains to pure logic. The task of clarifying ideas pertaining to pure logic – such as concept, object, truth and proposition, matter of fact and law, and so forth – leads inevitably to just the same questions, which, moreover, one must take in hand anyhow, because otherwise the essence of the clarification itself that one strives for in phenomenological analyses would remain unclear.[13]

Such a set of problems requires analyses which *in fact* are not psychological analyses in the usual sense. But, yielding to the traditional classification, which in addition to the objective sphere of cognition knows only the sphere of psychological immanence, Husserl designates these analyses as "psychological analyses." Soon after the appearance of Volume II of the *Logische Untersuchungen*, Husserl recognized that this designation was not appropriate for the actual intent which guided these investigations and, beginning in 1903, in an article in the *Archiv für systematische Philosophie*, he protested against his own designation of phenomenology as descriptive psychology, a designation which can only lead the reader into error. Actually, psychological description is an *empirical* description of psychic *facts*. Beyond this, by seeking to maintain the positivism of the fact, psychology remains a party to numerous speculative "presuppositions" it is unaware of. On the other hand, phenomenology's

13. *Log. Unt.*, Vol. II, first edition, p. 9.

descriptions do not concern mental processes, or classes of mental processes, belonging to empirical persons, since it knows nothing, and presumes nothing, about persons, about Ego and others, about my mental processes and those of others. Concerning such things it asks no questions, attempts no determinations, makes no hypotheses. Phenomenological description looks at what is, in the strictest sense, given, at the mental process as it is in itself. . . . For an epistemology and for any philosophy whatever that are free from contradiction it is, however, downright decisive that at last we make the fundamental essential division between, on the one hand, purely immanental phenomenology and criticism of cognition, which keeps itself free from all suppositions going beyond the content of the given,[14] and, on the other hand, empirical psychology, which, even where it merely describes, makes such suppositions, and that accordingly we do not, as is usual, confound the questions of epistemo-critical origin and the questions of psychological origin.[15]

In the second edition of *Logische Untersuchungen,* appearing in 1913, Husserl removes the reference to descriptive psychology and on the contrary places emphasis on the apriori character of his descriptions. The phenomenology of cognition has to do with mental processes "as such,"

it speaks of perceptions, judgments, feelings, and so forth, *as such,* and of what belongs to them a priori, with unconditional universality, precisely as *pure* single particulars subsumed under *pure* species; it speaks of what is to be discerned exclusively on the basis of the purely intuitive apprehension of "essences" (essential genera, essential species).[16]

Thus one arrives at an opposition between the matter-of-fact and the datum as it is grasped in its essence by intuition, which opposition had meanwhile been unknowingly obscured by theories. Therefore one cannot interpret the second volume of the *Logische Untersuchungen* as a relapse into the psychologism which the first volume attacked. In addition, it is significant that in the first edition of this second volume, though designating phenomenology as descriptive psychology, Husserl

14. On phenomenological description cf. *infra,* pp. xlv ff.
15. "Bericht über deutsche Schriften in den Jahren 1895–99, No. III," *Archiv für systematische Philosophie,* IX (1903), 399–400.
16. *Log. Unt.,* Vol. II, Pt. I, p. 18.

does try to reconcile the new orientation of his investigations with the antipsychologistic thesis of the *Prolegomena:*

> Phenomenology is descriptive psychology. Therefore the criticism of cognition is, in its essentials, psychology or at least is to be built only on the basis of psychology. Therefore pure logic too is founded on psychology. To what end, therefore, the whole battle against psychologism?
>
> To this objection, which no attentive reader of the *Prolegomena* can think of raising, we shall of course reply with what we have already indicated in § 2:
>
> The necessity of *such* a psychological founding of pure logic, namely a strictly descriptive one, cannot divert us from seeing the mutual independence of the two *sciences*, logic and psychology. For pure description is a mere preliminary to theory; it is not theory itself. . . .
>
> As it is epistemologically of quite unique significance to separate the purely descriptive exploration of cognition-processes, which is not concerned with any interests of theoretical psychology, from properly psychological research, which aims at empirical explanation and genesis, we do well to speak of *phenomenology* rather than of descriptive psychology.[17]

Even if one remains in the first edition of the *Logische Untersuchungen,* one still must not interpret phenomenological descriptions as psychological descriptions in the usual sense. In any case, the second edition leaves no uncertainty on this point. Husserl feels himself freed from the hypothesis of psychologistic interpretation (for which his first manner of expressing himself was somewhat responsible) to such an extent that he no longer insists on the *preliminary* function of descriptive phenomenological investigations vis-à-vis the establishment of a pure logic.[18] Meanwhile, the tendency to interpret phenomenological descriptions as psychological descriptions is maintained, and many studies which claim to be Husserlian

17. *Log. Unt.*, Vol. II, first edition, p. 18.
18. For example, a simple comparison of the beginning of § 5 of the first edition (p. 15) and that of the second edition (p. 15) is sufficient to reveal the evolution of Husserlian thinking: "With that, we are referred to a series of preparatory analytic labors, to make possible a formal logic and, first of all, a pure logical theory of forms . . ." (first edition). "With that, we are referred to a series of analytic investigations, to clarify the constitutive ideas for a pure or formal logic and, first of all, the ones relating to the purely logical theory of forms . . ." (second edition).

phenomenology are no more than simple psychological descriptions. If this is how things stand, we believe that it is because the notion of the *concrete,* which Husserl refers to, has often been poorly understood. The call to the concrete is, actually, often interpreted as a return to particular "factualness." As a matter of fact, however, Husserl wants to start from the concrete and thus to follow a *natural* order of investigation:[19]

> Thus the Objects that pure logic intends to explore are given at first in verbal attire. To speak more precisely: they are given [as it were][20] as embedded in concrete psychic processes that, in the function of *significational intention*[21] or else of *significational fulfilling* (in the latter function, as illustrative or else evident-making intuition), correspond to certain lingual *expressions* and, with these, make up a *phenomenological unity.*
>
> . . . Not the psychological judgment (that is: the concrete psychic phenomenon), but the logical judgment (that is: the ideal statement-signification, which is *one,* over against the multiple, descriptively very diverse, mental judgment-processes), interests [primarily and properly][22] the [pure][23] logician. . . .
>
> But, even though phenomenological analysis of concrete processes of thinking does not belong to the originally proper domain of pure logic, it is indeed indispensable to the furthering of pure logic's research.[24] For, provided that it is to become ours as an object of research and is to make possible the evidence of the apriori laws grounded in it, everything with which ⟨pure⟩ logic is concerned must be given in concrete fullness.[25]

Hence, at the start, in order not to break up a *natural unity,* it is necessary to take the propositions of logic in their "grammatical clothing" and to consider the mental processes of the sphere of expression. But the phenomenological clarification

19. *Log. Unt.,* Vol. II, Pt. I, p. 5 (first edition, p. 4).
20. Inserted in the second edition [Cairns's translator's note].
21. First edition: "the function of signification" [Cairns's translator's note].
22. Inserted in the second edition [Cairns's translator's note].
23. Inserted in the second edition [Cairns's translator's note].
24. First edition: "even though the analysis of ideal objects, and not the phenomenological analysis of concrete processes of thinking, belongs to the originally proper domain of pure logic, the latter analysis is indeed indispensable to the former" [Cairns's translator's note].
25. First edition: "in a subjective realization" [Cairns's translator's note].

must next denounce the ambiguities and uncertainties of language which entrap distracted thinking. It is necessary to strip away the equivocations attaching to language and masking the signification of pure logic. Starting from the concrete, the logician will "extract the components that interest him."

Something else which has contributed to the psychological interpretation of phenomenological investigations is the fact that the notion of intuition as Husserl uses it in his logical researches has often been conceived of as a sensuous intuition. And yet one of the main themes of the Sixth Investigation is devoted to the distinction between sensuous intuition and *"categorial" intuition*. When Husserl employs the word intuition in the expression "categorial intuition," it is to indicate opposition to the empty thinking which is satisfied to use a language unanimated by a truly present content. But one must not forget that categorial intuition is not the intuition of the real, sensible, objects; rather it concerns categorial objects, that is to say, ideal or irreal objects resulting from categorial activity, such as relations, wholes, grammatical categories of disjunction, conjunction, etc. In broadening the ordinary sense of "intuition" and "perception," one can say that categorial objects can be *perceived* in an *intuitive* manner when they are "themselves" presentiated and not only represented in an empty thinking. There is an intuition of the universal which, while different from empty conceptualization, still must not be confused with the intuition of the individual.[26]

Starting in 1901, with Volume II of the *Logische Untersuchungen*, we are confronted with investigations of an entirely new style. Even though focused on subjectivity in its activity of cognition, they cannot be assimilated, except improperly, to psychological investigations. But this novelty itself soon required that the principles which directed the method of the investigations be deepened and justified. The *Logische Untersuchungen* was for Husserl, in his own words, a "breakthrough" (*ein Werk des Durchbruchs*) — not an end but a beginning.[27] The investigation of both the sense and the method of the new phenomenology implies an enlargement of

26. Cf. Sixth Investigation, Chapter 6: "Sensuous Intuition and Categorial Intuition."

27. *Prolegomena*, Foreword of the second edition. p. viii.

the horizon of investigation. Phenomenology is revealed to have a bearing beyond the properly logical sphere where it found its point of departure. Hence Husserl formed the project of exposing for what they were the method and the problems of phenomenology considered in all their breadth and wrote the *Ideen zu einer reinen Phänomenologie und phänomenologischen Philosophie,* of which only the first book was published, in 1913. With the *Ideen* such an advance in thinking was made that a revision of the *Logische Untersuchungen* was required. But to raise the *Logische Untersuchungen* to the level of the *Ideen* would have involved a total resetting of the *Logische Untersuchungen,* i.e., a new work. Husserl made a compromise solution, which the unsystematic character of the "investigations" permitted. He reworked the former edition without essentially altering its style. He improved upon particular points, corrected hastily taken positions, such as that toward descriptive psychology, and allowed conceptions to remain that he no longer approved of but which retained a kind of propaedeutic interest.[28]

Under these conditions, the problems of logic could not be fundamentally rethought and could not profit from the development of a fully self-conscious phenomenology. Husserl also engaged in a much more profound reworking of the Sixth Investigation, the importance of this investigation being such that he could say, rightly, that it prepares the way for a phenomenological clarification of logical evidence.[29] But during the course of the printing he felt that he had to renounce this radical recasting, which required work whose difficulties he had underestimated, and he decided, finally, to republish the Sixth Investigation in the same spirit of correction that guided the rewriting of the first five investigations. After this second edition of the *Logische Untersuchungen,* Husserl turned away from problems of logic. He explains the reasons for his silence. In the first place, a period of idleness followed the intensive work he had put into the publication of the *Ideen* and the republication of the *Logische Untersuchungen.* Next, during the years that followed World War I he was incapable of bringing to the phenomenology of logic that "passionate interest" with-

28. Cf. *ibid.,* Foreword of the second edition, p. xi.
29. *Log. Unt.,* Vol. II, Pt. II, Foreword of the third edition, p. iv.

out which, he tells us, it was impossible for him to do fruitful work.[30]

Only with *Formal and Transcendental Logic* in 1929 did Husserl resume the examination of logical problems. With a refined method, Husserl rediscovered his first interests. This work exemplifies a mastery of thinking which Husserl had not attained until then. In the *Logische Untersuchungen* Husserl is seeking his philosophical way; in the *Ideen* he had to uncover for the reader for the first time an enormous and complex field of problems. By contrast, in *Formal and Transcendental Logic*, setting out from a well-determined set of problems, Husserl is able to present in a *systematic* manner to a reader already familiar with the phenomenological point of view the step-by-step development of this set of problems. But there is more to it. Thanks to the new themes introduced by the *Ideen*, not only can Husserl face the task of a radical grounding of logic but also, despite the particular character initially presented by the object of his study, he finds in this radical grounding an access route to the more general problems that a philosophy must confront. *Formal and Transcendental Logic* teaches us that radicalism and universality go hand in hand. In addition, to the extent that the Husserlian analyses press deeper and deeper into the problems of logic, new aspects of the phenomenological method appear. Also, *Formal and Transcendental Logic* appears to us to be the most revealing book on the method and intent of phenomenology. Investigations, provisional expositions of the broad lines of phenomenology, meditations, lectures – these are Husserl's other works. *Formal and Transcendental Logic* is a *book – the* book by Husserl.

We shall see the fundamental role of "subjective" investigations within *Formal and Transcendental Logic*. Logic can be grounded only by a transcendentally subjective logic, and from this fact the "truths-in-themselves" are relativized anew. But before one can interpret this subjective orientation as a return to psychologism, one must recognize that *Formal and Transcendental Logic* takes up the struggle against psychologism within a horizon much broader than Husserl's original horizon. *Formal and Transcendental Logic* triumphs over psychologism within the framework of a *theory of reason*. Yet it could be objected that Husserl uses certain expressions

30. *Ibid.*, p. 111.

that imply a surreptitious return to psychologism, such as the expression intentional *life*. To this one can reply that language does not know the phenomenological reduction and so holds us in the natural attitude. But is not philosophy precisely the power to transcend language? Can it not imbue language with a new thought? The notion of intentional life has a sense for transcendental phenomenology. It signifies that the intentionality of every *cogito* is multiple and that it is not exhausted by the description of its actual *cogitata*. Every ⟨actual⟩ intentionality has a horizon of potentialities. The transcendental analysis of consciousness can be a concrete investigation of this entire totality of actualities and potentialities without losing, as a result, its specifically transcendental character.

In taking Husserl's antipsychologism as a clue in characterizing the major traits of Husserl's conceptions, we do not claim, of course, to reduce phenomenology to this single antipsychologistic aspect, no matter how fundamental it appears. We mean, rather, to exclude beforehand the hypothesis of a psychologistic interpretation, the danger of which seems to us to be ever renascent.

In closing we should like to say something of the spirit in which we have undertaken this commentary on *Formal and Transcendental Logic*. We have sought to maintain the most direct contact with this book and thus with phenomenology. This is the reason—and it is the only reason—why we have abstained from using the critical expositions of phenomenology that exist. In order to respect the systematic character of the book, we have limited ourselves to a purely internal criticism, and in particular we have on principle avoided reference to unpublished manuscripts. Our commentary follows Husserl's exposition chapter by chapter in order to learn from an austere thought and from an ever-renewed effort.

Introduction

A SCIENCE WORTHY OF THE NAME must justify each of its steps. One can characterize science in this way without presupposing any particular theory of science. But if one asks for the justification involved, one quickly sees the diverse and opposed conceptions of science that can be formed. The answer to such a question indicates the orientation not only of an epistemology but even of an entire philosophy. For Husserl, only a justification that reaches pure and truly first principles can attain the dignity of genuine justification. Such an affirmation marks the absolute radicalism which is evident throughout Husserl's philosophy. In Husserl's eyes, the technical success of the organization of a science can never be considered as a justification for the well-groundedness of that science. Science must "give accounts" and do so in terms of radically first principles. Hence there is no need to wait for the ideal of genuine science to be separated through a comparative abstraction from actually constituted sciences. Only the pure idea of science can give the existing sciences a true "existence" by imposing their norms and prescribing their ways. The ethic of scientific justification can adopt the Kantian formula: It is a sad thing to deduce *what one must do* from *what is*. Only the "possible" can ground the actual.

But if the sciences are in no condition to teach us by their accomplishments, where is the pure idea of science to be derived from? For Husserl there is a *theory* of science which must distinguish the apriori possibilities to which a science must conform in order to be a true science. Hence a logic conceived as a *Wissenschaftslehre* [theory of science] will have

the "mission" of becoming the pure theory of possible science. Can traditional logic undertake this task of becoming the science of science? If, when it began in the Platonic dialectic, it was aware of this mission, bit by bit logic fell behind just those sciences which it was supposed to precede and guide. In their development and specialization the sciences encountered more and more complex and differentiated organizational tasks. An immense "positive" undertaking awaited them, and they let themselves be absorbed by this positivity without fully satisfying the spirit of "critical self-justification." What is more, they tended to deprecate the logical activity of grounding, which they judged sterile in comparison with the activity of constructing, which formed always new and richer theoretical organizations. But, as Husserl remarks, logic itself was an "accomplice" in this situation and betrayed its mission as the science of science. No matter what philosophical position one holds, one cannot deny logic's abandonment of this ideal of becoming a *Wissenschaftslehre*. We do not believe ourselves unjust in saying that traditional logic is a discipline completely separate from science. And if we turn toward modern logic, we are obliged to recognize its increasing tendency to become a particular science which develops by borrowing its methods – more exactly, its demonstrative style – from mathematics. The science of science, on the contrary, which is to provide the absolute grounds for all of the sciences, must be a universal science. Already by the fact of its universality, the science of science is differentiated from the other sciences which are special sciences. But, in addition, the special sciences are only "one-sided" sciences, for their outlook is only from their particular object-provinces. They are *directly* focused on objective cognition, and the attitude of the scientist can be called a "positive" and "straightforward" *(gerade)* attitude. The science of science, on the contrary, must reinforce the objective attitude of the scientist with a reflective attitude, for it cannot reach a true justification of cognition without the reflective examination of the subjective activity of cognition itself.

But does a clear consciousness of method not lead us deep into the cognitive activity in such a way that one could say that science itself produces the reflective concerns in its theme? Methodical control, for Husserl, is not, properly speaking, a consciousness of subjective activity. The formation of methods,

the application of methods, the very supervision of this application—these make up parts of a simple intellectual technique.
Husserl speaks of "the blinders imposed by their method, as
an inevitable consequence of the exclusive focusing of each
[science] on its own particular province" (4),* and he denounces

> the self-forgetfulness of the theorizer who, in his theoretical pro-
> ducing, devotes himself to the subject-matter, the theories, and the
> methods, and accordingly knows nothing of the inwardness of that
> producing—who lives in producing, but does not have this pro-
> ductive living itself as a theme within his field of vision (15).

Science, even the most characteristic theoretical science, e.g.,
mathematics, is, for Husserl, only a technique, for in studying
only its objective province, in studying only the "products of
its conscious production," it remains engaged in a one-sided
understanding, it lacks "insight into the *ratio* of its accomplished production" (3). In a word, the theoretical science is no
more than a *theoretical technique*. A theoretical technique.
If the reader wants to remain true to the style of Husserlian
thinking, he is obliged to take upon himself this strange association. The true theoretician would be he who practices this universal science of science. The mathematician himself "is not
in truth a pure theoretician, he is an ingenious technician." [1]
  Yes, the mathematician, like every man of science, is only
a technician. And often those who see in phenomenology a
"disavowal of science" fail to notice the constant admiration
that Husserl had for the accomplishments of science. The
sciences have established "highly differentiated methods." The
"much-to-be-admired sciences of Nature" operate according to
a method "which has proven itself." And Husserl says explicitly
in the *Krisis:*

> Naturally I am quite in earnest when I continue to call Galileo the
> foremost among the supremely great discoverers of the modern age;
> and naturally I am also quite in earnest in admiring the great dis-
> coverers of classic and post-classic physics and their thinking, which
> far from being merely mechanical, is indeed a most astonishing

---

*[Numbers in parentheses refer to page numbers in the English
translation by Dorion Cairns of Husserl's *Formale und transzendentale Logik,* forthcoming from Martinus Nijhoff, The Hague.—Translator's note.]
  1. *Prolegomena,* p. 253.

productive thinking. This thinking is not at all depreciated by the above-given clarification of it as *techné*.[2]

The facile criticisms of modern detractors of technique that we are accustomed to hearing are never to be found in the writings of Husserl. Technique bears the mark of man.

But if science has the mark of human ingenuity, how does it happen that Husserl can so often speak of "scientific naïveté"? Naïveté or ingenuity? It seems that one must choose. Husserl foresaw this objection in saying that with scientific naïveté one has to do with a "naïveté of a higher order" in contradistinction to the naïveté of everyday life. The naïveté of science is a naïveté "in the good sense of the term," as he says in the *Logische Untersuchungen*.[3] But is the very notion of degrees of naïveté *acceptable*? It seems that naïveté can be denounced only when one transcends it; but is it not abolished at the same time that it is denounced? Actually, phenomenology recognizes different *levels* of thinking. Science raises us above the kind of thinking that goes on in everyday life, and phenomenology raises us above scientific thinking. Even when one has reached the phenomenological attitude, one still finds different levels of investigation, for the procedure of phenomenology is an ascent from one level to a higher level. The phenomenologist is a new man and does not shed his naïveté all at once. The demand for absolute radicalism implies a relativism in its approach. Husserl will go so far as to say that phenomenological investigations "take on a painful and yet unavoidable relativity, a provisional-ness, instead of the definitiveness for which we were striving: Each investigation, at its own level, overcomes some naïveté or other, but is still accompanied by the naïveté of its level." [4] We can reach full consciousness of our cognitive activity only by stages.

This full consciousness is designated by Husserl with a phrase heavy with ethical resonances: *total self-responsibility.* The genuine science that would pursue the pure idea of science to its sources would assume this self-responsibility. But how can modern science allot the reflective tasks within a horizon of culture which has no concern for them? How can this radical reflection be initiated when, on the one hand, without a bad

2. *Krisis*, p. 53.
3. *Log. Unt.*, Vol. II, Pt. I, p. 22.
4. *FTL*, p. 270.

conscience, the existing sciences have betrayed the ancient Platonic ideal of science, and, on the other hand, logic, by letting itself be dominated by the fruitful development of the sciences, has itself become simply another special science? Development of the sciences, decommissioning of logic – that is the scientific situation of modern times. Therefore, where are the *motivational* powers which will move us from the positive scientific attitude to the reflective phenomenological attitude? Husserl is hardly explicit on this point. After telling us that the sciences are at fault for not understanding the one-sided character of their productions and that logic is not performing its proper function, Husserl simply says that "the present condition of European sciences necessitates radical investigations of sense" (5). It must be understood that one can discern nothing that can occasion a will to abandon the "natural" attitude – the attitude of positive science – as long as one remains in that attitude. But we do see that the philosophical calling is essentially a will to self-investigation, a will to self-responsibility, and that this requires even the philosopher to lift himself out of the natural attitude. "We cannot separate genuine humanity and living with radical self-responsibility, and therefore cannot separate scientific self-responsibility from the whole complex of responsibilities belonging to human life as such" (5). Science has a human function which goes beyond theory. The scientific vocation "must find its place within the highest practical idea, that of an all-embracing ethical life."[5] And striving to attain an ultimate understanding of ourselves is a way also of inquiring into the true sense of science.

But if we have perceived how to rediscover the ancient ideal of science, another question still confronts us: How was it possible to lose this ideal? We must recognize that *Formal and Transcendental Logic* does not pursue the internal articulation of this ideal or give the external motives for it.

> Science in the form of special science, has become a kind of theoretical technique. . . . Thus modern science has abandoned the ideal of genuine science that was vitally operative in the sciences from the time of Plato; and, in its practice, it has abandoned radicalness of scientific self-responsibility (3–4).[6]

5. *Ibid.*, p. 33.
6. We will find the same type of explanation again in the *Krisis*.

Actually, the question that Husserl takes up is a question that quickly orients him toward a living task: *How* can we re-institute the ancient ideal and constitute "genuine" sciences? By what method do we attain the universal *Wissenschaftslehre?*

> Now, however critical and skeptical our attitude toward our scientific culture as it has developed historically, we cannot simply abandon it, with no more reason than that we lack an ultimate understanding of it and are unable to manage it by virtue of such an understanding (5).

> We need only make clear to ourselves, by observing our present scientific and cultural situation, the necessity of radical and universal investigations of sense (6).

The reader who has learned the Husserlian lesson of radicalism may be surprised at this way of considering the existing sciences. But before justifying this paradoxical starting point, let us go along with Husserl as he examines different possible ways that we could take in a radical sense-investigation.

1. We might be tempted to consider the contemporary philosophical doctrines, which usually center about the problems of the theory of cognition. Then, by carrying out a criticism, we could ascertain the failures and extract the fruitful insights of these doctrines. But, in the "confused" situation of contemporary philosophy, that would be a "completely hopeless" undertaking, and in the Introduction to the *Cartesian Meditations* Husserl is specific:

> Instead of a serious discussion among conflicting theories that, in their very conflict, demonstrate the intimacy with which they belong together, the commonness of their underlying convictions, and an unswerving belief in a true philosophy, we have a pseudo-reporting and a pseudo-criticizing, a mere semblance of philosophizing seriously with and for one another. This hardly attests a mutual study carried on with a consciousness of responsibility, in the spirit that characterizes serious collaboration and an intention to produce objectively valid results. "Objectively [*objektiv*] valid results" — the phrase, after all, signifies nothing but results that have been refined by mutual criticism and that now withstand every criticism. But how could actual study and actual collaboration be possible, where there are so many philosophers and almost equally many philosophies? To be sure, we still have philosophical congresses. The philosophers meet but, unfortunately, not the

philosophies. The philosophies lack the unity of a mental space in which they might exist for and act on one another.[7]

2. Within this Introduction, Husserl can only indicate the Cartesian way of "meditations on first philosophy" that he takes a few months later in his *Cartesian Meditations*. The *Meditations* of Descartes himself were animated by a philosophical radicalism that can be taken as a model and revived, assuming that the present situation is analogous to that which Descartes encountered in his youth.[8] Unfortunately those meditations were guided by unperceived "prejudices" which defeated the attempt at the absolute grounding of cognition.[9]

3. *Formal and Transcendental Logic* will take another way, "suggested precisely by the historically given relation of the idea of genuine science to logic as its antecedent norm" (7). Then we turn from the sciences to logic. It is a question of considering and examining the existing logic as one finds it, in order to rediscover its true function as norm of science, and, through this logic, to rediscover what as such the genuine sciences are.

The objection of nonradicalism that can be made against such a manner of proceeding is all the stronger since it concerns not only the sciences but also the logic which must normatively ground these sciences. Husserl himself formulates this objection: "Thus we are presupposing the sciences, as well as logic itself, on the basis of the 'experience' that gives them to us beforehand. Because of this, our procedure seems not to be at all radical" (8). Husserl soon justifies himself; but if we take him on his own terms, he does so in a rather allusive fashion:

Whether sciences and logic be genuine or spurious, we do have experience of them as cultural formations given to us beforehand and bearing within themselves their meaning, their "sense": since they are formations produced indeed by the practice of the scientists and generations of scientists who have been building them. As so produced, they have a final sense, toward which the scientists have been continually striving, at which they have been continually aiming. Standing in, or entering, a comunity of empathy with the scientists, we can follow and understand—and carry on "sense-investigations" (9).

7. *CM*, p. 5.
8. *Ibid.*
9. Cf. *infra*, p. 155.

This remains a mute text if taken without its horizon of understanding, if not reinserted into the theory of intentionality,[10] for every consciousness is a consciousness of something, is directed toward an "object." A relationship between the processes of consciousness and the object is involved that implies a reciprocity. There is a correlation which indissolubly links the consciousness and its object. It is not without reason that Husserl employs the same word—*intentional*—to characterize both the mental process which relates itself to the object and the very object of this *"intentio."* [11] When we employ the word *object* in a general way, we have in mind the correlate of a process of consciousness and not necessarily the thing, the object of external perception. And, remaining within the sphere of interest of *Formal and Transcendental Logic*, we want precisely to consider the relationship between the activity of thinking and the thought formed in this activity, e.g., the relationship between the judging and the judgment judged. From the fact of this intentional connexion our judgments reveal the activity of thinking which gave them birth. They have long been dead significations from which all living intention has been withdrawn, but they can be "reactivated"; by questioning them, we can revive the subjective activity which engendered them.[12]

Thus cultural forms, such as the existing sciences, once questioned, can yield the living intention which constituted them. But an objection comes to mind. This intention is not itself a full consciousness of what genuine science must be. Modern science, by affirming a false autonomy in relation to an activity of reflecting and grounding, does not have the idea of genuine science within it. It claims to be science, but it is not truly science. Its naïveté derives from this.

> The sense of our whole meditation implies that sciences, as these facts of Objective culture, and sciences "in the true and genuine sense" need not be identical and that the former, over

10. On the theory of intentionality, cf. Q. Lauer, *La genèse de l'intentionnalité dans la philosophie de Husserl* (Paris, 1954).

11. Cf. *Log. Unt.*, Vol. II, Pt. I, p. 97, n. 1.

12. On the possibility of reactivation, cf. "Ursprung der Geometrie," *Revue internationale de philosophie* (15 January 1939), No. 2, pp. 203-25.

and above being cultural facts, involve a claim, which ought to be established as one they already satisfy.[13]

But this claim, in its very naïveté, is the mark of a demand for scientificness, and "science as an idea—as the idea, genuine science—'lies,' still undisclosed, precisely in this claim."[14] Under these conditions, starting from this scientific claim, we can hope to rediscover the idea of genuine science. Hence science as it exists can be a *clue* for our reflection.

> Even though we must not take any position with respect to the *validity* of the de facto sciences (the ones "claiming" validity)—i.e., with respect to the genuineness of their theories and, correlatively, the competence of their methods of theorizing—there is nothing to keep us from "immersing ourselves" in the scientific striving and doing that pertain to them, in order to see clearly and distinctly what is really being aimed at.[15]

The teleological idea that governs all scientific activity gradually comes to light: the scientist not only makes judgments but also grounds them. We see that in this there is a simple claim and that science as it exists does not exist to a sufficient degree to guarantee an ultimate criticism of cognition. But in the will to ground we grasp an intention which, when questioned, can lead us to the genuine ideal of the criticism of cognition.

Thanks to an "investigation of sense" (*Besinnung*), we can correctly carry out such an inquiry. What is to be understood by this denomination *Besinnung*? Husserl almost always employs the expression *radikale Besinnung* as if there were an inseparable connexion between the two terms. Yet the notion of *Besinnung* can be truly understood only if one refers to the two poles of the intentional relation: the consciousness and its object. Let us restrict ourselves to the sphere of judgment. To investigate sense is simultaneously to be fully aware of our activity of judging and to make the true sense which is the correlate of this activity appear.

In this connexion, we should like to point out an equivocation involved in the vocabulary of intentionality. On the one hand,

13. *CM*, p. 9.
14. *Ibid.*
15. *Ibid.*

intentionality is the fundamental property of consciousness: "The word intentionality signifies nothing else than this universal fundamental property of consciousness: to be consciousness *of* something; as a *cogito*, to bear within itself its *cogitatum*." [16] Every *cogito* has an intentional object. The judgment, for example, is the intentional object, the intentional sense, of the activity of judging. But let us consider the activity of judging more closely. Often we make judgments whose exactness we have not verified; these are simple meanings or opinions *(Meinungen)*. We opine or mean *(meinen)* that the things are thus and so, but without having verified that the things are just as we imagine them to be. Then the meaning remains "empty"; in order to become true, it must be "fulfilled" by means of a confrontation with the things. We translate *"erfüllen"* with "fulfilling," following an already established tradition. But this translation omits an important aspect of the signification of this word. *Erfüllen* means to fulfill an empty form, but it is also "to fulfill" a condition, to satisfy a requirement. When we form an opinion, we expect that the things will be as we think of them.

Thus the distinction between empty meaning and fulfilled judgment appears. And within the framework of that distinction the term *intentional* is this time reserved for characterizing the meaning; the meaning is the result of a simple *intentio* which must be confirmed in what follows by "fulfillment" *(Erfüllung)*. The judgment is only an intentional sense which is not yet fulfilled. Once fulfilled, the judgment is no longer an anticipatory opinion; it is there "in person" *(selbst)* as a true judgment, sanctioned by an adequation to the things. One deals no longer with the intentional sense but with the sense itself. In truth, this equivocation in the employment of the term intentional is less perceptible in *Formal and Transcendental Logic* than in earlier works because here Husserl willingly employs the expression *vermeint* instead of *intentional* in order to characterize the judgment as opinion. The opinion is a "meant" Object *(vermeintes Objekt)*.[17]

16. *Ibid.,* p. 33.

17. [Where, following Cairns, I use *meant*, it was necessary in French for Bachelard to use a neologism: *intentionné*. With slight omissions the note on this translation is retained, since it has bearing beyond the problem of translating *vermeint.* — Translator's note.] We were tempted to employ the Scholastic expression *mental object*. But

To investigate sense is precisely to transform the judgment that is a simple opinion into a fulfilled judgment.

Sense-investigation [*Besinnung*] signifies nothing but the attempt actually to produce the sense "itself," which, in the mere meaning, is a meant, a presupposed, sense; or, equivalently, it is the attempt to convert the "intentive sense [*intendierenden Sinn*]" (as it was called in the *Logische Untersuchungen*),[18] the sense "vaguely floating before us" in our unclear aiming, into the fulfilled, the clear, sense, and thus to procure for it the evidence of its clear possibility (9).

In the activity of meaning, we judge in a confused manner, *far from the things.* Only contact with the things can bring evidence of clarity. Hence, in the investigation of sense, we must come back to the "datum" itself, "to the things themselves" *(zu den Sachen selbst).* As Fink remarks, the latter is not a happy expression; it can lead to erroneous interpretations: "That is to say: The watch-word: 'Back to the things themselves!' is, for Husserl, as far from expressing the program of a 'naïve realism' as it is from expressing that of a speculative determination of the concept of being." [19] On the one hand, actually, "the things" are not necessarily the things of the external world, for they can be numbers, judgments, and so on. All the same, on frequent occasions Husserl sought to prevent a grossly realistic interpretation:

The "itself given" [*Das "selbst-gegeben"*] we do not identify with the "given originaliter," the given "in person" [*mit dem "originär-gegeben," dem "leibhaft"*]. In the definitely characterized sense, "given" and "itself given" are the same; and we use the re-

---

this expression does not allow us to account for the distinction between the judgment which is only *vermeint* and the fulfilled judgment. The fulfilled judgment is not held in view; still the expression mental object as synonym for the expression intentional object taken in the broad sense could lead to mistakes, as Husserl remarks in the *Ideen* (p. 168). Take a perceived object as an example: If one considers the *cogitatum* correlative to the act of perception, there would be danger in calling it a mental object, for this term leads us to believe that the mental object is a duplicate in the mind of the effective, real, object. This is not the case, for the perception is a consciousness of a *reality.*

18. Husserl's note: *Logische Untersuchungen,* second edition, Vol. II, Pt. I, pp. 50 ff.

19. E. Fink, "Das Problem der Phänomenologie Edmund Husserls," *Revue internationale de philosophie,* No. 2 (1939), p. 237.

dundant expression only to exclude *givenness in another sense*, in which it is said ultimately of everything objective [*von jedem Vorstelligen*] that is given in the objectivation [*in der Vorstellung*] (but perhaps "in an empty manner").[20]

Hence it is not necessary to understand by thing only the perceptual datum.

Nor is it a question, when one adopts the return to the things, of confining oneself dogmatically to a speculative theory which decides in advance what the things are, what being is. One must seek to uncover what the things are. The things are not offered to us in naïve immediacy. Sense-investigation is not content with expressing what it sees at first glance. It is the uncovering of a true sense initially hidden behind a confusion of manners of givenness. It is *sense-explication (Sinnauslegung)*. Taking the example of judgment, we see that usually we judge in a confused fashion, whether when yielding to another's authority we repeat a judgment formulated by someone else — when, for example, without actively rethinking it, we repeat a mathematical demonstration which we once understood and have learned by heart — or whether a vague idea comes to mind, etc. Then it is a question of clarifying these "empty meanings" and transforming them into genuine fulfilled judgments.

But in order to understand the true sense of any *cogitatum*, it is not enough to study the correlative processes of consciousness which are *actual*. Potential mental processes are implied in the intentionality of actual mental processes. The intentional functions intermingle; the data themselves cannot be considered in isolation from their milieux and only in the manner in which they are given. Every determination calls for a richer and more specific determination. Sense-explication is sense-enrichment *(Sinnesbereicherung)*, as *Erfahrung und Urteil* says.[21] Hence every intentionality has a *horizon*[22] which sense-investigation must progressively explicate.

20. *Ideen*, p. 126.
21. *Erf. u. Urt.*, p. 141.
22. Cf. *CM*, p. 45: "The horizons are 'predelineated' potentialities. We say also: We can ask any horizon what 'lies in it,' we can explicate or unfold it, and 'uncover' the potentialities of conscious life at a particular time. Precisely thereby we uncover the objective sense meant implicitly in the actual cogito, though never with more than a certain degree of foreshadowing."

Thus sense-investigation must delve in the "ultimate depths" of the sense. It is at once *Enthüllung* (uncovering) and *Vertiefung* (deepening). What is more, this *Vertiefung* is not motivated by simple curiosity, which would make it a matter of prolonged patience. Rather, it obeys a will to confirm, to correct, to justify, to ground – in a word, a will to know.

> Radical sense-investigation, as such, is at the same time *criticism* for the sake of original clarification. Here original clarification means shaping the sense anew, not merely filling in *(Ausfüllung)* a delineation that is already determinate and structurally articulated beforehand. . . . [T]hen original sense-investigation signifies a combination of determining more precisely the vague indeterminate predelineation, distinguishing the prejudices that derive from associative overlappings, and cancelling those prejudices that conflict with the clear sense-fulfillment [*mit der besinnlichen Erfüllung*] – in a word, then: critical discrimination between the genuine and the spurious (10).

Sense-investigation is a return to the anticipatory meanings in order to see whether they can be confirmed or, on the contrary, canceled. Actually, the life of cognition is made from anticipations, from precomprehensions, which are hasty and still vague but fruitful; they enable us to move ahead, and they enable us to return to these anticipations critically. Sense-investigation is also "reactivation" of the evidences which were once alive and which are later "sedimented." It is the clarification of *origins*. But one must not believe that the word origin in itself indicates a chronological origin. Beginning in the *Prolegomena* Husserl uses the word *Ursprung* habitually. When he assigns the investigation of the categories of logic as one of the tasks of logic, he soon specifies that it is a matter of "insight into the essence of the concepts in question and, methodologically, a matter of fixing unambiguous, sharply distinguished, verbal significations. These ends we can attain only by making the essence [present intuitively in an adequate intuition]."[23] Investigations into "origins" are investigations into *genuineness*. They are searches for radical grounds.

In works before *Formal and Transcendental Logic* Husserl repeatedly insists upon the descriptive character of the phe-

23. *Prolegomena*, p. 244 [passage added in second edition (Cairns's translator's note)].

nomenological method. Here, on the contrary, the term *Besinnung* comes to replace the term *Deskription* (or the equivalent term *Beschreibung*), even though Husserl does not forbid the employment of the latter. If this is how things stand, it is because the notion of *Besinnung* implies the notion of criticism and because *Formal and Transcendental Logic* gives criticism a fundamental role within the phenomenological method, a role that it did not have previously. Even so, criticism appears not only to have a controlling function but also to have a *constituting* function. No concept, no theory, can receive the seal of approval unless it has been grounded by criticism, by the ultimate criticism that the phenomenological *Besinnung* performs.

Nevertheless, Husserl does not deny the descriptive style which in his first works he had vindicated for the phenomenological method. In effect, then, description remains the first stage at which phenomenology begins. For the rest, phenomenological description is far from what is usually understood to be description. It is not a simple empirical description but rather a "pure" description. It does not have objects before it which are "pregiven." As we will see, phenomenology is not a science of fact but rather an apriori science of essences; more precisely, it is a science that investigates *essential types*. But under these conditions one may wonder why Husserl retained the term description to characterize the method of an apriori discipline. In fact, if the term description can provoke confusion on the part of psychologists who believe that they can appreciate phenomenological "descriptions," in turn it can also prevent misinterpretation on the part of the defenders of the Apriori; actually it indicates the distance which separates phenomenology from the other apriori sciences. Phenomenology is an apriori science, *but it is not deductive.* We believe it possible to affirm that it is this negativity that Husserl primarily meant to indicate by designating phenomenology as a descriptive science; i.e., phenomenology is called descriptive *because* it is not deductive.

Husserl worked in mathematics, and he always retained the demand for strictness or rigor, the desire to attain a legitimate objectivity through the Apriori. He wants to inaugurate a philosophy which also would be an apriori and strict science. But he understands that philosophy must have its own methods and

that it can protect the ideal of strictness while abandoning deduction, the strict method par excellence. In reading "Philosophy as Rigorous Science" we see with what vigor Husserl affirms this conviction:

> Because in the most impressive of the modern sciences, the mathematico-physical, that which is exteriorly the largest part of their work, results from indirect methods, we are only too inclined to overestimate indirect methods and to misunderstand the value of direct comprehensions. However, to the extent that philosophy goes back to ultimate origins, it belongs precisely to its very essence that its scientific work move in spheres of direct intuition. Thus the greatest step our age has to make is to recognize that with the philosophical intuition in the correct sense, the phenomenological grasp of essences, a limitless field of work opens out, a science that without all indirectly symbolical and mathematical methods, without the apparatus of premises and conclusions, still attains a plenitude of the most rigorous and, for all further philosophy, decisive cognitions.[24]

To us this passage is of the first importance, since it unifies two opposed teleologies into a common purpose: direct intuitive apprehension and scientific Aprioriness. This paradoxical union gives phenomenological description its own style.

But how can this paradoxical union be actualized? Husserl himself wonders: "A descriptive eidetics—is that not something utterly preposterous?" If this question comes immediately to mind, it is precisely because one is still taken with the ideal of the demonstrative style of mathematics. Husserl continues:

> . . . as the mathematical disciplines are the only ones that at present can uphold efficaciously the idea of a scientific eidetics, at first we are far from thinking that there can be eidetic disciplines of another sort, non-mathematical ones, fundamentally different in their whole theoretical type from those with which we are acquainted.[25]

But from the point when one begins to consider the sphere of study chosen by the phenomenologist, one is seriously obliged to ascertain that he is dealing with "objects" of a species entire-

24. "Philosophy as Rigorous Science," in Edmund Husserl, *Phenomenology and the Crisis of Philosophy*, translated, with an Introduction, by Quentin Lauer (New York, 1965), p. 147 (hereafter referred to as "Philosophy as Rigorous Science").

25. *Ideen*, pp. 132 f.

ly different from the objects of mathematics. Geometry, for example, has essences as a point of departure (the circle, the straight line, etc.) which it can *define* in an *exact* manner by means of fixed concepts. On the contrary, "the attempt to determine a process of consciousness as an identical object, on the basis of experience, in the same fashion as a natural Object — ultimately then with the ideal presumption of a possible explication into identical elements, which might be apprehended by means of fixed concepts — would indeed be folly." [26] A process of consciousness can only be studied by means of a description which respects the eidetic characters discovered by intuition. Thus the phenomenological method is in no way inferior to the deductive methods. A method has no value in itself; it must be used in its proper province of application. The objects of phenomenology are concrete objects which *must* be intuitively grasped. The phenomenological method does not consist in deducing, in "explaining" *(erklären)* by theories; it consists rather in seeing the things as they are, in "elucidating" *(aufklären)*.[27] If it is recalled that, in order to see the things, it is not enough just to look at them, that it is necessary to seek in order to see better, that it is necessary to uncover, to explicate, to clarify, then one already understands that descriptive tasks can be reconciled with critical tasks.

Accepting this, and readily agreeing that the nature of the subject matter of phenomenology imposes upon it a method entirely different from the deductive method, one can still be skeptical about the possibility of erecting a true science with such "flowing" data to start with. Husserl does not contest that it is impossible univocally to determine the individual objects of the phenomenological sphere. But if one cannot "define" the flowing *concreta* in an *exact* manner,[28] at least, when one elevates one's gaze toward the more and more general essences, one can bring scientific determination into play; one can determine these essences in a *strict* manner.

> Thus we describe, and thereby define, in *strict* concepts the generic essence of perception as such or ⟨the essence⟩ of subordinate species such as perception of something physical and perception of animate beings; likewise the generic essence of memory as such,

26. *CM*, p. 49.
27. *Log. Unt.,* Vol II, Pt. I, p. 20.
28. Cf. *Ideen*, pp. 139–40.

empathy as such, willing as such, and so forth. Prior to these, however, stand the highest universalities, mental process as such, *cogito*[29] as such, which already make comprehensive descriptions possible.[30]

And if one can describe in a pure and strict manner, it is because in intentional life "an essentially *necessary* conformity to *type* prevails and can be apprehended in strict concepts." [31]

In this way, therefore, eidetic description is one of the differences in style between the new apriori science which is phenomenology and the mathematical sciences.[32] Husserl affirms this continuously during the period of *Formal and Transcendental Logic* with the same cleanness as before. But with this book he imposes on himself a new phenomenological step which is an essentially critical step and no longer a merely descriptive one. Here again the phenomenological method sets itself apart from the method of objective science, for phenomenological criticism is set apart from scientific criticism in that it is a criticism that discovers orginal genuineness, that unmasks all prejudices, and that, by clarifying intentional horizons, determines the true bearing of evidences.

Let us now indicate the itinerary of the sense-investigation which sets out from traditional logic in order finally to arrive at the idea of the science of science taken in a genuine and radical sense. This point of departure, as we have indicated, can seem to ruin every claim to radicalism, and only the appeal to the intentional relations between constituted thought and constituting activity ⟨of thinking⟩ overcomes such an objection. If this objection is even stronger when one has not only the existing sciences but also the existing logic as starting point, at least logic has the advantage of being a better base for intentional inquiry than the other sciences. Actually, the original sense is more visible in logic than in the sciences. The systematic establishment of an architecture of thought is very neatly manifest in formal logic. And "even through such widely divergent

29. In all editions: *cogitatio* [Cairns's translator's note].
30. *Ideen,* p. 140.
31. *CM,* p. 49.
32. Cf. "Nachwort zu meinen *Ideen . . . ,*" *Jahrbuch für Philosophie und phänomenologische Forschung,* XI (1930), 553 (referred to hereafter as "*Nachwort*").

presentations and, indeed, distorting caricatures it has pre-
vailed, with an essentially identical core of unrelinquishable
content" (8). To be sure, the specific sense of its formal character has not been grasped with full consciousness. And it will be
precisely the task of the sense-investigation to distinguish the
immanent teleology which remains confused for the very persons who are guided by it.

The orientation of traditional logic remains essentially "objective," unilaterally focused on the object, toward thought-formations *(Denkgebilde)*. Hence the investigation of sense will
be obliged in the beginning to restrict itself to this one-sided
point of view. But in Husserl's style of thinking, a "beginning"
compromises nothing, even in the sphere of logic. By gradually
distinguishing the sense belonging to traditional logic, sense-
investigation uncovers the presuppositions of logic which reveal it to be a "naïve" logic, one that never dreamt of questioning
what it declares to be a matter of course. Sense-investigation
will then be led to criticize the evidences of logic, hence to return to the constituting subjective activity and to the clarification of this activity. The subjective orientation of this criticism
will then come to support the exclusively objective orientation
of the theme of traditional logic. But there is no reason to interpret problems referring to subjectivity as problems of natural
human subjectivity, hence as psychological problems. The problems that the phenomenological criticism of logic deals with
are the problems of transcendental subjectivity. Thus one comes
to a logic which "descends into the depths of transcendental
interiority." Only then can the sense of science in its true Objectivity be fully understood.

> Only a science clarified and justified transcendentally (in the
> phenomenological sense) can be an ultimate science; only a tran-
> scendentally-phenomenologically clarified world can be an ul-
> timately understood world; only a transcendental logic can be an
> ultimate theory of science, an ultimate, deepest, and most uni-
> versal, theory of the principles and norms of all the sciences (16).

The reader may be surprised that a way exists that leads
from formal logic to transcendental logic. If he is trained in
the mathematical disciplines, he will not understand that one
could wish for a horizon other than that of axiomatized mathematical logic. If he is a philosopher, he will not understand

that one can take such a formal logic into consideration, even as a simple way of entry, when one wants to institute a truly philosophical logic which, after a fashion, renders the problems of formalism *declassée*. Does Husserl not say that the "historically existing logic, with its naïve positivity, its way of obtaining truths as objects of naïve straightforward evidence, proves to be a kind of philosophic puerility" and that "it lacks in itself that originary genuineness by virtue of which it might achieve ultimate self-understanding and self-justification" (13)? But it is exactly the merit of Husserl's book that it succeeds in *going beyond* formal logic, not simply in setting it aside. This is the only example we have encountered in the philosophical literature of a "criticism" of formalism that does not proceed in a poorly informed spirit of criticism. The objections to formalism ordinarily made usually exemplify an ignorance and an intellectual sloth which destroy at the root the value of their arguments. The reader already disposed against formalism will happily take over Husserl's conclusions. But Husserl would be the first to denounce the naïveté of this laughable bias. Does he not say in the *Prolegomena:*

> Not the mathematician, but the philosopher, steps outside his natural sphere of competence, if he resists the "mathematizing" theories of logic and is unwilling to hand over his provisional foster children to their natural parents. The disparagement with which philosophic logicians like to speak of mathematical theories of inferences alters in no respect the fact that in the case of these, as in the case of all strictly developed theories (one must, it is true, take this word in its genuine sense), the mathematical form of treatment is the only scientific one, the only one that affords systematic closedness and completeness, that affords a view of all possible questions and the possible forms of their solution.[33]

Hence, on the one hand, Husserl sets himself apart from the logicians of philosophical orientation who disdain mathematical logic; he never fails to emphasize the "stimulating" power of the mathematical methods of the modern theories of deduction. On the other hand, while recognizing the necessity for a mathematization of logic, he does proclaim the rights of a genuine philosophical logic. We have seen that his first conception of such a logic, as it appears in the *Prolegomena,*

33. *Prolegomena,* p. 253.

has evolved and that the subjective focus of subsequent phenomenological investigations has given him more profound philosophical grounds. But after the *Prolegomena* Husserl emphasizes the necessity of a philosophical discipline of logic as a discipline that goes beyond the tasks of mathematics. He speaks of a division of labor between mathematicians and logicians (§ 71). The construction of theories, the solution of methodological problems, etc., must remain within the province of the mathematician. But the mathematician is only a technician of theory. Only the philosopher can initiate a radical criticism and thus penetrate the essence of theoretical cognition. Meanwhile, the mathematical spirit has an inventive power which should not be misunderstood by anyone who encounters its achievements. On numerous occasions Husserl speaks of a scientific *instinct*, which, however blind it be to the investigation of origins, is a sure guide for the mathematician. In any conflict it is better to be on the side of the mathematicians than on the side of intemperate philosophers. "The memory of Berkeley's battle against the infinitesimal calculus ought to serve us as an admonition to trust the mathematical instinct, which at first is uncritical but, in the principal features, guides us safely," Husserl writes in his second article in the *Archiv*.[34] One can even discern from chance remarks a nostalgia in Husserl for the constructive power which the logician can use against hasty criticisms by philosophers: "That is actually done then by the mathematicians, while excluding the specifically philosophic problems and in, so to speak, a naïvely dogmatic manner, without concerning themselves with the philosophers' objections—in my opinion, to the benefit of science";[35] and even: "for the genius of mathematics was right, as always, about the matters at issue; even though its logical self-understanding was faulty."[36] Often, in addition, the logician who has been trained in mathematics has, if we may say so, a mathematical "superego," with all that this implies in the way of admiration and vindication. But it is not necessary to give more importance than is appropriate to this psychological dimension of the problem of the relation-

34. "Bericht über deutsche Schriften in den Jahren 1895–1899, No. II," *Archiv für systematische Philosophie*, IX (1903), 258.
35. *Log. Unt.*, Vol. II, Pt. I, p. 340.
36. *FTL*, p. 94.

ship between mathematics and logic, and it should be kept first in mind that for Husserl the technical elaboration of theories, no matter how ingenious and perfected, must necessarily be completed by a fundamental philosophical clarification.

Preparatory Considerations

HUSSERL DOES NOT BEGIN his book with an examination of traditional logic, as one might expect, but, in a "more primitive" manner, with the significations of the word *logos*. Why were these Preparatory Considerations not indicated on the line of reflection so neatly traced in the Introduction? Actually, these Preparatory Considerations enable us to gain an advance understanding of the interest pertaining to traditional logic. It is important for Husserl to present a revelatory center for the inquiry as quickly as possible. One must first understand a little, in order then to understand better, in order finally to understand well.

Husserl distinguishes two groups of significations for the word logos: The first group includes not only discourse but also the sense enclosed in discourse and also the "sense-bestowing" act. In the second group, logos has the signification of reason — scientific reason in particular. These different significations are going to "guide" us and enable us to form an initial notion of what a science of the logos can be.

To begin with, Husserl places his examination on the level of the second group of significations by going along with the traditional conception of logic, and this is indicative of the general perspective of *Formal and Transcendental Logic*. At its highest level, logical thought is from the start considered as the science of the logical in the emphatic sense, as the science of the rational and, even more specifically, of the scientifically rational. The interest that is active here is an in-

terest relating to science.[1] This rather abrupt setting-up of the problem will have for its counterpart a regressive search that will lead us to a rediscovery of the lower levels of thinking activity. The specific character of "rationality" having been set up as the fundamental problem, it will first be a matter of envisaging the specific character of thought in general so as to circumscribe it. But every thought worthy of the name, that is to say, every communicable thought, is given to us through language: "Our first concern, therefore, is not with bare acts of thinking and bare thoughts, but is above all with statements, stated thoughts. This leads us back to the first group of significations of the word logos" (19). Now the natural function of discourse is to express something, for "the speaker's practical intention is obviously not directed ultimately to the mere words, but is directed 'through' them to their signification. The words carry significative intentions; they serve as bridges leading over to the significations, to what the speaker means 'by' them" (22). A provisional concept of thinking is then disengaged as embracing all the processes of consciousness in which this significative intention is formed and which are truly "sense-bestowing." Yet not all mental processes are sense-bestowing. Only the sphere of the acts of the ego taken in the specific sense, including those of secondary passivity, is to be retained for consideration.[2]

Now that we have characterized thinking in general, we are to "delimit" thinking on the level of logic understood as theory of scientific reason. The acts bestowing signification are then the acts where judgments are constituted—judgments which are ordered or *coordinated* in certain ways in order to form the *unity* of a *theory.*

But does this initial delimitation of logic as theory of the scientific logos, even though of a provisional character, not beg the question? Husserl explicitly replies to such an objection:

1. *Erfahrung und Urteil,* a "genealogy of logic," moves in the opposite direction, and not until the last part does it begin considering the logical activity which is the center of interest in *Formal and Transcendental Logic.*

2. Husserl terms secondary passivity that passivity which is founded on an original activity (e.g., the passivity of a judgment that comes to mind without its original evidence).

Because scientifically judicative reason, in the manner characteristic of a highest level, presupposes all the lower levels of productions effected by thinking and, when taken concretely as a theme of inquiry, includes them all, the reference to science, and therefore the conception of logic as theory of science, involves no restriction; it simply has the advantage of directing attention to the highest final idea of judicative reason (28).

For the moment, we cannot appreciate how well-grounded this reply is, since we do not yet know the type of dependence that obtains between the highest level and the lower levels. Hence let us keep this reply in mind provisionally and say in advance that it is one of the keys to understanding of Husserl's thought.[3]

Before specifying the notion of logic thus understood, let us emphasize a function of language which Husserl returns to in numerous writings: Thanks to language, "A maximally durable documentation of the results, in the Objective cultural world, is also relevant to this purpose" (27). The *Logische Untersuchungen* mentions this original function of *Dokumentierung,* exercised by language, which *Formal and Transcendental Logic* insists upon. Language is what enables thought to acquire an intersubjective status, to be a durable *acquisition* to which one may refer at any time: "Only in this form [namely: the form of statements] do truth and, specifically, theory become the abiding possession of science." Thanks to language, thought is "recorded in documents" (*urkundlich verzeichnete*).[4] But it is not necessary to believe that this *Dokumentierung* alienates the spirituality of thought. To be sure, the words incorporate (*verleiblichen*) thought, "they carry it incorporated in them." But this embodiment of thought is itself "animated" (*beseelt*) by fusion with thinking. In addition, the incorporation of language is itself, taken in itself, "so to speak a spiritual corporeality [*eine geistige Leiblichkeit*]" (21). Actually, it is necessary that the word as sensible phenomenon be distinguished from the word as grammatical formation. I can easily pronounce or write a word of the latter sort several times, and, when I do so, I will say that I pronounce or that I write the *same* word, which thus appears as an *ideal unity* distinct from its multiple material reproductions. *A fortiori* we will consider the word as an expression fulfilled by a sense.

3. Cf., *infra*, pp. 144 f. and 212 f.
4. *Log. Unt.*, Vol. II, Pt. I, pp. 1, 3, 95.

There is an ideality to language that can be characterized by the fact that "language has the Objectivity proper to the objectivities making up the so-called spiritual [*geistige*] or cultural world, not the Objectivity proper to bare physical Nature" (20). And if the logician is interested in language, it is precisely in language under the perspective of its ideality. Yet Husserl only indicates these linguistic problems in order quickly to "exclude" them.

But one can wonder why Husserl so rapidly sets aside the problems of language that he judged it necessary to introduce. Actually, as we have just pointed out, *Formal and Transcendental Logic* is a book that goes straight to the primary problems. It only considers

> the primary purposes of theoretical reason, which lie on the significational side and consist in the attainment of truths. . . . In our further considerations pertaining to the systematic clarification of the idea of logic, we shall address ourselves exclusively to the significational side of scientific locutions — that is to say: purely to judicative reason itself and the formations it produces (27).

However secondary the problems of language are for the logician, it is normal that they occur to him, for "the statement-formations are the first to make their appearance in his field of consciousness among its prominences" (27). The expression is a *thematic index*. Hence we are to let ourselves be guided by this index if we want to follow a *natural* investigative procedure. But the expression is *only* an index which of necessity refers beyond itself to the themes of logic properly so-called. Hence, after this brief excursion into the problems of language, *Formal and Transcendental Logic* returns to the themes of logic as its true thematic goals.

If logic is not content to be a simple methodology with the various methods of the special sciences as its subject matter, if, instead, it wants to be the theory of the *principles* of science, it must distinguish what is *purely* universal. It must be an *apriori* science which breaks with empirical "factualness" in every respect. But the universal it is concerned with is not only the pure universal but also the *formal* universal. An apriori "universality" can be related to a material, to a *hylé* (thought in pure universality). Then one is involved with a "contingent Apriori," contingent because it is connected with the contin-

gent domain of this or that *hylé* (as is the case when one considers, for example, an apriori proposition about sound in general). On the other hand, the Apriori pertaining to logic is a "formal Apriori"; the properly logical concepts are "form-concepts" *(Formbegriffe)*,[5] which have no reference to materials of cognition in contradistinction to "material" concepts *(sachhaltige Begriffe)*, such as, for example, the concept of sound.

But not only is what is called "formal logic" formal, but also any logic whatever "in its universal and (as universal) its only philosophic sense" (29). Then we encounter an astonishing expression from Husserl: "Reason itself, including theoretical reason in particular, is a form-concept" (29). Is this not a devaluation of reason, every form-concept being only an *empty* concept? On the contrary, we will see that the formal is made valuable. We come to the broadest possible sense of formal, one that concerns not only the structural character of constituted thought but also the very structures through which subjectivity necessarily manifests itself in its rational activity. This new conception of the formal considers "forms as principles" which are the states *(Bestände) essentially necessary* to a rational subjectivity in general, without which this latter could not be thought. Now rational subjectivity is required by one of these necessities to refer to a *hylé* as the foundation for the possible experiences that are necessarily presupposed for the activity of judging. Also the concept of *hylé* is itself a form-concept. But, on the other hand, it is not essentially required of subjectivity to operate on one or another *hylé*, be it a color, a sound, or whatever. Hence the Apriori of the rational structures must necessarily refer to a *hylé*, but it can be considered as independent of every *hylé*. This formal Apriori is the Apriori belonging to pure reason, or, as Husserl says, "introducing an old word that tended blindly in the same direction" (30), it is an "innate" Apriori. Then formal logic is no longer only the theory of the possible forms of theory, according to the con-

5. *Philosophie der Arithmetik* already employs the term *Formbegriffe*: "With full legitimacy the concepts something and one, plurality and cardinal number, these concepts that are the most universal and the most void of content, may be designated form-concepts or categories" (p. 91). On the distinction between *"sachhaltige Begriffe"* and *"Formbegriffe"* cf. *Erf. u. Urt.*, § 85, pp. 407–8.

ception of the *Prolegomena;* it is, according to *Formal and Transcendental Logic,* "the science in which pure theoretical reason accomplishes a complete investigation of its own sense and perfectly Objectivates itself in a system of principles" (31), which is a "complete system of this formal Apriori in the most fundamental sense" (30). We can estimate the length of the road traveled by Husserl after the *Prolegomena* by opposing the following two affirmations. In the *Prolegomena* he writes that, far from taking concepts of the understanding and reason as "mythical" concepts, he takes them as "simple indications meant to orient us toward the form of thinking and its ideal laws, which pertain to the logic and not to the empirical psychology of cognition."[6] And in the *Cartesian Meditations,* which are of the same period as *Formal and Transcendental Logic,* he writes: "Reason is not an accidental de facto ability, not a title for possible accidental matters of fact, but rather a title for an all-embracing essentially necessary structural form belonging to all transcendental subjectivity."[7] Thus the formal assumes a dignity which gives it full rights within the sphere of transcendental philosophy. And henceforth we will see outlined the unity which connects the problems of formal logic in the traditional sense with the problems of transcendental logic.

Husserl ends these Preparatory Considerations by emphasizing what he calls the "two-sidedness" of logic. What traditional logic studies are concepts, judgments, deductions, theories, etc. – in a word, "thought-formations" *(Denkgebilde).* From a theoretical viewpoint, logic, at its highest level, considers that which makes for the *systematic unity* of the totality of theoretical truths constituting a theory. Thus conceived, logic is therefore exclusively focused upon the results of thinking. But if logic intends to be the ultimate understanding of science, it must not limit itself to this objective focus. It must direct its examination equally toward the forms of cognizing subjectivity. These forms are "deeply hidden." Only a reflective attitude will enable us to unveil them. To be sure, by the very fact of its normative interests, traditional logic refers to subjectivity. But the activity of thinking is then brought in only through normative regulation: How must one operate in order to arrive at such and such a *result?* No genuine description is called for. The

6. *Prolegomena,* p. 214.
7. *CM,* p. 57.

logician's interest remains fixed upon the objective result, and subjectivity, properly speaking, is not thematized. Even when logic comes to problems of the justification of theories and hence to the subjective problems of evidence, it considers these problems only as transient themes which are to lead to the validation of objective results. Here the logician conforms to the style of the sciences. Actually the sciences develop exclusively on the theoretical plane. The important thing for the sciences is always to understand better and better the provinces with which they are occupied, seeking all the while to eliminate any intrusion of the subjective into their objective themes.

In emulation of the sciences, logic has hence developed with a focus solely on the primary theme of Objectivity, even though it must have a two-fold theme and hence a subjective theme. But what is much more serious, logic has not been fully aware of the exclusiveness of its interest. Its theme has not been "consciously and purely" related to the logical formations; logic has not understood that its normative and practical interests are secondary, that its essential interest is to be purely theoretical. It has found a way to be a one-sided discipline and at the same time to present a "hybrid" character by masking its objective preoccupations by normative interests that lead it into a superficial subjective study.[8]

The *Prolegomena* has the merit of grasping the objective problems of logic in their purity. But it does not foresee the transcendental dimension of subjective research, and it would consider every systematic subjective examination a relapse into the psychologism against which it struggled. On the contrary, after having resumed the examination of the essential structures of traditional objective logic, *Formal and Transcendental Logic* is going to devote itself to the examination of the two-fold theme of logic in the genuine sense.

8. Husserl does not mean by this that logic should not have normative functions. Logic is *essentially* pure logic, theoretical logic, but it has normative functions derivatively; not that it *is* normative, but rather that it *becomes* normative. Cf. *FTL*, § 7, and *Prolegomena*, Chaps. 1 and 2.

Part I

The Structures and the Sphere
of Objective Formal Logic

[A.] The Way from the Tradition to the Full Idea of Formal Logic

1 / Formal Logic
as Apophantic Analytics

PART I OF *Formal and Transcendental Logic* is
devoted to the study of traditional formal logic, a study that will
make the pure delimitation of the specific sense of this logic
possible and that will result in an extension that fully com-
pletes it.

Logic is considered under the Aristotelian perspective in
the first chapter. Thus understood, logic is located in the formal
sphere and is designated, as it was by Aristotle, by the name
"analytics" to distinguish it from a logic that deals with material spheres of cognition governed by "synthetic" laws. And
since it has the assertion, the predicative judgment, for its
theme, it is more precisely designated by the name "apophantic
analytics" (from *apophansis:* assertion). In order to delimit
this apophantic formal logic in a distinct fashion, let us recall
the distinction between categories of signification and categories of the object introduced by the *Logische Untersuchungen.*[1] Husserl makes explicit reference to them in Chapter 2
of *Formal and Transcendental Logic.* The signification-cate-
gories include concepts "pertaining to the essence of the proposition"[2] — for example, the concepts of concept, proposition,

1. *Prolegomena,* Chapter 11, in particular p. 244; see also Vol. II,
Pt. I, Fourth Investigation and *Ideen,* pp. 22 ff.
2. *Ideen,* p. 24.

[3]

subject-form, predicate-form, nominal form, adjective form, etc. The proposition is considered as a simple signification.[3] One does not seek to study *through it* the object of which it speaks. These categories of signification have the categories of the object—for example, the concepts of object, unity, plurality, number, property, relation, identity, equality, totality, whole and part, state-of-affairs,[4] and so on—for *correlates*. In effect, one can say that an object has this or that property, is identical with this or that other object, or forms a totality with other objects.

Formal logic can be situated on either the level of the signification or the level of the object. In the first case it would be a matter of apophantic analytics, which studies the judgment as propositional form; in the second case it would be a matter of ontological analytics, which studies the object in general from the purely formal point of view. Later we will show the relations between these two formal disciplines. At the stage of the first chapter, we remain within the framework of apophantic analytics alone. In order to avoid confusion, notice that Husserl often calls apophantic analytics simply "analytics," remaining in the Aristotelian tradition, which has never known formal ontology. But as we shall see, formal ontology is also an analytics, for in no way does it consider the content of cognition, the materially determinate objects.

The first chapter opens with a key notion, that of the *stratification* of logic. To classify the problems of logic, to arrange and hierarchize the tasks that logic must take up, is the usual thing. But logic itself remains a theory situated on one plane only. Logic is a *unified* theory, and this unity confers on logic the dignity of a science that can master the totality of its prob-

3. It is necessary to understand clearly in what sense Husserl employs the term signification. "Signification" has no place here as the correlate of "expression" but must be understood as the correlate of "object." We say that the proposition, the subject-form, etc., *are* significations, *not* that they *have* a signification.

4. The state-of-affairs (*Sachverhalt*) is the objective correlate of the judgment, just as the affair or thing (*Sache*) is the objective correlate of the concept. But the notion of state-of-affairs gives rise to much more complex problems than would appear from this rapid characterization. It can be completely accounted for only when numerous phenomenological distinctions are brought in. (We introduce these below; cf. pp. 148 f.

lems. In contrast to this, *Formal and Transcendental Logic* insists on the clarifying power of a separation of logic into several theories that are *founded* one *upon* another. In the first place, at the fundamental level, there is a pure morphology of judgments; next comes the logic of non-contradiction; lastly the logic of truth. This stratification was already outlined in the *Logische Untersuchungen,* but, by Husserl's own admission, in a still rudimentary form. In order to appreciate the new distinctions made by *Formal and Transcendental Logic* better, let us see how the stratification of logic is presented in the former work.

The goal of the Fourth Logical Investigation is to show that one can distinguish and *separately* consider an *elementary* logical stratum upon which the remainder of the logical edifice is founded. This fundamental stratum, called the *pure morphology of significations* or the *pure logical grammar,* is characterized by the following problems: How can significations be put together to make a new signification, and how can this be done without considering the objective validity of these significations? Translated into non-Husserlian language: How can one put propositional expressions together—propositions and elements of propositions—in such a way as to obtain a more complex expression that has a unity, and how can one do so on the basis of the simple form—and without considering the sense—of these expressions? Hence, according to *apriori forms,* the laws of this elementary logical stratum determine which significations belonging to the different categories of signification are unified to form a *unitary* signification and not a *chaos* of significations. From the normative point of view, these laws are precisely intended to prevent assemblages of signification "devoid of sense"—simple unorganized heaps which Husserl calls nonsense *(Unsinn).* In the Husserlian terminology this term "nonsense" characterizes what is unacceptable on this first logical stratum in a *specific* manner. Now current usage confuses under the term nonsense (or expressions without signification, expressions devoid of sense) things very different from the ones phenomenological analysis means to distinguish.[5] We commonly say, for example, that we utter a series of words devoid of sense when we say: "King but

5. *Log. Unt.,* Vol. II, Pt. I, pp. 54 ff. (First Investigation).

where seems and";[6] but we say equivalently that the expression "a round square" is devoid of sense. Husserl reserves the word nonsense to designate the first type of expression without signification. Each word taken separately has a sense, but the totality of words does not form a genuine proposition. Every nonsense is excluded from the morphology of significations because, properly speaking, it is not a signification. On the contrary, the expression "a round square" has a sense for this first logical stratum; it is a well-formed unity, and one must go beyond the level of morphology in order to characterize what it is that makes it an expression "devoid of sense." This denomination — "devoid of sense" — then has a new sense. Hence the phenomenologist must not scorn ordinary language, filled as it is with equivocations, if he wants to make the essential distinctions.

Thus with morphology there appears a theory in its own right. But what does it teach us? Rules, we must say — which goes without saying. What does it forbid? Pure nonsense, the utterance of which would never occur to anyone. Husserl is the first to recognize that the systematic search for all the possible forms of signification and all the possible forms of their connection has no practical value. But taking such a state of affairs as a pretext for denouncing the vanity of this area of study is to recognize only practical value and to remain blind to properly theoretical value. The most modest teacher of logic experiences a very common resistance to pure theory when he encounters the peremptory and banal question: But what use is there for all these subtleties of the logical apparatus? The pure morphology of significations has no practical value, and that is that. But, Husserl says, the theoretical interest attaching to it is "all the greater."[7] "All the greater" — this is a provocative ex-

---

6. We adopt the material examples that Husserl uses. But of course the *pure* morphology of significations must in principle consider only *formalized* expressions, expressions where all reference to the material of cognition is excluded. This *pure* morphology is to be based on formalized expressions such as *A and B* (well-formed expression), *A non B* (nonsense), A and B designating, e.g., propositions. In the same way that the most primitive requirement, when we express ourselves, is to respect coherence on the level of language, so too in logical language the most primitive requirement is to respect coherence on the level of formalized language, a coherence whose rules are provided by the pure logical grammar.

7. *Log. Unt.*, Vol. II, Pt. I, p. 332.

pression, but it loses its paradoxical ring for those whose lives are devoted to theoretical interests. Every mind acclimatized to the style of logic will gladly welcome this revindication of the exclusively theoretical interest. But for Husserl it is not only the logician who can give himself over to such an interest in pure theory; it is also, and above all, the philosopher who is, by his calling, theoretician par excellence.[8]

Once this level is completed, the study of the elements and structures of signification reaches a new set of problems on a higher level—problems which involve questions of the *possible truth* of significations. In the first logical stratum only the coherence of logical language was under consideration. Now questions of properly logical coherence, coherence regulated by the laws of logic in the strict sense, appear; the laws of non-contradiction, *modus ponens,* etc. At this level only those significations whose constituent significations are mutually *compatible* and capable of leading to truth are relevant. The coherence of logical language is a condition for properly logical coherence, but it is not a sufficient condition. In addition, the constituent significations must not contradict one another.

The laws of the first level protect us against nonsense; the laws of the next higher level protect us against formal (or analytic) *countersense (Widersinn)*, against formal absurdity. The choice of examples could mislead the reader, for those Husserl offers in the Fourth Investigation are all examples of material (or synthetic) countersense, examples where the concrete intervenes, such as: "a round square," "wooden iron," "all squares having five angles." Formal countersense is a purely formal incompatibility, abstraction being made from all material of cognition, such as "All A's are B's, including some that are not B's." [9] By and large, the examples given in the *Logische Untersuchungen* are material examples, while those given in *Formal and Transcendental Logic* are usually formalized. This is because the *Logische Untersuchungen* are "investigations" that want to "stimulate thinking" and take examples which by their material character are easier to understand. On the other hand, *Formal and Transcendental Logic* is a systematic work, and here there is no fear of imposing an abstract form of exposition upon the reader. But when it is a question

8. *Ibid.*, p. 341.
9. Example from *FTL*, p. 71.

of differentiating between nonsense and countersense, the conclusions are the same, whether one takes a material or a formal countersense for an example. The propositions: "All squares have five angles" and "All A's are B's, including some that are not B's," are both admitted by pure morphology. They are not nonsensical. Considered according to their propositional structure, they are "honorable propositions" (*ehrliche Sätze*). But they are countersensical and must thus be excluded from the sphere of logic above the morphology.

This second logical sphere, the sphere of logic properly so-called, is not studied in the *Logische Untersuchungen*. One of the tasks of *Formal and Transcendental Logic* is to study this higher sphere, which itself is divided into two strata. In the *Logische Untersuchungen* it is envisaged only in opposition to pure morphology, which is the central theme examined. The original plan of the Fourth Investigation is to prove that one can separately consider a logical theory which is essential to logic but does not raise questions of non-contradiction. To consider the morphology as a theory in its own right was a new conception that authorized a special study restricted to that theory and permitted clarification of numerous problems, e.g., the relation between logic and grammar.

> Nothing else has so greatly confused discussion of the question of the correct relationship between logic and grammar as has the continual confounding of the two logical spheres that we have distinguished sharply as the lower and the upper and have characterized by means of their negative counterparts: the sphere of nonsense and the sphere of [formal][10] countersense.[11]

We can say that logic has nothing in common with grammar if we understand by logic the sphere of the higher level. But the situation is completely different if we consider the sphere of the lower level. To be specific, in the Fourth Investigation Husserl willingly designates the morphology of significations with the expression *pure grammar*. There is, according to Husserl, an explicable Apriori in language itself, an Apriori that is not to be confused with a group of general characteristics distinguished in comparative grammar or historical studies. The idea of a universal grammar, so dear to the rationalism of the

10. [Inserted in the second edition (Cairns's translator's note).]
11. *Log. Unt.*, Vol. II, Pt. I, p. 341.

seventeenth and eighteenth centuries, reappears in Husserl. "Likewise in the grammatical sphere there is a fixed measure, an apriori norm, that must not be transgressed";[12] "language has not only physiological, psychological, and culture-historical, but also apriori foundations." [13] Hence the apriori laws of the structural compatibility of significations proclaimed by morphology have a grammatical "bearing." To be sure, the grammatical rules for the connection of the parts of discourse relate, to a great extent, to entirely contingent usages which vary with the linguistic society. But besides these empirical factors there are the apriori universals which appear more or less distinctly in the laws of grammar. That a universal grammar has its place Husserl sees represented in the fact that one can, for example, pose this sort of question: How do German, Latin, Chinese, etc., express "the" categorial proposition, "the" plural, and so forth? It could be objected that Husserl takes for apriori characteristics precisely the characteristics which are common to several languages without, for all that, being "universal"; and it can further be objected that the universal invariants that one can distinguish are the basis for only a very poor science. But we do not want to revive the debate over the possibility of a "general and reasoned grammar," the more so because our lack of linguistic competence could only lead us to naïve and prejudiced judgments. We only want to discuss Husserl's philosophical options.

In *Formal and Transcendental Logic* Husserl rarely employs the expression "pure grammar." Must we see in this an evolution where the problems of language are concerned? Has he renounced the idea of a universal grammar? We believe not. In the *Cartesian Meditations*,[14] written the year that *Formal and Transcendental Logic* appeared, Husserl recalls the contribution of phenomenology to the building up of a general ontology of the objective world and includes pure grammar among the apriori sciences that phenomenology led to. On this point, what distinguishes the *Logische Untersuchungen* and *Formal and Transcendental Logic* from each other is their different approach to the themes of logic. The *Logische Unter-*

12. *Ibid.,* p. 336.
13. *Ibid.,* p. 338. [Part of a paragraph inserted in the second edition (Cairns's translator's note).]
14. *CM,* p. 138.

suchungen arrives at the themes of logic after numerous preparatory studies that thematize the problems of language. On the other hand, as we have seen, *Formal and Transcendental Logic* soon concentrates on the themes proper to logic. But this difference should not make us forget that if logic is a mediating theme in the *Logische Untersuchungen*, it is not only that. In particular, the center of interest of the Fourth Investigation is not the building up of a universal grammar, taken in all its breadth, but rather the building up of a pure grammar that can serve as a basis for logic. In the second edition of the *Logische Untersuchungen*[15] Husserl specifies that, in order to indicate the first stratum of logic, it would be preferable to substitute for the expression "pure grammar" *(reine Grammatik)*, employed in the first edition, the expression "pure logical grammar" *(rein-logische Grammatik)* in order to emphasize the restriction of this pure grammar to the logical sphere. This is because the pure morphology does not embrace the totality of the Aprioris relevant to universal grammar; Husserl says, for example, "to the relationships of mutual understanding among psychic persons—relationships that have so great an influence on grammar—there belongs in fact an Apriori of their own." [16] In the Introduction to the Fourth Investigation, and in a sentence added in the second edition, Husserl does not even trouble to explain what the Aprioris outside the sphere of logic could be: "Here the extent to which yet other spheres of an Apriori belonging to pure grammar can be brought to light lies outside the limits of our interest." [17] If, meanwhile, during the course of the Fourth Investigation Husserl considers the problems of pure logic in their universality, it is because he had to give new force to the idea of an apriori grammar—an idea that had been abandoned by the linguists of that period, whose whole concern was with the empirical methods of comparative grammar. He wanted to react against the tendency in his own era, an era where the sense of the Apriori "threatened, almost, to atrophy." For Husserl, it is necessary to "learn by heart" that "here, as everywhere else that philosophic interests are active, it is of

15. *Log. Unt.*, Vol. II, Pt. I, p. 340.
16. *Ibid.* [Part of a paragraph inserted in the second edition (Cairns's translator's note).]
17. *Ibid.*, p. 295. [A sentence inserted in the second edition (Cairns's translator's note).]

the greatest importance sharply to separate the Apriori." [18] The atrophy of the Apriori is a true philosophical malady.

The only time in the course of the *Formal and Transcendental Logic* that Husserl refers to the denomination "pure logical grammar" employed in the *Logische Untersuchungen,* he does so with care to avoid absolutely any confusion with an empirical grammar. And he adds with a condensation which the very slow exposition of the Fourth Investigation often lacks: "[I]t is . . . not without reason that people often say that formal logic has let itself be guided by grammar. In the case of theory of forms, however, this is not a reproach but a necessity – provided that, for guided by grammar (a word intended to bring to mind *de facto* historical languages and their grammatical description), guidance by the grammatical itself be substituted." [19]

Let us now return to the stratification of logic in the more elaborate form given it in *Formal and Transcendental Logic.*

First level: Pure morphology of judgments. – *Formal and Transcendental Logic* repeats in their broad outlines the series of tasks that the Fourth Investigation establishes for the pure morphology of significations. Notice that Husserl has replaced the term signification with the term judgment. He does not explain this change in vocabulary, but the reasons for it are clear. To employ the term judgment is to adhere to a strictly logical terminology, which is appropriate to the scope of *Formal and Transcendental Logic.* Also, without denigrating the demand for essential distinctions, this employment preserves the notion of signification, more normally correlated with the notion of expression than with the notion of object.

Judgments may be classified according to their simple forms. One classification of the different forms of judgments leads us to see that among themselves these forms have relationships of *subordination.* There are *fundamental* forms (e.g., the form S *is* p[20]), from which one can engender the other forms by *derivation.* Hence the morphology is to indicate the funda-

18. *Ibid.,* p. 337. [Part of a much longer passage substituted in the second edition for fifteen lines of the first edition (Cairns's translator's note).]

19. *FTL,* pp. 70–71.

20. If one limits himself to the categorial judgment, it is necessary to say that there is only one truly fundamental form: S *is* p. For ex-

mental forms of judgment and their internal structure and to examine the processes by which the other forms can be derived from these fundamental forms. Next, the fundamental forms of *connexion* between forms of judgments considered this time as unanalyzed totalities are to be established (e.g., the conjunctive connexion between two judgments A and A'). With this notion of the connexion among forms of judgment, the notion of operation appears in a quite natural manner. It is a curious thing, however, that the term *operation* is not employed in the Fourth Investigation to designate these modes of connexion, even though Husserl relates them to arithmetical operations. On the contrary, the notion of operation is here brought to the fore. It even comes in among the forms of judgment: "the form 'S is p' is more original than the form 'Sp is q,'" which is an operational transformation of it, namely by the operation of converting a predicate into an attribute" (52). Thus, in a general way, the concept of operation can be understood as a *guiding concept* for the investigation of forms, forms deriving one from another by operational transformations. If, for example, we consider two forms of judgment of any sort A, A', the result *A and A'* from the conjunctional connexion of these two forms is still a form of proposition that in its turn can be subjected to the same operation and enter into conjunctional connexion with a third form of any sort A'', which yields *(A and A') and A''*, and thus *in infinitum*. Thus a law is extracted that dominates the whole of morphology: *every operational law carries with it a law of reiteration*. From the fact that operations can be reiterated, one can construct the infinity of possible forms. But the notion of operation can be extended, and then one can "take the point of view of operation so broadly that one regards even the fundamental form 'S is p' as an operation: the operation of determining a determinable substrate, S. Similarly, one will then regard every modalization as a form-productive operation that transmutes the sense in a certain manner" (52). But as J. Cavaillès correctly remarks:

> Husserl is concerned neither with explicitly bringing out an internal justification for the unity of the notion of operation thus understood, nor a principle of diversification that connects the

---

ample, S *is not* p is considered by Husserl not as a fundamental form on a par with the form S *is* p but as a variant of it; cf. *Erf. u. Urt.*, p. 353.

rather heterogeneous aspects that it assumes, such as those of simple apophantic combination (conjunction and disjunction) and modalization.[21]

To be sure, Husserl recognizes in a brief remark that the concept of operation extended to modalization is separated from the narrow concept of operation by the fact that "modalization is plainly not a matter of arbitrary transmutation" (52). An "operation" taken in the usual sense of an abstract operation can be performed without restriction. One can put various operations together arbitrarily, and one can perform arbitrary reiterations. This is not the case with modalization.

Second level: The logic of non-contradiction or logic of consequence.—Above the level of morphology is the level of the science of all possible forms of true judgments. It being given that this second discipline envisages only *possible* forms of true judgments—hence the conditions for the truth of judgments—we are not yet on the level of a truth-logic; we are "concerned merely with whether the judgment-members included in a whole judgment, no matter how simple or how complex it may be, are 'compatible' with one another or contradict one another and thereby make the whole judgment itself a contradictory judgment, one that cannot be made 'properly'" (54). This logical discipline is to exclude formal countersense such as "All A's are B's, including some that are not B's" (71). Husserl reserves the name pure analytic (*pure Analytik*) for this discipline, which constitutes the second level of formal logic taken in its totality and is designated as analytic in the broad sense. Here Husserl indicates a *restriction* on the word pure (*pure* in German), a restriction to the second level of logic (or, if one wants, to the whole made up of the first and second levels, the first being the condition). When he speaks of *pure* analytics (*reine Analytik*), he wants to emphasize the formal purity of the analytics, whether the analytics be taken in a broad or a narrow sense.[22] The *Logische Untersuchungen* does not

21. Jean Cavaillès, *Sur la logique et la théorie de la science* (Paris, 1947), p. 45 [our translation].

22. It happens that Husserl uses in the same sentence the expressions *pure Analytik* and *reine Analytik*. We have attempted to render this distinction in French by translating *pure Analytik* as *pure analytique* and *reine Analytik* as *analytique pure*. [In Cairns's English translation the original German is given in square brackets after the English phrase "pure analytics." (Translator's note.)]

recognize this analytic in the narrow sense as itself a discipline solely concerned with questions of non-contradiction, quite apart from the question of truth; on the level above that of pure logical grammar, possible truth is a problem just as much as the compatibility of significations. From the *Logische Untersuchungen* to *Formal and Transcendental Logic* there is a clear shift in interest indicating a progressive differentiation. The task of the *Logische Untersuchungen* is to justify the description of structures as a discipline in itself, without reference to the demands of coherence and possible truth. Then the task of *Formal and Transcendental Logic*, with the results of the *Logische Untersuchungen* taken into account, is to distinguish a logic of non-contradiction quite apart from any question of possible truth. A judgment can be non-contradictory without being a true judgment. Appendix III tells us that

> the fundamentally essential part of the doctrine stated in the main text is, in my opinion, the thesis that, as they function in the whole of formal analytics, compatibility, contradiction, . . . can and must be defined in a pure sense, one that contains no reference to the truth or falsity of the judgments.[23]

Husserl also calls this level of logic the logic of consequence. The laws of deduction originally arise from this level. In deductions one can consider the analytical relationships of implication and exclusion without bringing in the notions of truth and falsity as themes.[24]

Third and last level: The logic of truth. — Hence we must rise once more to a higher level in order to reach a formal logic of truth which establishes *the formal laws of possible truth.* From now on Husserl allots the tasks of such a formal truth-logic. Since non-contradiction is the condition for possible truth, it is initially of value to explore the sphere of non-contradiction. Moreover, and above all, the logic of truth is the terminal point of formal logic, and at this highest of levels we see the difficulties that the relationships between formal logic and transcendental logic give rise to. Hence the formal logic of truth comes to deal with problems that are, so to speak, terminal, something which presupposes a prior penetration.

23. *FTL,* p. 332.
24. We will soon return (p. 23) to this denomination of the logic of consequence.

Actually, the "mere predelineation of the separations with which the last sections are concerned, separations that must be made in formal logic, is not enough. There is need of more penetrating substantiations" (56). *Formal and Transcendental Logic* then becomes oriented toward its first subjective investigations. Investigations of grounds, so far as they necessarily refer to noetic intentionality—for the logical formations originate in categorial activity—are directed into subjectivity. A phenomenological sense-investigation must then explicate the different evidences[25] corresponding to the three levels of logic in order to be able to understand absolutely the necessity and bearing of this stratification. Thus the objective logical theory can only be grounded if one considers it as the correlate of the subjective activity of cognition.

A judgment can be given in very different subjective manners:

1. It can be completely vague and confused, as is the case when a vague idea comes to mind.
2. It can also be a distinct judgment—and this is what must, properly speaking, be called a judgment. The distinct judgment can also be said to be explicit, for the process of distinguishing *(Verdeutlichung)* which transforms a judgment from a vague state to a distinct state is a process of explicating.

What complicates the relationships between confused judgments and distinct judgments is the fact that the difference between confused and distinct already appears on the level of language. Take the case of reading without concentration. One can read in such a way as to follow the distinct organization of a sentence without truly *thinking* of what one is reading. Distinct reading, empty thinking. Hence the judgment can be distinct on the level of language while the corresponding thought is not distinct. If the language is a true language, it carries a distinct organization in it. But when there is a jumble of words—the nonsense proscribed by morphology—then it is the language which is confused. This "distinctness" of lan-

25. We shall see later that the Husserlian theory of evidence in its fundamental character allows for various degrees and types of evidence.

guage deriving from grammatical organization is revealed to us by the organization of the sounds themselves:

> The verbal sounds have their indications, which, in themselves, refer interdependently to one another and are built one on another. The sounds conjoin to make the unity of a word-formation, which in turn consists of relatively self-contained formations. Each of these is bearer of a unity of indication; and the whole is a self-contained unity, which has noetically the phenomenological characteristic of associative self-containedness and on the parallel side (noematically) the phenomenological characteristic that consists in the self-containedness of an indicated "significational" unity, built correspondingly out of indicated formations (57).

This is why Husserl says that "the whole support of form-construction is *speech*" (70) and that, "without the definite articulation of vague judgments by means of the sensuous articulations of verbal signs, no theory of forms, no logic whatever, would be possible—and, of course, no science either" (71). Thus the very rhythm of language is an invitation to think distinctly. Are we to recognize in this that logic depends on the sensible side of language in such a way that in its totality the logical edifice is in continuity with an irreducible "factualness"? Let us look more closely at the role of this organization of the sounds of a sentence. An associative synthesis makes a unity from a cluster of sounds. This synthesis proceeds passively and "indicates" its progress to thinking. Thus the passive synthesis of the sounds of language has a preconstitutive role. This passive synthesis is not referred to in the *Logische Untersuchungen*. At the time it was written, association did not have for Husserl the fundamental role it came to have later.[26] On the other hand, *Formal and Transcendental Logic* always emphasizes that passive syntheses precede activity in the proper sense. If, within the concrete situation of the activity of judging, one takes the place of a being who judges, one sees that he does not judge in an active way to begin with, that he does not initially judge "in the proper sense." In the concrete situation, he begins with a vague opinion that has become equivocal through some association, or passively he listens to someone who is speaking. He who reads, for example, lets himself go along with the rhythm of reading without continually accom-

26. Cf. *infra*, Part II, Chapter 6.

panying his reading with an active thinking, without rethinking the judgments he reads. "In ordinary reading, we by no means have, combined with that, an accompanying articulation of actual thinking, of thinking produced from the Ego, member by member, in synthetic activity" (56). All reading in its first stages is to some extent a distracted reading.

As we have said, language is an "index," but it is not only this. Thanks to the passive synthesis of sounds, "this course of thinking proper *is only indicated* (by the passively flowing synthesis of the sensuous verbal sounds) as a course of thinking to be performed" (56). The "sensuous" organization of the sounds of language is definitely a condition for starting, but it is no more than a preface to the activity of thinking in the proper sense. And the fact that logic is separated into levels permits it to become independent of these initial conditions without denying them.

3. In the process of explicating the thinking that renders an initially vague judgment distinct, there is no question of a possible adequation to the things. This is why Husserl frequently uses the word *opinion* ⟨or meaning⟩ instead of the word judgment in order the better to indicate that it is a matter of judgments presumed to be true, the confirmation of whose truth is at that time not proposed. But if we place ourselves in the perspective of adequation, then a new manner of the givenness of the judgment appears, which Husserl calls the mode of *clarity*. When what is judged "through" a judgment comes to be given "in person," when the judgment is recognized as a true judgment due to its contact with the things ⟨or affairs⟩ "themselves," then the judgment is not only distinct but is also *clear*. "To judge explicitly is not *per se* to judge with 'clarity': Judging with 'clarity' has at once clarity of the affairs . . . and clarity of the predicatively formed affair-complex in the whole judging." [27] Thus distinctness and clarity are no longer the two criteria of evidence; each is a criterion of an evidence.

27. *FTL*, p. 61. As an example of a distinct but unclear expression Husserl several times cites the expression "regular decahedron" (cf. *FTL*, p. 284; *Log. Unt.*, Vol. II, Pt. I, p. 55; *Ideen*, Book III, p. 101). On the one hand, the expression *"regular decahedron"* is distinct on the level of language; it follows the grammatical rules of the connection of the substantive and the adjective. On the other hand, the thought of a regular polygon of ten sides, enclosed in this expression, can be rendered distinct. But such a regular polygon is a mathematical coun-

Here, as Husserl says, "two evidences become separated" (60): evidence of distinctness and evidence of clarity, the evidence of clarity being an evidence on a level higher than that of distinctness. The process of distinguishing would explicate the confused judgment, the process of *clarifying* would in turn bring about the fulfillment of the distinct judgment. Hence we see the precise sense we are to give to the Husserlian notion of clarification *(Klärung)*. Clarification is only to be understood in the perspective of an adequation.

Let us now come back to the stratification of apophantics. Pure analytics in the strict sense, that is to say, the logic of non-contradiction, is singularly occupied with distinct judgments. On the one hand – in fact, at the stage of coherent thinking – the problems of adequation remain outside the framework of analytics in the strict sense. The evidence of clarity is not involved. Only the evidence of distinctness is required. Hence the fundamental question of analytics can be formulated: When are judgments as such, of any sort and of simple form, possible within the unity of a more complex judgment and according to what relations? In this it is thoroughly understood that, when we say "judgment" without qualification, we understand the distinct judgment, the judgment "proper," which is the theme of analytics in the strict sense.

Problems of the evidence of clarity are presented only on the level of truth-logic. The separation between the logic of non-contradiction and the logic of truth is grounded in the separation between the evidence of distinctness and the evidence of clarity. But we need to avoid the absurdities that the interpretation of such a separation might lead us into. In the first place, by introducing the problems of adequation to the things, we still do not leave the framework of purely *formal* considerations. When we read (in the pure analytics) that we must never "go beyond distinct evidence, [but] we go beyond this apriori sphere, as soon as we ask questions concerning truth" (65), it is necessary thoroughly to understand that we do, to be sure, go beyond the apriori sphere of the evidence of dis-

---

tersense. Actually, according to a mathematical theorem, there are only five species of regular polygons: the tetrahedron, the cube, the octahedron, the dodecahedron, and the icosahedron. If we think "in the light of the things," we cannot think the notion of a regular decahedron.

tinctness, but we do so in order to reach the *sphere, also apriori,* of the evidence of clarity. The *formal* position of a logic of truth is neatly explicated by Husserl: "What then does it signify, to seek formally universal eidetic insight concerning possible judicial truth?" (65). To take a stand concerning the *actual* truth of the judgment, it would be necessary to consider the "stuff" of this judgment. How do we recognize whether a judgment is true if we do not concretely know the things spoken about in it? But this is not the problem of the *formal* logic of truth, for that logic considers only the *possible* truth of the judgment. On the other hand, by including the problems of adequation to the things in its theme, the formal logic of truth does not leave the framework of apophantics. To be sure, a true judgment is a judgment that has an adequate relation to the object. But the object is not thematized, and the problems of formal ontology are not entered into. "The predicate truth does indeed relate to judgments and only to judgments" (65).

But what have we gained, then, in going beyond the logic of non-contradiction and the sphere of the evidence of distinctness, if we are forbidden to take a stand concerning the actual truth of the judgment and effectively to arrive at a cognition of the object? In truth, nothing substantial is acquired with a formal logic of truth. Properly speaking, a new domain is not explored. Only the perspective of examination is changed. New *thematic interests* emerge. It is a question of exchanging "the theoretical focusing on mere judgments for the *focusing on cognition*" (65), that is to say, the attitude in which one is interested not only in judgments considered in themselves but also, by means of them, in a cognition of the object. Hence a *change in focus* is called for when we pass from the logic of non-contradiction to the formal logic of truth. Furthermore, only reference to the corresponding subjective modes of evidence can truly ground the separation between these two disciplines. Hence, in this subjective investigation, the superiority of truth-logic to the logic of non-contradiction can be appreciated. By attaining the formal logic of truth I do not *know* more —I *am* in another way. Hence I know better. I know that, beyond the questions to which the second discipline of logic is limited, there are other questions to be raised by another discipline. What is more, this new discipline is not juxtaposed to

the first one but is superior to it, since it studies judgments not taken as ends in themselves but in their true *purpose*. To judge is to judge in order to know:

> Now the judgments are thought of from the very beginning, not as mere judgments, but as judgments pervaded by a dominant *cognitional striving*, as meanings that have to become *fulfilled*, that are not objects by themselves, like the data arising from mere distinctness, but passages to the "truths" themselves that are to be attained (65).

This change in focus is indicated at the level of language by a substitution of the vocabulary of truth for the vocabulary of non-contradiction and consequence. The principle of *modus ponens*, for example, is enunciated in the logic of non-contradiction in the following form (and, in this form, it is also the genuine *deductive* principle):

From the two judgments: "If M, then N" and "M," the judgment "N" follows analytically.

Stated in logic of truth:

If between any two judgments "M" and "N" there exists an immediate relationship of antecedent to consequent, then the truth of the antecedent entails the truth of the consequent.

Hence Husserl has distinguished the three manners of the givenness of the judgment: one can judge in a confused fashion, a distinct fashion, and in a clear fashion. The process of distinguishing which brings the judgment from confusion to distinctness and the process of clarifying that brings the judgment from simple distinctness to clarity appear as two essentially different processes. Meanwhile Husserl tells us that the first and second modes of judgment "obviously have *a relationship similar*" (69) to that which exists between the second and third modes. Fundamentally, only clarification is "fulfillment." The judgment is fulfilled only when it is evident in relation to the state-of-affairs. But in a certain sense the notion of fulfillment can be transposed. Let us consider a distinct but empty judgment. Once clarification is carried out, we say that we are dealing with the *same* judgment which was empty and now is fulfilled. Now consider a confused judgment. If we have succeeded in rendering it distinct, we say that we are dealing with the *same* judgment, formerly confused and now distinct. Hence in the two cases there is an analogous process of

identification, an identifying "synthesis." If one pays attention to the terminus of the *cognitional* striving, that is to say, the possible possession of the things themselves *(Selbsthabe)*, one says that a judgment that is only distinct is empty. It is from this point of view — which is the original point of view — that one must understand the passage in *Erfahrung und Urteil*[28] where it is said unreservedly that *Verdeutlichung* (distinguishing) in its specific Husserlian sense is an "explication within *empty consciousness*." Certainly, however, in a very relative sense, we can already consider the stage of distinctness as a terminus. The intending that is linked to an interest which is uniquely attached to coherence, which stops at the level of theory as systematic totality of coherent statements, has distinctness as its terminus. And it is in this entirely relative sense that the following affirmation by Husserl is to be understood: "Confused judging bears within itself — not always, but (as we have said) in the nexus of a theoretical interest — an aiming, which is directed to the distinct judgment and which, if it attains this, becomes *fulfilled* therein" (69). In an absolute sense one can only speak of the fulfillment which leads the distinct but empty judgment and the clear judgment to coincidence *(Deckung)*. But in an analogous fashion one can say that there is a "parallel fulfillment-synthesis that effects the coincidence of a confused and distinct judgment" (69). Even in this latter case one can also speak of a giving of the things themselves — understanding, of course, that here the "thing" ⟨or "affair"⟩ is the judgment as such and not its objective correlate. The judgment which is only distinct can only be a judgment presumed to be true; it is not a clear judgment but only an opinion; nevertheless, it is there "in person" and not masked by a confused manner of givenness. In sum, we see that on the level of simple distinctness we can employ — in a purely relative manner, it is true — the language which applies *stricto sensu* to the sphere of clarity *(Erfüllung, Selbsthabe, Deckung)*.

But the identifying synthesis must be conceived even more broadly. In the most favorable cases it can happen that a confused judgment can be made distinct and clear. In this case we say that we are dealing with the *same* judgment, first in the manner of confusion, then in the manner of distinctness, and finally in the manner of clarity. Thus a concept of judg-

28. *Erf. u. Urt.*, p. 142.

ment is distinguished "that is unaffected by the differences among confusion, distinctness, and clarity" (70); Husserl calls this the broadest concept of judgment. Husserl feels authorized to take this broadest concept as the basic concept from the fact that "the concept of the confused judgment embraces, in a certain manner, all judgments in the broadest sense, including those that can be made distinct and those that can be made clear" (70). This affirmation can be surprising when one thinks of the new things that the passage from the first level of logic to the second, and the passage from the second to the third level, represent. How is this "in a certain manner" to be understood? Does it mean that every confused judgment can be made distinct and clear? We have seen that one proceeds by anticipation in meaning; the opinion needs to be confirmed in order to become a true judgment, and, even before clarification, it often needs to be explicated in order to become a merely distinct meaning. But far from being confirmed, this anticipation can be canceled. A place must be kept for this eventuality. The expectation of truth can be deceived: "I thought that things would be thus and so. Now I see, however, in the presence of the things, that they are otherwise." Now, even in this case, one can say that one has clarified one's meaning, but *negatively*. If the confused judgment "includes" the distinct judgment and the clear judgment, it does so not only because the confused judgment contains, like a promise, the distinct judgment and then the clear judgment, but also because the confused judgment often is a clear or a distinct judgment that has *become* confused. "When this [broadest concept of the judgment] is taken as a basis, there corresponds to each insightfully cognitive judgment, and to each distinct judgment (in view of the essential possibility—and, genetically, the constant necessity—of its becoming confused), a like judgment, or rather the same one, in the confused mode" (70).

The broadest concept of judgment just distinguished is the concept belonging to the domain of morphology. Actually, this discipline does not have to consider the problems of distinctness or, *a fortiori*, those of clarity. "The free construction of forms knows as yet no restraining contradictions" (70). It goes without saying that one cannot assert that the vague judgment is the theme of morphology. A logical dis-

cipline, even of the most elementary level, cannot consider the vague judgment as such. All that one can say is that it abstains from presenting problems of distinctness. To this abstention corresponds *conscious* abstraction — we use Husserl's own term[29] — from the differences between confusion, distinctness, and clarity, an abstraction from which the broadest concept of judgment results. The indistinct judgment that the logic of non-contradiction excludes can hence be retained among the judgments that are acceptable for morphology, always on the condition that it respects the laws of the organization of the language of logic.

Husserl indicated the different levels of formal logic in a descriptive classification at the beginning of the present chapter. Next, thanks to an investigation conducted into evidence, he was able to indicate three different concepts of judgment: judgment taken in the broadest sense, the distinct judgment, and the clear judgment, which appear to be the concepts belonging respectively to morphology, to the logic of non-contradiction, and to the logic of truth. Thus the phenomenological analysis of the different evidences in which the judgment can be given has enabled him to clarify "from the most originary sources" and hence to ground the analysis of apophantics into three disciplines on different levels.

REMARK. — Husserl calls the second level of logic the logic of non-contradiction or the logic of consequence. In Appendix III Husserl explains this double appelation by specifying the relationships between the lawfulness of non-contradiction and the lawfulness of consequence [*Konsequenz*]. Every negation of a necessary formal consequence is a contradiction. The formal law of contradiction thus includes that of deductive consequence. The concept of consequence is then "subordinate a priori to the most universal concept of non-contradiction" (331). But we can define the concept of consequence in a much broader fashion.

The concept of *"Konsequenz"* is a very general one, which comprises not only "logical" consequence, *Konsequenz* in the pregnant sense of necessary analytic consequence [*Folge*], but also consistency, *Konsequenz* in the sense of unitariness in, so to speak,

29. *FTL*, p. 70.

accidental temporal *sequence* [*Folge*], namely of judgments meant in succession but yet *unitarily,* judgments that (as we see when we pay precise attention to their form) are mutually compatible.[30]

In sum, by going along with the ambiguity of language, one can take the expression *consequential (Folge) proposition* in the double sense of *proposition* that analytically flows from an antecedent proposition and *proposition* that follows another proposition in such a way that the totality of propositions remains coherent. If one takes the concept of consequence in a sufficiently broad sense, it then appears as the primordial concept to which the concept of contradiction can be related secondarily. "Thus any judgments whatever make up a system of *Konsequenz*—in this sense—if on 'more precise inspection' they go together for the judging subject, to form the unity of a combined judgment within which no judgment contradicts any other." [31] If one takes the concept of consequence in such a broad way, and if one even takes the concept of non-contradiction in such a way as to include the "trivial" non-contradiction of two judgments which do not contradict each other but have "nothing to do with each other," one can take the expressions *logic of non-contradiction* and *logic of consequence* as synonyms and designate the expressions of the second level of formal logic with either of them indifferently. Throughout the text the concepts of non-contradiction and consequence are taken in this broad sense, so that they respectively extend to trivial non-contradiction and to consequence in the sense of a "consequential" series of judgments that meanwhile do not necessarily flow one from another.

30. *Ibid.,* p. 332.
31. *Ibid.*

2 / Formal Apophantics, Formal Mathematics

DESPITE ITS STRATIFICATION, apophantics nonetheless retains an internal *unity*. This unity derives from the strictly formal perspective in which it is situated, for, abstracting from their "material," it considers judgments only from the formal point of view. Apophantics can be fully understood in its specificity only if one distinguishes its formal sense with an absolute *purity*. But, simultaneously, its field of action is neatly circumscribed and its limits are established. In our opinion, one can go so far as to say that it is a fear of recognizing its own limits that has, for so long a time, kept formal logic from absolutely assuming its formal character. In fact the "limits" of formal logic are not restrictions that would give rise to a sense of impotence; they are rather determining factors which on the one hand enable us to carry out the formal program and on the other hand force us to see that there can be other logical tasks. "[F]ormal logic cannot be the whole of logic: the full and − in a new and richer sense − formal theory of science." [1] This is simply an allusion to transcendental logic, but it obliges us to raise a question which cannot be answered until later: In what sense can one say that logic in general is still formal? To what extent can one speak of the formal that

1. *FTL*, p. 73.

leads us into a dimension other than that of the formal in the usual sense?

If we remain within the limits of the formal in the usual sense, it seems that we have a completely finished logic whose hierarchical organization and internal unity are equally well grounded. And yet Husserl tells us that "no matter how certain we have become of the self-containedness of analytic formal logic, this discipline itself still presents us with great problems" (73). With these new problems we see an *extension* of formal logic that takes us beyond the framework of apophantics. An investigation of the sense of the teleological idea obscurely governing traditional logic enabled us to discern the specific sense of apophantics with full clarity. Now an investigation of the sense of the common goal striven for by the various mathematical disciplines that can be called "formal" mathematics leads Husserl to encounter these new problems, the problems of formal ontology. When clearly understood, the rapprochement between formal mathematics and traditional logic brings out a kinship which authorizes a synthesis of these two disciplines. Thus we rediscover the Leibnizian ideal of *mathesis universalis*.

The reasons that caused Husserl to envisage this synthesis between logic and mathematics are very different from those that actually governed the rapprochement between logic and mathematics as it occurred in the nineteenth century. But in order to understand better how Husserl sets up this problem, let us first see how this rapprochement is in fact constituted.

Traditional logic and traditional mathematics are completely separate, as much by their spheres as by their demonstrative techniques. An evolution was necessary in both mathematics and logic for the kinship between them to emerge. A new conception of mathematics was very gradually developed in a systematic fashion during the second part of the nineteenth century which emphasized the *relations* between mathematical objects without considering the proper *nature* of these objects. Let us take an example that Husserl uses several times, that of whole numbers and addition. Let there be two whole numbers of any sort a, b; they obey the relation $a + b = b + a$, which expresses the commutativeness of arithmetical addition. Now we can bring our attention to bear upon

this property of commutativeness in itself and abstractly consider an operation that possesses this property. In the same way we can envisage other properties, such as that of associativity, which arithmetical addition also obeys: $a + (b + c) = (a + b) + c$. Then, by obliterating all reference to the mathematically "concrete," we can speak of a set [*ensemble*] S of objects $x, y, z \ldots$ regarding which we suppose a relation to be defined such that it obeys purely formal laws—

$$\begin{cases} x \oplus y = y \oplus x \\ x \oplus (y \oplus z) = (x \oplus y) \oplus z \end{cases} \tag{I}$$

—x, y, z being three objects of any sort whatever belonging to the set S. Thus we have characterized an *abstract* operation $\oplus$ uniquely defined by the properties of associativity and commutativeness. Starting from this axiomatic system (I), we can develop an entire theory that applies only to the formal properties codified in these axioms and that in no way depends on the "concrete" nature of the elements $x, y, z \ldots$ or on the concrete sense that is given to the operation $\oplus$.

Then one can ask what we have gained by placing ourselves on a purely abstract plane and abstaining from any reference to the concrete.[2] In the first place,

> a concrete theory, reasoning about well-determined objects, has the fatal tendency to apply itself to all of the properties of these objects; now, very often, we see, after a more or less uneven analysis, that certain of these properties are perfectly useless and, in fact, play no role in the construction of the envisaged theory.[3]

Hence by ascending to the abstract level, one can discern the

2. By concerning ourselves with only so simple and fragmentary an example as the one we have started with, it is difficult to prevent the following skeptical objection from arising: What good is this abstract apparatus? From such an example one can receive the impression that the abstract formulation is a simple transposition that uselessly splits the concrete statement, a concrete statement that, moreover, is immediately understood as an entirely natural evidence. In reality, to sense the fecundity of this abstract thought, one must delve into all the complexity of the various intersecting abstract mathematical structures.

3. Roger Godement, "Les méthodes modernes et l'avenir des mathématiques concrètes," in F. Le Lionnais (ed.), *Les grandes courants de la pensée mathématique* (Paris, 1948), p. 323.

mechanism of the various deductive implications, seeing the determining role of this or that property – in a word, discerning the essential. When we reason about such a concrete province, the totality of our mathematical knowledge weighs upon our intellectual behavior. On this level of abstract mathematics – which alone enables us to distinguish views of *structures* – our concrete knowledge must remain "our private affair," as the logician Tarski says.[4] Thus one could say in Husserlian language that there is a parenthesizing of the concrete that consequently enables us to understand it better. In fact, once we are in possession of such an abstract structure, we can search for other concrete actualizations that can fit this structure, beyond the one that originally gave birth to it. For example, the axiomatic system (I) is also satisfied by the vectorial addition of the vectors of the plane. Hence abstract mathematics gives rise to unexpected rapprochements among entirely heterogeneous concrete provinces and thus leads to a considerable extension of the province of validity of the concrete results. One would want very definitely to give precedence to the concrete system from which one actually began. To this the mathematician may legitimately reply:

> It is not deniable, certainly, that most of these forms have as origin a well determined intuitive content. However, it is precisely by deliberately emptying them of this content that we know how to give them all the efficacy that they potentially have and that we prepare them to receive new interpretations and to completely fulfill their role of elaboration.[5]

We have pointed to the possibility of the formation of abstract theories in algebra. We find other types of abstract theories in set-theory [*ensembles*] that appears at the end of the nineteenth century: Cantor's theory of numbers and the combinational calculus already adumbrated by Pascal.

Hence we see in what sense we can speak of abstract mathematics in contrast to "concrete" mathematics – we should even say "formal" mathematics in order to use the Husserlian denomination presently involved.

Now let us turn to logic. Over the centuries it has shown

4. A. Tarski, *Introduction to Logic* (New York, 1946), p. 122.
5. N. Bourbaki, "L'architecture des mathématiques" in *Les grands courants de la pensée mathématique*, p. 47.

such stability that, with Kant, one can say that "by all appearances it is finished and closed." It is necessary that logic adopt a new ideal of intelligibility if it is to escape the framework within which it has been traditionally situated since Aristotle. This ideal of intelligibility is one of mathematical rigor and certainty. About 1850 the attempt was made to transpose the methods of mathematics, more especially the methods of arithmetic, ⟨into logic⟩ and to establish a logical "calculus." Could one not "add" the logical classes, "multiply" them, hence "calculate" with classes, form equations where, as in mathematics, one would eliminate the terms? Similarly, could one not "calculate" with propositions? This was the spirit in which Boole formed an algebra of logic which he introduced in 1847 with his book *The Mathematical Analysis of Logic, Being an Essay towards a Calculus of Deductive Reasoning.* This algebra of logic is distinguished from the algebra of the mathematicians in that it is powerless. To multiply classes is to consider the common part of these two classes, as the logician says. To multiply a class by itself results in the class itself, which can be written $X \times X = X$, an algebraic equation that is satisfactory in ordinary algebra only when $X = 0$ or $X = 1$. Thus one can say with Husserl that "the calculus of arithmetic becomes reduced to the 'logical calculus,' if one thinks of the series of cardinal numbers as limited to zero and one" (78). These initial attempts at "mathematizing" logic were, subsequently, transcended, and logicians turned, not toward a simple transposition of the calculus of algebra, but toward the deductive elaboration of logic in the demonstrative style of mathematics; this in turn gave way to logistic ⟨or symbolic logic⟩, which was not truly developed until the beginning of the twentieth century. Besides, in the period of the algebra of logic, abstract mathematics was not yet systematically envisaged; as a result, the profound sense of the algebra of logic could not be attained.[6] In fact,

6. The plurality of algebras, defined as abstract structures, which we have just characterized, were discoverable only because of the new conception of abstract mathematics. Actually the algebra of logic is found to be a concrete interpretation of an abstract structure which is one "algebra" among others and which the mathematician calls *Boolean algebra.* Boolean algebra is differentiated from other algebras specifically by the fact that it does not have power—that it is "impotent," as the mathematician says.

it was not until the theories which systematically study the formal relations among mathematical objects were constituted that the kinship between mathematics and formal logic appeared in all its clarity. "Only someone who is not acquainted with mathematics—as a modern science—and who judges of it by Euclid and Adam Reise, can still adhere to the general prejudice that the essence of the mathematical lies in number and quantity." [7] and can hence consider mathematics as having a domain completely separate from that of logic.

In addition to the late discovery of the purely formal, Husserl draws attention to another factor that has contributed to hiding the unity of formal apophantics and formal mathematics. This is the misunderstanding of the objective status of logical formations. Actually, judgments form a "specific Objective field of apriori ideality" (81), as do numbers, geometrical forms, etc. "Even after the development of a formal mathematics and its enlargement to include the calculus of logic, most logicians were unable to see an internal connexion between the themes of mathematics and the themes of logic" (82). In order to grasp this internal connexion, it is not enough to see that the domain of logic can be dealt with by methods analogous to those that govern the mathematical domain. One must also recognize in the logical formations (judgments, deductions, etc.) the same status of ideal Objectivity that one recognizes in mathematical formations (numbers, geometrical forms, etc.). Since the situation is "in principle the same" for mathematical formations and logical formations, how does it happen that they are ordinarily considered in different ways? The reason, Husserl says, is that in mathematics

> one had the continual support of the sensuous configurations, spatial and temporal, which furnished examples and drew attention to the Objective side from the start; though at the same time they masked the irreality of the mathematical configurations. The constructions, sets, number-formations, and so forth, made with real objects as representative examples, furnishes products that might be taken as real (as real figures, real solids, real sets, real numbers); whereas the like is not the case with products of judicative actions (82).

There we have "a deeply rooted difficulty . . . of abstracting

7. *Prolegomena*, p. 252.

thematically from the judging activity" (81), the judgment not being objectivated in the sensuous examples that can be considered as real objects.

Furthermore, the "philosophically minded logicians" usually do not take into account the fact that the concepts of mathematics need a clarification analogous to that which the concepts of logic call for and that there are parallel difficulties in mathematics and logic. "It never actually came to a serious philosophic exploration of the origin of the concepts fundamental to formal mathematics" (83). This is a reproach whose severity is surprising in view of the importance of investigations into the "foundations" of mathematics. But in Husserl's eyes these are not genuinely philosophical investigations since they are inseparable from the objective perspective of the theoretical technique. A "philosophical" exploration of the origin of fundamental concepts must go back to the sources of the subjective activity that constitutes these concepts.

Hence, where the relationships of the theme of formal logic and the theme of formal mathematics are concerned, the philosophical logicians and mathematicians are cheaply satisfied; the former proclaim an absolute separation between mathematics and logic and thus give themselves the right to ignore the problems that mathematics gives rise to, while the latter believe themselves done when they are able to reach a unity which has its source in a simple theoretical technique. Thus once more we see Husserl reject both the science whose interests remain subject to a "positivistic" naïveté and the philosophy that ends by ignoring the accomplishments of this positive science.

Therefore Husserl does not study the rapprochement between logic and philosophy from the technical point of view. For him there is no question of putting the positivity to work and seeing what technical reorganization is required in order that mathematics and logic can be considered within a synthetic unity. "Great as such an interest may be, it falls far short of the philosophic interest: the interest in uncovering the teleological structures immanent in the final idea of a theory of science" (75). In the preceding chapter, starting from traditional logic, Husserl had isolated such a teleological structure, that of formal apophantics. Proceeding in the same manner, starting from formal mathematics, he is going to isolate another

structure of the theory of science through an intentional analysis, that of formal ontology.

These two intentional analyses have different situations at
the outset. Traditional logic is a unified discipline, but it is not
fully aware of its characteristic sense. As for formal mathematics, it includes a diversity of theories, each of which has, to
be sure, undergone a high degree of technical elaboration;
but, according to Husserl,[8] there is no awareness of its unity.
The task of the philosophical sense-investigation is to bring
out this unity of formal mathematics by discerning its fundamental thematic concept, and to do this by inquiring into the
intention that directs the accomplishments of formal mathematics. Let us consider one of the theories of formal mathematics, e.g., set theory [*la théorie des ensembles*]. A set
E is regarded as given or defined when a property characteristic of its elements is stated, that is to say, a necessary and
sufficient condition for an entity to be an element of E; then we
have established the property of belonging [*appartenance*]
$a \in E$, which expresses that a is an element of E and is stated:
"a belongs to E."[9] Hence we can say, as Husserl does, that the
determining concept of set theory is the concept of *element*.
Now let us consider another discipline of formal mathematics:
the theory of cardinal numbers. This time the determining concept is that of *unit*. But when we think of element and of
unit, in both cases we think of an entity of some sort, an object *in general*, without any concrete determination; and
because we think of the object with this universality, we can
set up a theory that is concerned only with formal relations.
Reviewing the other formal mathematical theories, we see
that each of them, in its manner, is concerned with the object
in general, with "anything whatever" as Husserl says.

> This gives rise to the idea of an all-embracing science, a formal
> mathematics in the fully comprehensive sense, whose all-inclusive
> province is rigidly delimited as the sphere of the highest form-
> concept, any object whatever (or the sphere of anything-whatever,
> conceived with the emptiest universality), with all the derivative
> formations generable a priori in this field (77–78).

8. Husserl's opinion here should be revised in light of the present
stage in the development of formal mathematics.
9. Cf. P. Dubreil, *Algèbre* (Gauthier-Villars, 1946), Vol. I, p. 1.

Let us take the example of set theory. What are the derivative forms, the variants, of the anything-whatever that it thematizes? These forms are totality, part (subset), collection of sets, intersection of sets—all forms that can be conceived without reference to concretely designated objects. "Accordingly it is natural to view this whole mathematics as an *ontology* (an apriori theory of objects), though a *formal* one, relating to the pure modes of anything whatever" (78). Hence formal ontology, as the *Ideen* says, is "an eidetic science of any object whatever [*eidetische Wissenschaft vom Gegenstände überhaupt*]." [10] Thus it is distinguished by its theme from formal apophantics, which itself is the apriori formal science of the judgment, more precisely of the predicative judgment, of apophansis. Apophantics has to do with the categories of signification (concepts of proposition, of concept, etc.), while formal ontology has to do with categories of the object (concepts of property, quality, relation, identity, equality, unity, totality, whole and part, etc.).

Apophantics and formal ontology being thus distinguished on the basis of their fundamental themes and not by their techniques, it is then a question of rethinking their relationship on a plane other than the plane of technique. To be sure, apophantics can be treated mathematically, and one can speak, for example, of the algebra of logic. And one must not lose sight of the fact that

> the methodically perfect development of this analytics (as soon as it becomes concerned exclusively with the signified judgments) necessarily leads to a formal apophantic "mathematics": Once anyone has become acquainted with deductive technique, as practised in modern mathematics and mathematical analysis generally, he must see forthwith (as Leibniz was the first to see) that proposition-forms can be treated in the very same manner and that one can "calculate" with them just as one can with numbers, quantities, and the like—nay more, that this is the one manner in which a universal theory of propositions (as essentially a deductive theory) can be built (76).

Formal logic must be a "mathematizing logic," as the *Prolegomena* says in the Foreword of the first edition.[11] But if

10. *Ideen*, p. 22.
11. *Prolegomena*, p. vi.

we want to examine apophantics and mathematics according to their thematized intention, we must go beyond the technical plane of method.

The relationships between apophantics and formal ontology will be studied systematically in Chapters 4 and 5. But from now on Husserl gives one the feeling that they present problems more complex than the thematic separation of the two disciplines would lead one to believe. "Formal ontology and formal apophantics, despite their expressly different themes, must be very intimately related and are perhaps inseparable" (79). In fact, to judge is to bring judgments to bear upon objects, to state the properties of these objects. Ultimately all categories of the object in formal ontology (any object whatever and its derivative forms) exist only insofar as they play a role in judgments. What is more, the operation of "nominalization" (which sets up a corresponding nominal element for each proposition and for each partial form that can be distinguished within the proposition) makes these categories of the object appear as *constitutive elements* of the proposition. Let us, for example, consider the judgment "S is *p*." One can "nominalize" the predicate *p* and say "the quality *p* is appropriate to S." Then one judges about the *quality p*. And the category of quality appears as a structural element of the proposition. Hence, through the intermediary of the operation of nominalization, we see the interaction between apophantics and formal ontology. The *Ideen* emphasizes this:

> Thought of as determined exclusively by the pure forms, the concepts that have originated from "nominalization" are formal-categorial variants of the idea of any objectivity whatever and furnish the fundamental conceptual material of formal ontology, including all the disciplines of formal mathematics. This proposition is decisively important for the understanding of the relationship between formal logic, as a logic of the apophansis, and the all-embracing formal ontology.[12]

Thus logic truly has two aspects, an apophantic aspect and a formal ontological aspect. With apophantics and formal ontology, we have, properly speaking, not two correlative sciences but rather two correlative aspects of one identical science: formal analytics, for the correlation between proposition and

12. *Ideen*, p. 249.

object appears within the very sphere of the proposition.

The notion of formal ontology is specifically Husserlian. Husserl does recall certain of Bolzano's sentences which "would seem to promise a definition of formal ontology" (85). Actually, Bolzano distinguishes mathematical disciplines such as the theory of numbers and combinatory theory from mathematical disciplines such as geometry and mechanics. Only the disciplines of the first group have laws which "are applicable to all things without exception" (85), while those of the second group have laws that relate to concretely determined mathematical objects, spatial forms, forces, etc. It would seem that this is precisely Husserl's distinction between formal mathematics and material mathematics. Nevertheless, Bolzano has not seen the exact sense of the relationships of dependence between formal mathematics and material mathematics:

> But when he thinks of the universal, thing, as the highest genus, under which the superordinate concepts belonging to geometry and coordinate disciplines stand as particular genera, resulting from division, it becomes plain that he has failed to see the difference between the empty form, anything-whatever, as the highest genus whose subordinate differentiations are likewise empty forms, and the universal region, the possibly factually existent [*des möglicherweise Daseinden*] (the real in the broadest sense), which is differentiated into particular regions (85).

This criticism which Husserl makes, though rapid, is a fundamental criticism which is decisive for understanding the formal. Actually, one does not grasp the characteristic sense of the formal if one confuses generalization and formalization. As is said in the *Ideen*, "generalization is something totally different from formalization, which plays so great a rôle in, for example, mathematical analysis; and specialization is something totally different from de-formalization, as a filling out of either a logico-mathematical empty form or a formal truth." [13] Inside the formal sphere, just as within the material sphere, we have to do with more or less general concepts, hence with relationships between genus and species. But the relationships between the formal and the material are not the relations of genus to species. They are rather relationships of *subordination*, and this is what is difficult to understand, since we

13. *Ibid.,* p. 26.

habitually think of subordination according to the model of the relationships of particularization. Actually, however, formal ontology has a status entirely apart from that of the material ontologies. Let us turn to the notion of region, which Husserl alludes to here and which he introduced in the *Ideen*.[14] Communities of essence cut the totality of concretely determined individuals up into regions (such as the regions spatial form, sensible quality, etc.). Inside each region one finds a hierarchy of concepts that subordinates the less general to the more general; for example, the concept triangle is subordinated to the concept spatial form. Such regions in turn can be subordinated to more general regions. Then the question arises: Can one speak of a formal region? In the *Ideen* Husserl says:

> Instead of speaking simply of regions, as we have up to now, we shall therefore be inclined to speak of material regions and to rank the "formal region" alongside them. But, if we adopt this manner of speaking, some caution is needed. . . . The so-called "formal region" is therefore not something co-ordinate with the material regions (the regions pure and simple); properly it is, not a region, but the empty form of any region whatever: it has all regions, with all their materially filled essential particularizations, not alongside it, but (even though only formaliter) *under* it.[15]

Hence, though Bolzano has clearly seen that there is a subordination here, by interpreting it as a simple subsumption of the less general under the more general, he fails to do justice to its sense. "This subordination of the material to the formal manifests itself in the fact that formal ontology contains the forms of all ontologies without exception (all ontologies 'proper,' all 'material' ontologies) and prescribes for material ontologies a formal structure common to them all. . . ."[16] Now we understand the sense of the reproach Husserl offers to the Aristotelian ontology: "Aristotle had a universal ontology of realities only; and this was what he accepted as 'first philosophy.' He lacked formal ontology, and therefore lacked also the cognition that formal ontology is intrinsically prior to the ontology of realities."[17]

Let us be clear that for Husserl formal ontology is by no means located within a metaphysical horizon. It is precisely

14. *Ibid.*, p. 9.
15. *Ibid.*, pp. 21 f.
16. *Ibid.*, p. 22.
17. *FTL*, p. 80.

because of the fact that echoes of substantialist metaphysics attach to the word ontology that Husserl did not originally decide upon the denomination "formal ontology." *Formal and Transcendental Logic* says simply:

> To the best of my knowledge, the idea of a formal ontology makes its first literary appearance in Volume I of my *Logische Untersuchungen,* in connexion with the attempt to explicate systematically the idea of a pure logic—but not yet does it appear there under the name of formal ontology, which was introduced by me only later (86).

But in the *Ideen* he is more explicit on this point:

> At that time [namely: the time of the *Logische Untersuchungen*] I did not yet venture to take up the expression ontology, it being objectionable for historical reasons. I designated this investigation [namely: Investigation III. Contribution to the Theory of Wholes and Parts] as part of an *"apriorische Theorie der Gegenstände als solcher* [apriori theory of objects as such]"— a phrase that Alexis von Meinong contracted to make the word *"Gegenstandstheorie* [object-theory]." Contrariwise I now hold it to be more correct, in conformity with the changed times, to revive the old expression ontology.[18]

The idea of a formal ontology, far from being a response to metaphysical concerns, arises from the examination required by a logic that incorporates formal mathematics. As Husserl remarks at the end of Chapter 5 of *Formal and Transcendental Logic,*

> the task of formal ontology can be undertaken directly from the very beginning, without starting from the idea of a theory of science. In that case the question of formal ontology is: What can be stated within the limits of the empty region, object as such? . . . Obviously the whole of formal mathesis will then accrue.[19]

18. *Ideen,* p. 23, n. 1. The word *ontological* is used in the *Prolegomena* (p. 234). Husserl speaks of "ontological" sciences in contrast to "nomological" sciences. But, as we will see, the ontological sciences are nothing but the concrete sciences (such as geography, history, and natural history), and the nomological sciences are nothing but the abstract theoretical sciences (mathematics, for example). Husserl adopts the terminology of von Kreis, which appears to him more proper than the usual terminology for differentiating these two types of science in a regular manner.

19. *FTL,* p. 148.

This, however, is not Husserl's itinerary. He arrives at the idea of a formal ontology by inquiring after the sense that logic conceived as theory of science must have, and he arrives there in the *Logische Untersuchungen* as he does in *Formal and Transcendental Logic*. However, in the *Prolegomena*, the theory of science is elaborated with focus entirely on the *objective* ideal content of the sciences, while in *Formal and Transcendental Logic* a new dimension of investigation presents itself—one which is focused on the subjective problems of constitution and which alone makes possible a true justification of the distinctions seen in the objective focus. Formal logic is neatly characterized in the *Prolegomena* as at once formal apophantics and formal apriori theory of the object, but the inseparability of these two aspects of logic is not elucidated, since the exclusively objective orientation of the *Prolegomena* is not broad enough in scope to bring us a final understanding of the relationships between formal apophantics and formal ontology.

Meanwhile we can retain the description of the apophantical and ontological tasks of a theory of science which the *Prolegomena* gives, with the understanding that the relationships between apophantics and formal ontology are to be the object of a sense-investigation capable of revealing to us the "intentions" of these two disciplines.

There are three successive tasks which fall to logic conceived as apophantics and formal ontology:

1. It is the task of logic to make evident the primitive concepts that essentially pertain to a theory taken in its pure sense; these concepts fall into two groups:[20] the categories of signification and the correlative categories of the object.

2. The task that follows consists in distinguishing the laws that are grounded in these two groups of categorial concepts and which refer to Objectivity. We have two sorts of laws depending on whether they are grounded in the categories of signification or in the categories of the object. These laws consist of theories: where the signification is concerned, the theories of deduction (e.g., syllogistics), and where the object is concerned, the apriori theories of any object whatever, that is to say, of formal ontology

20. Cf. *supra,* p. 4.

(e.g., the pure theory of number is grounded in the concept of number).

3. With these two tasks it could seem that logic has reached the goal set for it, that of being the theory of theories. But if one takes the development of formal mathematics into consideration, a third and final task for logic is recognized, that of inquiring into the possible *forms* of theories. At this level we rediscover the duality between the plane of signification and the plane of the object. At the same time that it becomes the theory of the possible forms of *theories*, logic becomes the theory of the possible forms of the *provinces* of objects.

Formal and Transcendental Logic can only touch upon the first two tasks characterized in the *Prolegomena,* but the third task will be the theme of Chapter 3. That *Formal and Transcendental Logic* resumes the study of this third task gives rise to problems concerning the nature of the architecture of logic brought to light in this book. Actually, we have come, thanks to the first chapter, to a division of apophantics into three levels, the highest of which is the formal logic of truth. Now *Formal and Transcendental Logic* takes over the three tasks of logic characterized by the *Prolegomena* and gives a special place to the third task. Then we are led to wonder what the relationships of these two hierarchies are and what privileged role the theory of the possible forms of theory has. In order to simplify the discussion, we remain in the apophantic focus, remembering that at any moment we can reinforce it with the ontological focus. The distinction between apophantics and formal ontology in fact indicates a duality of correlative focuses that do not clash with the preceding distinctions.

Actually, only the first hierarchy is a *structural* hierarchy, for it concerns the division into *levels* in the proper sense, while the second hierarchy is a hierarchy of *tasks* that accords with the complexity of the organization of theories. The first level of logic, i.e., morphology, has as its task precisely the first of the tasks designated by the *Prolegomena:* To make evident the primitive concepts and the elementary forms of connexion that constitute the "grammatical" architecture of any theory whatever. But there is no reason to believe that such a correspondence can be established between the second level and the second task or between the third level and the third task. The second task,

viz., the task of making evident the laws that come together in theories, can be considered solely from the viewpoint of the logic of non-contradiction or from the viewpoint of the logic of truth. As for the accomplishment of the third task, viz., the constitution of the theory of the possible forms of theories (or, as *Formal and Transcendental Logic* often says more briefly, the theory of deductive systems), it carries out a *renewal* of logic in relation to its traditional form. This renewal alone was under consideration in Chapter 1, where the stratification of logic was explored.

> But, in consideration of the fact that a completely novel type of mathematical analysis had shot up in a mighty theoretical-technical development during the nineteenth century, and because of the need of making clear the still utterly confused logical sense of this analysis, I saw yet a third and highest task for a formal logic or formal theory of science (90).

Actually, to arrive at a theory of the possible forms of theory, one must learn to consider theories only from the point of view of form, and one must have had contact with the formal mathematics which studies the forms of relations, relations among objects without concrete determination, which studies the "abstract" structures of theories. Hence it is logic — in the broad sense that incorporates formal mathematics — which is capable of undertaking this third task. But this *extension* of logic is at the same time a *transcendence* of logic which raises us *above* the traditional problems. In fact, to constitute the theory of the possible forms of theory is not to study particular theories as to their form; rather, it is to think directly on the level of pure form, to consider the possible forms of theory in themselves and to take them as the immediate objects of study.

In Chapter 3 of *Formal and Transcendental Logic* Husserl characterizes this theory of the deductive forms as "the highest level of formal logic." The term "level" can mislead us. Actually the three disciplines — pure morphology of judgments, logic of consequence (or of non-contradiction), and logic of truth — were distinguished in the first chapter as the different levels of formal apophantics. To avoid all confusion, it would be neater to say that apophantics has its highest task in the constitution of a theory of the forms of theories. A simple glance over the Table of Contents even increases the possibility of confusion.

Let us examine more closely the titles of §§ 13, 14, 15, 28.

§ 13. The theory of the pure forms of judgments as the first discipline of formal logic.
§ 14. Consequence-logic (logic of non-contradiction) as the second level of formal logic.
§ 15. Truth-logic and consequence-logic.
§ 28. The highest level of formal logic: the theory of deductive systems; correlatively, the theory of multiplicities.

We see that the term "level" is not used in the title of § 15 to designate the logic of truth. But this is a mere lack of symmetry in the editing, and only a reader who adheres to the terminology of the Table of Contents could believe that the third level of stratification announced in the Introduction is the theory of deductive systems and not the logic of truth. Actually, if Husserl has designated the theory of deductive systems as the highest level of formal logic, it is not only because this task is a supreme task but also that it can only be the task of a discipline on a level higher than that of traditional formal logic. Thus *Formal and Transcendental Logic* takes up the notion that already appears so neatly in the *Prolegomena*, the notion that this task involves us in a group of entirely new problems which go beyond the problems envisaged until now. The *Prolegomena* would indicate, in fact, that the propositions established to regulate the connexions of forms and to regulate the various transformations of these forms, etc. – in a word, the propositions constitutive of the theory of the forms of theories – "will have manifestly another content and another character than the axioms and theorems of the theories that one encounters while about the second task," or even that "[logic] points beyond itself to a supplementary science which deals a priori with the *essential species (forms) of theories and with the laws that state the relations among those species.*" [21]

The stratification of logic established in the first chapter took into consideration only traditional logic, as we have said. Now we must note the fact that at this highest level the distinction between the logic of non-contradiction and the logic of truth can also be established and in exactly the same way as

21. *Prolegomena*, p. 247.

traditional logic. In other words, the theory of the forms of theory can also be developed equally as well from the point of view of the logic of non-contradiction as from the point of view of the logic of truth.

Thus Chapter 3 of *Formal and Transcendental Logic* succeeds in integrating the program of logic sketched in the *Prolegomena* into the logical frameworks fixed by Chapter 1. In *Formal and Transcendental Logic* Husserl says:

> In one respect, we have made essential progress by our present investigation, namely in that we were able to establish, in Chapter 1, the fundamental triple stratification of logic. . . . On the other hand, we were still behind the *Logische Untersuchungen* in Chapter 1, since consideration of the results obtained in that earlier essay has now required us to recognize a higher level of problems, the aforesaid entirety-problems or "multiplicity"-problems, and to regard them as the theme of a higher discipline, though one that is still formally logical.[22]

22. *FTL*, p. 104.

3 / Theory of Deductive Systems and Theory of Multiplicities

WHAT ARE THE ESSENTIAL CHARACTERISTICS of the theory of the possible forms of theory?

As Husserl shows at the end of this chapter, the fact that a discipline is kept within the limits of *formal* logic imposes a limitation upon the notion of theory itself. It does not matter what theory the theory of the possible theory-forms is concerned with.

In order to specify the sense of this limitation, let us refer to the opposition between abstract and concrete sciences as the *Prolegomena*[1] envisages it. Every science is a group of truths that are interconnected in such a way that they form a *unity*. Science is not a simple accumulation of cognitions: "A group of chimerical cognitions surely does not authorize the expression chimerical science."[2] Something more is needed, an interconnexion and a unification of the cognitions. But this unification can have two extremely different sources. The unity can proceed from principles of explanation that reveal a fundamental lawfulness. Then the unity of the science is brought about by a *theoretical* unity; this is the case in sciences said to be "abstract." Husserl also proposes to call these sciences "explanatory" or even "theoretical" sciences. But there is

1. *Prolegomena*, p. 234.
2. *Ibid.*, p. 14.

[43]

another type of unity that derives not from the theoretical apparatus but from the "things" that the science in question deals with. Here the unity of the province is the only unifying factor. Such is the case in "concrete" sciences (geography, history, natural history, etc.). In order to emphasize the difference between these two unifying factors, *law* and *object*, Husserl adopts a distinction, suggestive of von Kries, between the *nomological* and the *ontological* which he applies to the sphere of the sciences. Hence he calls the theoretical sciences "nomological" sciences and the concrete sciences "ontological" sciences. In works written after the *Prolegomena*, Husserl abandons the term "ontological" for designating the concrete sciences, since, as we have seen, he employs this term for more precise purposes. However, he retains the term "nomological"; and in *Formal and Transcendental Logic* he employs it in preference to other equivalent terms.

What role does this separation of the sciences into two groups play in the development of a formal study that has as its object the structure of the sciences? It is evident that only "nomological" sciences can occasion a substantial study of form. In fact,

> when we practise formalization [on the concrete sciences] . . . and then we ask what combines all the emerging proposition-forms to make up the unity of a system-form . . . we come upon nothing but the empty universality, that such a science is an open infinity of propositions that hang together by virtue of their objects and can be united with one another at least as analytically noncontradictory. . . . Obviously we can become cognizant of the principle of unity in such sciences only by going beyond the analytico-logical form.[3]

On the other hand, the study of the *form* of a *nomological* science is a study which, one can say, has a content. The nomological sciences have a deductive apparatus that properly gives rise to formal logic, so much so that the forms of *theories* are restricted to the theory of the forms of *nomological* theories. But if this limitation is grounded in the nature of things and operates by itself, at least it must be "justified" by an explanation of what conditions it, that is to say, by an explanation of the formal design of the logical analytic. As *Formal and*

3. *FTL*, p. 102.

Transcendental Logic points out, this justification does not appear in the *Prolegomena*. There the undiscussed adherence to an *ideal* of science takes the place of justification. In the *Prolegomena* the true science is the specifically theoretical science, the theory that an explanation develops on the basis of fundamental principles. Under these conditions, logic as theory of science is conceived as a theory focused on the science par excellence, which is to say, as a theory of theoretical science. In *Formal and Transcendental Logic* Husserl certainly still subscribes to the affirmation of the *Prolegomena*[4] according to which all scientific cognition is radically grounded cognition *(Erkenntnis aus dem Grunde)*. But then he recognizes that there are grounding activities other than those of the nomological sciences. Phenomenology is the witness to this. At all events, to start off by setting up the nomological science as an ideal for all science is a "prejudice." The limitation of the universal concept of science, taken as theory in the broadest sense, to the concept of nomological theory had to appear in the *Prolegomena* as the solution to a *problem* that can be stated broadly: When can a theory be constructible a priori in the purely analytic sphere?

By having recourse to the distinction between abstract and concrete sciences, this justification of the narrow limits of the *Prolegomena* is somehow foreign to the procedure of *Formal and Transcendental Logic*, in which it appears only to the extent that Husserl wants to provide a *critical* complement to the *Prolegomena*, justifying it after the fact. The basic route that *Formal and Transcendental Logic* follows enables it along the way to come upon the notion of deductive or nomological theory without needing to proceed by elimination, i.e., by the elimination of the concrete sciences. *Formal and Transcendental Logic* begins with a provisional delimitation (which is quite different from an initial limitation that has not been justified) of logic as the science of the principles of the *logos* taken in its highest manifestation: reason in its scientific activity of judging. We have seen that logic thus conceived is formal and that it takes the universal principle as its general theme. "Formal logic" is then the point of departure for an intentional analysis that makes it possible to clarify the genuine sense of this logic. During the process of explicating this sense,

4. *Prolegomena*, pp. 231–33.

the idea of *mathesis universalis* appears. "In [*mathesis universalis*] occur, as the highest level, the deductive system-forms and not others. . . . By its own resources [logic] can attain only the cognition that . . . the propositions conceived with formal universality as jointly holding good for it have a constructional (deductive) system-form." [5] Husserl even specifies that "logic, as analytics, is not equipped with any ready-made distinction among sciences, like the usual distinctions between concrete (descriptive) and abstract ('explanatory') sciences or any other distinction that may be proposed" (103). The notion of nomological theory proposed in *Formal and Transcendental Logic* hence is not, properly speaking, conceived as the result of a "limitation"; rather it is conceived as the object of a *specific* study on the highest level of formal logic. If we have emphasized this valuable distinction from the *Prolegomena* — a distinction that *Formal and Transcendental Logic* wants to ignore — we are doubtless making a concession to traditional pedagogy, where the means for specifying a notion lie in that which distinguishes it from what it is not; but we also do so because, as it seems to us, the reading of *Formal and Transcendental Logic* needs to be a double reading. On the one hand, the results of the *Prolegomena* are not disavowed — they are even incorporated; and, on the other hand, these results are mastered by the method of intentional analysis — something still alien to the procedures of the *Prolegomena*. We must recognize that if *Formal and Transcendental Logic* profits from what the *Prolegomena* teaches by way of preparatory distinction-making, it also finds a more direct and more audacious way of reaching its objects, and, by going beyond the stage of "distinctness," it reaches the *clarity* of the things.

Hence the highest level of formal logic has the task of establishing the theory of the forms of nomological theories — more briefly stated, the theory of deductive systems. What is the *correlative* task — focused no longer on the theories but on their *objects* — going to be? "The objective correlate of the concept of a possible theory, determined only in its form, is the concept of any possible province of cognition that would be governed by a theory having such a form" (91). The mathematician calls a province of objects thus conceived a *multiplicity* (*Mannigfaltigkeit*). The dissociation of these two correlative

5. *FTL*, p. 103.

tasks would be artificial since a multiplicity is not only a mere "set" [*ensemble*] of objects but rather a set determined specifically by the fact that it is subject to a form of nomological theory. Let us be more specific. On the one hand, the multiplicity is not a set of objects determined in their concrete mathematical nature. On the other hand, as we have just said, it is not purely and simply a set—a set being quite simply defined as formed of elements capable of possessing certain properties. The multiplicity is a set of objects determined by the "operations" to which these objects are subject, these operations being themselves determined in a purely formal manner by the properties enunciated in the axioms, or, using an expression often employed by Husserl, in the elementary laws. "And these [elementary] laws determine, then, both the province and the theory that can be built or, stated more correctly, the theory-form" (91). Let us return to the axiomatic structure that we presented above[6] as an example of the theory of formal mathematics (a structure which the mathematician calls an Abelian demigroup). At the same time that this structure specifically characterizes a theory, it also determines a multiplicity of objects, viz., the multiplicity of objects $x, y, z \ldots$ subject to the operation $\oplus$, an operation which is determined in a formal manner by the two properties of commutativeness and associativity:

$$x \oplus y = y \oplus x$$
$$x \oplus (y \oplus z) = (x \oplus y) \oplus z$$

This is so, no matter what x, y, z, belonging to the multiplicity, are.

Hence we see to what extent the two correlative tasks—the cognition of the province and the constitution of the theory—converge from the moment it is decided that the cognition of the province is to remain within the purely formal framework. And, without respecting the correlative opposition between theory of deductive systems and theory of multiplicity, one can speak of the theory of multiplicity by including under this title the two correlative focuses.

We have had an example of a discrete multiplicity. If we consider continuous multiplicities, such as geometrical

6. *Supra,* p. 27.

multiplicities, we are dealing, however, with an analogous process of formalization. For example, Euclidean geometry can be related to a theory-form.

> Naturally this is done by that peculiarly logical universalization called "formalization," as a result of which all the materially determinate What-contents of the concepts — in the case of geometry, all the specifically spatial contents — are converted into indeterminates, modes of the empty "anything-whatever." Consequently the materially determinate system of geometry becomes changed into an exemplary system-form: To each geometrical truth a truth-*form* corresponds; to each geometrical argument or proof, an argument-*form* or a proof-*form*. The determinate object-province made up of spatial data becomes the form of a province; it becomes, as the mathematician says, a multiplicity (93).

This multiplicity is determined by the totality of the forms of the Euclidean postulates; hence it is determined by a deductive theory having a form deduced from Euclidean geometry by means of formalization.[7]

Having once performed this reduction to form in its purity, thinking can *keep* itself on this strictly formal plane. Then one comes "to view such system-forms as mathematical Objects, to alter them freely, universalize them mathematically, and particularize the universalities" (93). When one takes as object of study a system-form, one can "vary" it, one can start from it and obtain other forms, one can study the relationships that all of these forms have among themselves, one can discover a more general form to which they are subordinated, and so on. What is more, thinking *must* be kept on the formal plane if it is to uncover the profound structural kinship among the mathematical theories, a kinship masked by the heterogeneity of the material contents of these theories. Thus (and we address ourselves to those who criticize formalism so lightly) there is a true *life* of thinking which evolves on the plane of purely formal abstraction. This thinking life is called forth by a power of universalization and of rapprochement never encountered in the former mathematical orientation.

Hence, by thinking on the level of form, one can account for the plurality of algebras, of geometries, etc. — a plurality that can appear scandalous to a mind trained only in "concrete" mathematics.

7. Cf. *infra*, p. 55, Remark 1.

If we give the name Space to the well-known order-form of the phenomenal world, then naturally it is absurd to speak of "spaces" for which, for example, the axiom of parallel lines does not hold good. In the same manner it is absurd to speak of different geometries, if geometry is the name of the science of the space pertaining to the phenomenal world. But, if we mean by space the *categorial form* of world-space and mean correlatively by geometry the categorial theory-form of geometry in the common sense of the word, then space finds its place under a genus of purely categorially determined multiplicities, which is delimited by laws and with respect to which we shall naturally speak of space in an even more comprehensive sense. In the same manner the geometrical theory finds its place in a corresponding genus of theoretical complexes and purely categorially determined theory-forms, which we may then call, in a correspondingly amplified sense, "geometries" of these "spatial" multiplicities.[8]

We should like to use the expression *life* of formal thinking to indicate the mobile and free character that presides over the constructions of formal theories. As the *Prolegomena* says so profoundly: "With the spreading of the deductive and theoretical sphere, the free vitality [*die freie Lebendigkeit*] of theoretical research grows also."[9] And with *Formal and Transcendental Logic* one can say that "mathematicians went on in the above-characterized direction *without restriction. Unconcerned about theoretical sciences that were already given*, they *freely* constructed 'multiplicities' (forms of multiplicities) or, correlatively, forms of deductive sciences" (94). Still, there is no reason to take this freedom for arbitrariness; freedom in the construction of forms remains a *regulated* freedom. There are dependencies and subordinations among the forms of theories which one must respect in the "free" variation of forms. To be sure, Husserl speaks of "the danger of becoming lost in an excessive symbolism" (98). But in this there is no disdain for formal thinking as such. The danger, in Husserl's eyes, is that thinking lets itself be hypnotized by what is only a means of liberation with respect to content, i.e., by symbols, and that the theory of multiplicity then becomes "deductive games with symbols" (99). When, for example, one is dealing with equiform deductive theories, they must be considered in two different ways in order to avoid

8. *Prolegomena*, p. 251.
9. *Ibid.*, p. 248.

this purely deductive game. On the one hand, they must be thought of as *equiforms*. "Technically therefore it would be pointless to build each of them explicitly by itself, instead of deriving the relevant form of theories systematically from the common forms of axioms, once for all, at a higher level of formalization" (99). But, on the other hand, there must be added to this technical interest the *logical* interest that pursues *such and such* a theory-form, in which case it is necessary to consider the form of such a theory *in its own right* and to take it as a *possible* form of *actual* theory. We are obliged to think on two different levels, for if we are to reach a higher level of formalization we must remember that this higher level is founded on lower levels. However that may be, even when the "logical" interest backs up the technical interest, we remain within the properly *formal* sphere. Even in his expression, Husserl can emphasize this notion of *form*. When the mathematician speaks of a space of *n* dimensions, of Riemannian spaces, etc., he knows quite well that it is a question of a space in an enlarged sense, of a "space." But Husserl thinks that, instead of continuing to employ the term space in the usual sense, it would be neater to employ the expression *the categorial form of space:*

> To be sure, the usual locutions were and are unclear: Mathematicians talk, not about the categorial form ⟨of⟩ space, but about "Euclidean space." In referring to universalizations, they talk about *n*-dimensional spaces, about Riemannian and Lobachevskian spaces, instead of about universalizations of that categorial form ("three-dimensional Euclidean multiplicity"), which yield forms of "multiplicity"-types having *n* dimensions and further defined thus and so in respect of form. Just as unclearly, they talk about axioms, instead of about axiom-forms, and then go on to speak of theorems, proofs, and so forth, in referring to a formally universal deduction in which forms of principles are presupposed and the theorem-forms included in the principle-forms are derived — in forms of arguments and proofs (93–94).

Hence in verbal expression itself the notion of form must be emphasized if one wants fully to undertake the formal reduction of mathematical theories and, above all, if one wants to eliminate in advance all counter-sense on the part of those who remain strangers to mathematical technique.

Now let us be more specific about the fact that thus far we

have not subjected the deductive structure of theories to this formal reduction. A deductive theory derives its theorems from axioms asserted to be fundamental propositions. What can be said about the system formed by these axioms? Even if it is a *finite* system, is it permissible univocally to define the *infinite* group of objects which is the multiplicity correlative to this theory? Husserl calls such an axiom-system, capable of "totally and unequivocally determining" a multiplicity, a "definite" system (in German: *definit),* and he calls the correlative multiplicity a "definite" multiplicity.[10] Husserl writes:

> The axiom-system formally defining such a ["definite"] multiplicity is distinguished by the circumstance that any proposition (proposition-form, naturally) that can be constructed, in accordance with the grammar of pure logic, out of the concepts (concept-forms) occurring in that system, is either "true"—that is to say, an analytic (purely deducible) consequence of the axioms—or "false"—that is to say: an analytic contradiction—; *tertium non datur.*[11]

10. Cf. *infra,* p. 58, Remark 2.
11. *FTL,* p. 96. The notion of *definite* multiplicity is not studied in the *Prolegomena,* even though several sections are devoted to the idea of a pure doctrine of multiplicity (§ § 69–70). Yet, as Husserl indicates in a note to the *Ideen* (p. 136, n. 1), he used the concepts of "definite" multiplicity and "definite" system of axioms around 1890 (hence about ten years before the *Prolegomena*) in his unpublished *Untersuchungen zur Theorie der formal-mathematischen Disziplinen* [Investigations pertaining to the Theory of the Formal-Mathematical Disciplines]. "The concepts introduced here served me already at the beginning of the 1890's, . . . mainly for the purpose of finding a *radical* solution to the problem of the imaginary." The *Prolegomena,* conceived as an introduction to the phenomenological investigations of Volume II (cf. *Formal and Transcendental Logic,* p. 97), were oriented toward a philosophical systematization that set aside the purely technical problems brought up by the problem of using fictions [*les imaginaires*]. The notion of "definite" multiplicity appears explicitly in the *Ideen* (pp. 134–36), but without relation to the problems that Husserl originally confronted: "The multiplicities comprising all spatial formations have a remarkable fundamental logical property, indicated by the names 'definite' multiplicity and 'mathematical multiplicity in the pregnant sense,' names that we hereby introduce. . . . Such a multiplicity is characterized by the fact that a finite number of concepts and propositions, derivable in a given case from the essence of the province in question, completely and unambiguously determines, in the manner characteristic of purely analytic necessity, all possible formations belonging to the province,

Now a theorem established by Gödel in 1931,[12] i.e., two years after the appearance of *Formal and Transcendental Logic*, demonstrates that in elementary formal arithmetic (and hence in practically all mathematical theories) there exists an "undecidable" closed statement, that is to say, one which can be neither demonstrated nor refuted. Does Gödel's result destroy the conclusions reached by Husserl's reflection? Jean Cavaillès thinks so. "The adventure is particularly serious for the Husserlian conception of logic and mathematics. . . . The very notion of an isolable and masterable theory cannot be maintained."[13] Where the great majority of mathematical theories are concerned, we have the following facts before us. On the one hand, it is impossible to bring together any statements that would enable us to deduce or refute any proposition that one can formulate in the envisaged theory. On the other hand, theories branch out and intermingle. This lack of independence on the

so that, of essential necessity, nothing in the province is left open. . . . In the case of a mathematically definite multiplicity, the concepts 'true' and 'formal-logical consequence of the axioms' are equivalent." In *Formal and Transcendental Logic* Husserl resumes the notion of *definiteness (Definitheit)* in this spirit of essential characterization. Beginning with the *Ideen* the problems of logic in a general way are genuinely *integrated* into the phenomenological investigations. Actually, in the *Ideen* the problems of definiteness are dealt with only on the side. Definiteness enables us to characterize the abstract sciences *in contrast to the concrete sciences*. Husserl wants to show that the concrete "essential" sciences must not be conceived after the model of the abstract eidetic or essential sciences, whose type is represented by mathematics. Phenomenology, a concrete science of essence, is not a "geometry of mental life"; the stream of consciousness is not a mathematical multiplicity. On the contrary, the problems relating to the deductive sciences are the direct problems of *Formal and Transcendental Logic*. Thus, in the manner in which this one question of definiteness is treated we have an index of the intentions which govern Husserl's different works. The denomination *definiteness*, which Husserl used from the beginning of the century, appears later in the logical literature. Cf. Zermelo,"*Untersuchungen über die Grundlagen der Mengenlehre,*" *Mathematische Annalen*, LXV (1907), and "*Über den Begriff der Definitheit in der Axiomatik,*" *Fundamenta Mathematicae*, XIV (1929).

12. Kurt Gödel, "Ueber formal-unentscheidbare Sätze der Principia Mathematica und verwandter Systeme," *Monatschr. Math. Phys.*, XXXVIII (1931), 173–98.

13. J. Cavaillès, *Sur la logique et la théorie de la science* (Paris, 1947), p. 72.

part of theories has its effect upon their proper development, and from this fact, furthermore, we must renounce the simplifying schema of a theory which by itself would bring about a total cognition of its objects. Must we simply denounce the vanity of the notion of nomology as Husserl understands it? For him nomology par excellence is represented by a complete deductive theory, a "definite" one. Now such nomologies are exceptional. Can the exception play the role of norm? Can the dignity of "par excellence" survive application only to the exception? Thought through in its essentials, that is the situation. One can answer this question as Tran-Duc-Thao does: "The impossibility of reaching completeness for any system on a par with or superior to arithmetic simply signifies that the ideal cannot be actualized; but this does not destroy its value." [14] One must not lose sight of the fact that Husserl has clearly pointed to a "definite" nomology as the *ideal* of mathematical theory. But at the same time it must be recognized that he thought of this ideal as becoming actualized in mathematical technique. "The *ideal of 'mathematization'* . . . has great significance for the cognitive practice of all the 'exact' eidetic disciplines," [15] that is to say, for all deductive disciplines. Yet, basically, can we not think that the error of a confident naïveté in the face of an unactualized ideal fails to constitute an objection to that ideal as such? We can gain two things from an ideal not incorporated into the concrete: (1) it nevertheless can serve as a motivating force, e.g., in moral life, and (2) it cannot be excluded categorically by a specific sense immanent in an intellectual technique, as is the case with mathematics. If, true to the spirit of phenomenology, we inquire into the forward movement of Husserl's thinking, according to its intention, we see that the present mathematical technique has occasioned the emergence rather than the repudiation of the Husserlian ideal. For Husserl, as we have just emphasized, the notion of a "definite" deductive system does not remain on the level of the technical questions which motivated its introduction. This key notion allows us to think of the deductive ideal of *exhaustiveness* in its specificity. A "definite" system of axioms exhaustively defines the multiplicity which corresponds to it. Finally,

14. Tran-Duc-Thao, *Phénoménologie et matérialisme dialectique* (Paris, 1951), p. 35, n. 1.

15. *Ideen*, p. 18.

"nothing remains undetermined." [16] To be sure, it would be easy to take the existence of "undecidable" propositions in most mathematical theories as a pretext for demonstrating the chimerical character of the Husserlian ideal. But actually, if one considers the mathematician at work, one can say that he continues to be guided by this ideal of exhaustiveness. In this case, the ideal is not incorporated in schemata quite as simple as Husserl indicates. For him, as for all the axiomatizers at the beginning of the twentieth century, axiomatization is thought of as an antecedent grounding activity which makes it possible to bring together once and for all the fundamental statements required for developing the entire theory.[17] On the contrary, as D. Lacombe says, "for the present-day mathematician, axiomatization is no longer an *antecedent* concern that can even be left to others but is instead the very material of his everyday work. . . . The 'grounding-axiomatics' is transformed into a 'branching axiomatics'; or, if you will, axiomatization has moved from the static to the dynamic stage." [18] In the most modern mathematics determination is not attained strictly in accordance with an ideal of linearity but is rather due to the intersection of different structures. The ramification of theories is not an obstacle to determination. As D. Lacombe emphasizes again, one can discern in the theoretical entanglement numerous webs of implication, and the structure which develops in this way "is itself harmonious and passionate." [19] The Husserlian ideal of axiomatic grounding carried out once and for all is hence transcended, for it reveals a ponderousness that has become foreign to contemporary mathematical technique. This ponderousness is explained by the struggle that was necessary for axiomatic thinking to reach its origin. Axiomatic thinking had to bring about an entirely new spirit of systematization. On the other hand, one cannot form an absolute judgment about Husserl's characterization of the deductive sciences if one does not consider the fact that this characterization is basically inclined to separate the style

16. *Ibid.*, p. 135.
17. Cf. *ibid.*, p. 17: ". . . *die ein für allemal systematisch zusammengestellten Axiome.*"
18. D. Lacombe, "La géométrie de Hilbert et l'axiomatique actuelle," in *Structure et évolution des techniques*, Nos. 19–20, p. 8.
19. *Ibid.*, p. 9.

of these sciences from the style of concrete sciences such as phenomenology, though the apriori character is common to both sorts of science. This opposition between deductive and concrete apriori sciences led Husserl to accentuate the rigidity of deductive systematization: "The generic essence of the province of geometry, or the pure essence of space, is of such a character that geometry can be fully certain of governing by its method actually all possibilities and of doing so exactly." [20] What is more, the rigidity of the Husserlian ideal of deductive science is the price paid for an *enthousiasme de la raison* toward this power of systematization. This rational enthusiasm emerges on a splendid page in *Krisis:*

> The conceiving of this idea of a rational infinite universe of being, with a rational science systematically mastering it, is the unheard-of novelty. An infinite world, here a world of idealities, is conceived as a world in which objects do not become accessible to our cognition only singly, imperfectly, and as if fortuitously; on the contrary, a rational, systematically unitary method finally reaches—in its infinite progress—any object in its full being-in-itself. [21]

The mathematician can correct certain of Husserl's affirmations. For example, he can consider this vindication of uniformity false. Yet he betrays the purpose of his effort if he does not subscribe to a profession of faith which justifies the accomplishments of his everyday life.

REMARK I.—The notion of multiplicity was introduced into mathematics systematically by Riemann in a report which he read for his habilitation to the Göttingen philosophical faculty in 1854. The title of this report is "Ueber die Hypothesen, welche der Geometrie zu Grunde liegen [On the Hypotheses which Provide the Grounds for Geometry]." [22] Riemann was concerned with *continuous* multiplicities, being oriented toward them by his plan for clarifying the primitive data of geometry. We will quote several pages of this report in order

20. *Ideen,* p. 135.
21. *Krisis,* p. 19.
22. In Riemann's *Gesammelte mathematische Werke und wissenschaftlicher Nachlass,* published with the cooperation of R. Dedekind and H. Weber (Leipzig: Teubner, 1876), pp. 254–69. The present report was translated into French by J. Hoüel [and I translate therefrom (Translator)].

to reveal the nascent state of the formal considerations of contemporary mathematics:

> It is known that geometry admits as pregiven not only the concept of space but also the first fundamental ideas of constructions in space. It does not give these concepts more than nominal definitions, the essential determinations being introduced in the form of axioms. The mutual relations among these primitive data remain enveloped in mystery. We do not see clearly whether they are necessarily connected, or to what extent they are so connected, or even, a priori, if they can be so connected.
>
> From Euclid to Legendre, to mention only the most illustrious of the modern reformers of geometry, no one among the mathematicians or among the philosophers has cleared up this mystery. This is because the universal concept of multidimensional magnitudes, including as a particular case the extended magnitudes, has never been the object of a study. Consequently, I first set myself the task of constructing the concept of a multidimensional magnitude, beginning from the universal concept of magnitude. From this it will result that a multidimensional magnitude is prepared for entry into different metrical relationships, and it follows that space is only a particular case of a three-dimensional magnitude. . . . The concepts of magnitude are only possible when a universal concept exists which allows different modes of determination. Depending on whether or not it is possible to pass from one of these modes of determination to another in a continuous fashion, they form a continuous or a discrete *multiplicity*. Each one of these modes of determination in particular is in the first case called a point, and in the second case an element, of this multiplicity. The concepts whose modes of determination form a discrete multiplicity are so frequent that, given objects of any sort whatever, there is discovered, at least in the civilized languages, a concept which comprises them. On the contrary, the occasions which can give birth to concepts whose modes of determination form a continuous multiplicity are so rare in ordinary life that the loci of sensible objects and the colors are almost the only simple concepts whose mode of determination forms a multiplicity of several dimensions. Only in higher mathematics do the occasions for the formation and development of these concepts become more frequent.[23]

These pages account for the difficulty of reaching the abstract plane in the case of continuous multiplicities, for the

23. "Sur les hypothèses qui servent de fondements à la géométrie," trans. Hoüel (n.d.), pp. 1–3.

mind is restricted to a quite limited number of concrete continuous systems. The limited field of examples of continuity that the senses offer us does not suggest a *freedom of variation* which would authorize formal thinking to turn its back on the sensible datum. The process of universalization, which leads to multiplicities of n dimensions, begins in a complete *break* with sensuous experience. Not only is it necessary to adopt an exclusively mathematical standpoint in order to perceive the possibility of such multiplicities, but, beyond this, only "higher mathematics" presents the problems to which these multiplicities are adapted. In Riemann's report we see the moment when this break was truly made for the first time.[24] The novelty of this attitude is such that Riemann almost excuses himself for leaving the level of thinking habitual to the geometer:

> After having constructed the concept of an n-dimensional multiplicity and having discovered as the essential characteristic of such a multiplicity the property that place-determination can lead to n magnitude-determinations, we come to the second of the problems set up above, *viz.*, the study of the metrical relations to which such a multiplicity is subject and the sufficient conditions for the determination of these metrical relations. These metrical relations can be studied only in abstract concepts of magnitude, and their dependence can be represented only in formulae. On certain hypotheses, however, they are decomposable into relations which, taken separately, are subject to a geometrical representation, and thereby it becomes possible to represent the results of the calculus geometrically. Thus, in order to reach solid ground, one cannot, it is true, avoid abstract considerations in formulae, but at least the results of the calculus can then be represented in geometrical form.[25]

24. In his report Riemann indicates ([French] translation, p. 2) that for the elaboration of his theory of multiplicities of n dimensions he had no help from previous work "except some brief indications given by Mr. Gauss in his second *mémoire* on biquadratic residues. . . ." Cf. Gauss, "Theoria residuorum biquadraticorum, Commentatio secunda" (1831), published in *Werke* (Göttingen, 1856), II, 95–178; this sentence in particular appears the most significant (p. 110): "Si, a conceptibus quos afferunt varietates duarum dimensionum (quales in maxima puritate conspiciuntur in intuitionibus spatii) profecti, quantitates positivas directas, negativas inversas, imaginarias laterales nuncupavissemus, pro tricis simplicitas, pro caligine claritas successisset."

25. Riemann, *op. cit.*, p. 6.

Where discrete multiplicities are concerned, we are dealing with a different state of affairs. But the difficulty of taking up an abstract mode of thinking is no less great. True, as Riemann emphasizes, with diverse collections of objects we have numerous examples of discrete totalities which we can always name. Simple mathematical situations offer us an occasion to consider various operations with various properties. But this diversification is so much a part of the mathematically concrete that it is difficult to consider the formal *for its own sake*, independent of its concrete mathematical underpinnings. It is, so to speak, difficult to discern the universal in the particular relations and from them to arrive at the notion of an "abstract" operation. In sum, the ways in which the concrete mathematical relations keep us at arm's length from the abstract mathematical relations differ in the cases of the continuous and the discrete. The continuous concretum blocks us by its unity. But once we have broken away from this unity, we are immediately involved in formalizing universalization. Furthermore, the discrete concretum can make us think on the formal plane, but it is difficult to eliminate since it continually leads to a splitting of formal thought.

REMARK 2. — The currently employed term for designating the correctness of an axiomatic system is *vollständig* (which is usually translated as "complete").[26] Husserl refers to this term but is careful to employ another which is specifically his own: *definit* (which we translate by "definite"). But actually the expression *vollständig* is used with quite different senses in the literature of logic. Here we cannot explicate all the implications which exist among these diverse usages. We want to distinguish them only to avoid the confusions which Husserl seems not to have escaped. Actually he writes:

> Throughout the present exposition I have used the expression "complete system of axioms," which was not mine originally but derives from Hilbert. Without being guided by the philosophicological considerations that determined my studies, Hilbert arrived at his concept of completeness (naturally quite independently of my still-unpublished investigations); he attempts, in particular, to complete a system of axioms by adding a separate "axiom of

26. [The French usually use *complet,* but also use *saturé,* to render *vollständig.* (Translator's note based on original text and author's modification thereof.)]

completeness." The above-given analyses should make it evident that, even if the inmost motives that guided him mathematically were inexplicit, they tended essentially in the same direction as those that determined the concept of the definite multiplicity.[27]

Similarly in the *Ideen* Husserl notes: "The close relationship of the concept of definiteness [*Definitheit*] to the 'axiom of completeness' [*Vollständigkeitsaxiom*] introduced by David Hilbert for the laying of a foundation for arithmetic will be evident forthwith to every mathematician."[28] Now we shall see that the concept of definiteness is, contrary to Husserl's affirmation, totally different from the concept of completeness in the sense of the axiom of completeness introduced by Hilbert into the axiomatics of arithmetic and subsequently introduced by him into the axiomatics of geometry. Let us first review the various usages of the concept of *Vollständigkeit*.

1. An axiom-system can be called *vollständig* (in French one would say *sémantiquement complet*, "semantically complete") for a determinate province if it enables all of the valid formulae of this province to be deduced.

2. An axiom-system can be called *vollständig (syntaxiquement complet,* "syntactically complete") if the adjunction as an axiom of an expression not deducible from the axioms of the system considered renders them contradictory.

Husserl's affirmation whereby a "definite" axiom-system

> is distinguished by the circumstance that any proposition . . . that can be constructed in accordance with the grammar of pure logic, out of the concepts (concept-forms) occurring in that system, is either "true" — that is to say: an analytic (purely deducible) consequence of the axioms — or "false" — that is to say: an analytic contradiction — ; *tertium non datur*[29]

could lead us to think that Husserl had in view the syntactical completeness [*complétitude syntaxique*] which we have just formulated. But, on the one hand, the assimilation by Husserl of "true proposition" and "analytic consequence" (and the same with "false proposition" and "analytic contradiction") and, on the other hand, his first characterization — as much in the *Ideen* as in *Formal and Transcendental Logic* — of

27. *FTL*, pp. 96–7.
28. *Ideen*, p. 77, n. 1.
29. *FTL*, p. 96.

definiteness as the possibility of the exhaustive determination of a multiplicity show us that semantic considerations are equally implied and tend to have the same sense as Hilbert's affirmation that "the axiom-system of geometry suffices for the demonstration of all geometric propositions." [30] These two characterizations of definiteness are presented by Husserl as equivalent. We know now that semantic completeness does not by itself lead to syntactical completeness. Indeed, Husserl, not only here but elsewhere, despite his distinction of the two correlates *theory* and *multiplicity*, never came to distinguish between the *syntactical* and the *semantic*. If we recall that the syntactical-semantic distinction was systematically discerned by symbolic logic [*la logistique*] only much later, it is difficult to be harsh with Husserl.

3. Finally, Hilbert ("On the Concept of Number," 1899), introduced the *axiom of completeness* to which Husserl alludes. But this axiom concerns a particular property of a model of a formal system. If it satisfies the axioms of this system, a province of determinate objects (e.g., the rational numbers) on the basis of which the determinate operations are defined (e.g., ordinary addition and multiplication) is a *model* of a certain axiomatic system expressing the purely formal relations among formal objects ("objects of thought"). It can happen that the different models satisfying an axiomatic system are *isomorphic*, that is to say, a bi-univocal correspondence can be established among their elements – the properties defined by the axioms being left invariant. In this case the system of axioms is called *categorial* or, in the language of contemporary mathematics, *univalent*. Another question presents itself: Among the possible models of an axiomatic system is there one that is *maximal*, that is to say, is there a model to which one cannot add still more elements without making it cease to satisfy the axioms? Hilbert wanted to find such a maximal model for the theory of numbers. In order to exclude every model other than the maximal model, he introduced the *axiom of completeness*, which he expressed thus:

It is not possible to add another system of things to the number

30. Hilbert, "Ueber den Zahlbegriff," in *Grundlagen der Geometrie* (5th ed.; Leipzig and Berlin: Teubner, 1922), Appendix VI, p. 238 [my translation from Miss Bachelard's French. – Translator].

system in such a way that, in the system formed by their union, axioms I, II, III, IV (i.e., the axioms preceding the axiom of completeness) are all satisfactory sets [*ensembles*]; in short, numbers form a system of things which, if one retains the group of axioms, are not subject to any extension (*Erweiterung*).[31]

Let us designate by A the set of axioms I, II, III, and IV and by S the axiom of completeness. The rational numbers form a model for the axiomatic system A; the real numbers (that is to say, the rational and the irrational numbers) form another model of this system A. But the rational numbers cannot satisfy the system A + S because one can add the irrational numbers to them, which the axiom S prohibits. On the contrary, the group of real numbers cannot be extended. One can only add to the real numbers other elements of such a sort that the axioms A are still satisfied. Only the group of real numbers form a possible model of the system A + S. Thanks to the axiom S, Hilbert has excluded the rational model in order to retain only the real model. Thus, to say in this Hilbertian sense that the axiomatic system of reals is "complete" signifies that all models of this system susceptible of extension (the third sense of "completeness") are excluded.

Hilbert introduced an analogous axiom into the axiomatization of geometry: The elements of the geometry form a system of entities which, if one retains all of the axioms, is not amenable to any extension. The geometrical axiom of completeness played no role in the first edition of the *Grundlagen der Geometrie* (1899). Hilbert mentions it in a note written for the French translation by Laugel (1900): "Let us note that one can still add the following axiom (that is, the axiom of completeness) to the five preceding groups of axioms. It is not of a purely geometrical nature, and from the point of view of principles it merits special attention . . ." (p. 25). Only after the fourth edition of the *Grundlagen* does the axiom of completeness play an integral role in the system of axioms of geometry, and on page 23 of that edition Hilbert says that this axiom "now forms the keystone of the whole axiomatic system." The very special nature of this axiom (which speaks of the other axioms) and its late insertion into the axiomatic system of the *Grundlagen* has surrounded the signification of this

31. *Ibid.*, p. 240.

axiom with obscurity. And if one adds the equivocation which the very expression "axiom of *completeness*" is susceptible to, one understands the possibility of the confusion which Husserl fell into. Yet, only one year before the appearance of *Formal and Transcendental Logic*, Baldus devoted an important study to this axiom.[32] And in order to draw attention to the special sense of "completeness" within the perspective taken by Hilbert, Baldus, when he speaks in this sense of a complete system, takes care to specify that it is a question of a complete system *in the sense of the axiom of completeness,* or even *in Hilbert's sense.*

Finally, there is an essential difference between the two heterogeneous notions of completeness in the sense of the axiom of completeness (sense number three)[33] and syntactical completeness (sense number two), i.e., as Jean Cavaillès says, "between the closure of the field of the objects of a theory and the closure or completeness of its conceptual field." [34] On the one hand, the inexhaustibility of the model does not bring about the categoricity of the system considered. In the case of the axiomatic system of the *Grundlagen*, there is inextensibility and categoricity. But one cannot say in general that inextensibility implies categoricity. Baldus in particular has shown in his study that if one considers what J. Bolyai has called absolute geometry, i.e., the axiomatic system of geometry where the axiom of parallels is omitted, then one can, thanks to the axiom of completeness, obtain extensibility. But in the case of absolute geometry there are two inextensible models which are not isomorphic. On the other hand, categoricity does not, by itself, lead to syntactical completeness.[35] Gödel's theorem (1931) specifically shows that a categorial theory, such as elementary arithmetic formulated in a second-order logic, can

32. R. Baldus, "Zur Axiomatik der Geometrie: Ueber Hilberts Vollständigkeitsaxiom," *Mathematische Annalen*, C (1928), 321–33.

33. And in the sense of Husserl's investigations concerning imaginary numbers and the problems of the possibility of algebraic extension (cf. *FTL*, p. 97).

34. J. Cavaillès, *Sur la logique et la théorie de la science* (Paris, 1947), p. 72.

35. Cf. Church, *Introduction to Mathematical Logic*, I (Princeton, 1956); Fraenkel and Bar Hillel, *Axiomatic Foundations of Set Theory* (Amsterdam, 1958); and Roger Martin, *Logique contemporaine et formalisation* (Paris, 1964).

be syntactically incomplete (and at the same time semantically incomplete). Hence there are several breaks in implication between the notions of inextensibility and completeness, and, definitively speaking, one can say that between Hilbert's axiom of completeness and Husserl's concept of definiteness there are not the connexions affirmed by Husserl.

[B.] Phenomenological Clarification of the Two-Sidedness of Formal Logic as Formal Apophantics and Formal Ontology

4 / Focusing on Objects and Focusing on Judgments

WITH THE THEORY OF DEDUCTIVE SYSTEMS and with the theory of multiplicity we have reached the highest level of a fully developed logic, that is to say, traditional analytics with formal mathematics incorporated into it. The moment has come to examine thoroughly the relationship between the apophantic focus and the formal ontological focus of the analytics thus enlarged. Division B of Part I (Chapters 4 and 5) are devoted to this task.

We have already seen that apophantics and formal ontology are distinguished as correlates and that in changing our focus we pass from the propositions to their correlates, i.e., to the objects. This change of focus itself remains to be studied.

What are the objects for formal ontology? They are any objects whatever and not concretely determinate objects. They are universal objects thought by means of concepts such as property, unity, plurality, relation, totality, etc. These concepts are categorial concepts, "that is: concepts that have accrued through merely looking abstractively at the syntactical forms in which the object is apprehended at varying levels in syntactical actions, actions of judgment" (106). If it did not enter into a judgment, we could say that the anything-whatever, was a pure nothing. "In formal analytics, then, the object is thought of purely as an object of possible judgments" (106). Hence we

see that the relationship between the judgment and the universal object is an internal relation that appears within the sphere of judgment itself.

Moreover, the activities of thinking which produce judgment are of the *same nature* as the activities which produce number, totality, and all the other concepts derived from the anything-whatever. Even in the *Prolegomena* Husserl was struck by the relationships between the formality of arithmetic and the formality of logic, and he there demonstrated the analogy between counting and judging. But in these relationships *Formal and Transcendental Logic* sees much more than analogical relationships. Counting or combining are actually "form-producing activities" (107).[1] A morphology of judgments must deal with the forms of formal mathematics — such as whole and number — on the same plane as the forms concept, proposition, subject-form, etc. In this perspective, the formal mathematical formations make up an integral part of the apophantic sphere. Then Husserl extends the concept of judgment-formation in such a way that he applies it indifferently to number, whole, etc. And now this enlarged concept of judgment is just what Husserl refers to. In the beginning, formal ontology and apophantics appear as cleanly separated, the one definable as the formal science of anything whatever and the other as the formal science of the predicative judgment. The actual analyses assimilate the formations of formal ontology (whole, number, etc.) to the formations of judgment and show that the formal theory of judgment should include among its problems the problems of formal ontology, since "it is also true that nowhere but in the judgment does the empty concept Something make its appearance, the concept in which all ob-

1. In the *Philosophie der Arithmetik* Husserl took into account the formal character of the concepts in arithmetic: unity, plurality, cardinal number, etc., thus showing the mathematician's receptiveness to the formal. And, as we have already said, he called these concepts form-concepts *(Formbegriffe)*, or categories. "What characterizes them as form-concepts or categories is the circumstance that they are not concepts of contents belonging to a definite genus but, on the contrary, include in a certain manner each and every content" (*Philosophie der Arithmetik,* p. 91). However, these remarks are not exploited for a unification of formal mathematics and formal logic. What Husserl insists upon in the *Philosophie der Arithmetik* is that one cannot explain the genesis of the concept of number as one does, for example, the concept of color.

jects are thought by logic" (110). Hence it seems that we have a simple integration of formal ontology into apophantics and that actually, even where formal ontology is concerned, we remain within the framework of apophantics.

Remaining on the purely objective plane, Husserl has been engaged until now in distinguishing the sense of these close ties between formal ontology and apophantics. It is always a question of the concepts pertaining to these two disciplines. Husserl of course referred to the corresponding activities of thinking, but he considered them in an objective fashion while seeking the results they reached. Now he is going to introduce another direction of examination which is typical of a "phenomenological" investigation: the activity of thinking is going to be studied with respect to its *intention*. What is going to be inquired into is the interest which guides this or that type of thinking activity. It goes without saying that it is not a question of describing the different personal motives which can lead any one of us to interest himself in this or that discipline. That would be a psychological study. It is a question, rather, of bringing out the type of interest which *every man* who practices these disciplines *should have;* let us call it the interest *attached* to these disciplines. Then we can hope to understand their genuine tendencies.

Let us apply this direction of examination to logic. Logic, as theory of science, takes as its interests the interests of science. The interests of science are the interests of the *cognition* of a province, and a science is essentially oriented toward the cognition of the *objects* of its province. Now to cognize objects is to be able to determine them and to determine them predicatively. Interest in the object leads of itself to a predicative activity. Hence the function of the cognition of a science leads us to judging. But "in judging we are directed, not to the judgment, but to the currently intended 'objects-about-which'" (112). As *formal* theory of science, logic will therefore determine objects with a pure universality:

> Like the sciences themselves, analytics as formal theory of science is directed *to what exists [ontisch gerichtet]*; moreover, by virtue of its apriori universality, it is *ontological*. It is formal ontology. Its apriori truths state what holds good for any objects whatever, any object-provinces whatever, with formal universality, in whatever forms they exist or merely can exist — as objects of

judgments [*urteilmässig*], naturally: since, without exception, objects "exist" only as objects of judgments and, for that very reason, exist only in categorial forms (120).

Thus the theme of interest for those who judge is always the object. When we go back into the intention which governs the activity of judging, the situation hence appears to be the reverse of the one we characterized a moment ago. Formerly it seemed that we could only stay within a formal theory of *judgment*—even when it was a question of the anything-whatever and its derivative concepts. And now we see that, when we judge, we are always directed through the judgment to the *object*. Actually there is no contradiction here. We are concerned with one situation which is thought first in the mode of province and then is thought in the mode of *theme*. The thematic considerations open the way to what we are happy to call a *phenomenological epistemology*. This epistemology connects the two correlative notions of interest and theme by way of intentionality. Let us say in passing that they make the renewal of epistemology possible. In effect, the notion of theme is an analytical instrument which enables us to distinguish different sciences which have the same province. In another work we will show that sciences such as theoretical physics and mathematical physics—which are concerned with the same "things"—can be precisely differentiated by their thematic interest.[2]

But, where logic is concerned, must we stop here and say that formal logic has as its province the sphere of judgments and that it has anything whatever as its theme? Can we not ask just as legitimately, following the traditional characterization of logic, ". . . to what extent is the predicative judgment the privileged and central *theme,* and to what extent, therefore, is apophantic logic, i.e., the theory of judgment, necessarily the core of logic?"[3] What is gained is that in guiding ourselves with the function of the science of science, which logic has, we can affirm that it has an interest thematically oriented toward the object. But "there is possible at any time such a *shift* of thematizing interest that what then lies in the thematic field is not the particular object-province and the categorial

2. [Cf. Suzanne Bachelard, *La conscience de rationalité; étude phénoménologique sur la physique mathématique* (Paris, 1958).]
3. *Erf. u. Urt.*, p. 5.

objectivities formed out of it at higher levels,[4] but—as something other and sharply differentiated—what we call judgments
and their components, their combinations and other transmu-
tations" (121). Let us see under what conditions this thematic
shift can be effected. Let us grasp the activity of judging in its
concrete actuality; that is to say, let us follow it along *in its
course*. Each time we judge, we accord being-status to the objects about which we judge. Judging is always "having something 'before one' as existent [*etwas als seiend "vor sich"
haben*], whether one has it there intuitively or non-intuitively"
(121). In a concordant series of judgings [*jugements*], we continue to grant being-status to the *same* objects. It is specifically
the unity of the theme which gives a cohesion to the judging
as it progresses. It is the same theme which continues to have
status throughout the judgmental activity. But this being-
status must be guaranteed by a verification. Interest in cognition implies interest in verification; one "needs to convince
oneself 'by the affairs themselves' of 'how they actually are' "
(122). Before interest in verification arises, the objects of the
judgment are considered simply as existing and their existence
gives rise to no problems. Once this cognitional interest dawns,
simple existence becomes *meant (vermeint)* existence, existence as it is presumed. The meant needs to be confirmed in
order to be recognized as existing—existing no longer purely
and simply but *truly and actually*. Thus we re-encounter the
Husserlian distinctions between judgments which are only
meanings ⟨or opinions⟩ by which one presumes that the things
are thus and so and judgments *fulfilled* by contact with the
things ⟨or affairs⟩ themselves. The man of everyday life already has this sort of "aspiration" for verification, but in him
it is a haphazard affair. Moreover, his verifying activity is
short-lived: "The non-scientific thinker . . . 'merely looks and
sees' whether it is actually thus; and, if he sees, he is satisfied" (125). For the scientist, on the contrary, the activity of
cognition is essentially an activity of verification. He also
judges in a straightforward manner, just like the man on the
street; but he knows that these straightforward judgments can
have the dignity of "scientific" results only if he has confirmed their exactness by adequation to the things themselves.
The scientist acts *provisionally:* no scientific results without a

4. Cf. *infra*, p. 75, Remark 1.

criticism of these results. Hence straightforward certainty must be questioned. Beside the case where this certainty is confirmed stands the case where the existent is modalized and becomes doubtful, problematical, or even null. The intention, instead of being fulfilled, can be "deceived." Modalization acquires a more and more important place for Husserl as the study of judging takes precedence over the study of the judgment, for the very life of the judgmental activity leads to setting up the problem of modalization. *Formal and Transcendental Logic* reproaches the *Prolegomena* for having omitted this problem. *Erfahrung und Urteil* succeeds in enlarging the concept of modalization in such a way that the confirmed certainty is designated as a modalization of the straightforward certainty, of "simple" certainty, which further accentuates the force of the distinction between these two certainties as it is presented in *Formal and Transcendental Logic*. Once having introduced this broad concept of modalization, *Erfahrung und Urteil* can affirm that

> modalization is not a contingency that just *occasionally* enters into the complex of judgment; on the contrary, the sense of the striving of judgment cannot be understood at all except from the point of view of the transition through modalization and of the striving from modalization toward the certainty of believing and ascertaining.[5]

In the language of *Erfahrung und Urteil*, we could say that the scientist's criticism is essentially a modalization of the straightforward certainty, the certainty not "shattered" by doubt. But by undergoing criticism, the judgments come to be considered for themselves and to be thematized. "Scientific judging indeed forsakes the naïvely straightforward cognitional directedness to objective actualities that comes from the naïve having of them themselves in straightforward evidence, and continually makes the judgments thematic, the supposed objectivities as supposed" (129), and not the objectivities as simply existing.

We must emphasize this thematic shift, which is necessary if criticism is to take place. The straightforward attitude ignores the *problems* of adequation as problems. The person who judges in a straightforward and naïve fashion that "S is

5. *Erf. u. Urt.*, pp. 328–29.

p" does not dream of investigating whether things are actually that way; instead, he believes them to be so. The critical attitude, on the contrary, makes us aware that the question of adequacy *must* be raised. For the dogmatic "S is *p*" is substituted "I think that S is *p*; this is my 'meaning.'" This "meaning" ⟨or "opinion"⟩ requires confirmation; it needs to undergo verification in order to be called a true judgment. Hence criticism has for its end the return to the things ⟨or affairs⟩ themselves; this is to be done in such a way that upon contact with the things themselves we see whether they are actually what we think they are. But first we are led to examine the meaning *for its own sake*. In a certain sense, the discovery that the simple judgment of the straightforward attitude is only a meaning *detaches* us from the problems of adequacy. The judgment [*jugement*] is *only* a meaning; hence it owes nothing to the things it intends, and it can be studied as a simple meaning without our caring about the objective actuality to which it refers. We can carry out a study of the judgment while remaining on the plane of the simple judgment and not considering it as a judgment-about. Thus we can provisionally disinterest ourselves in any possible adequation. But this rupture is only provisional, and "it is obvious, on the other hand, that this procedure is subservient to determining the province itself, and that therefore the judged propositions are only intermediary themes" (129). Thus we see to what degree the notion of theme is a much more efficacious instrument of epistemological analysis than the notion of province. The notion of theme introduces a relativity which permits us to distinguish between primary and secondary themes or even between ultimate and intermediate themes.

Logic, as science of science, as the theory which serves as norm for science, must be, specifically, the instrument for the criticism of principles which grounds science in its genuineness. It must consider the judgments which make up a science as requiring criticism and authentication by this criticism. From the fact of this critical focus, logic thematizes the sphere of judgments considered in themselves. Its apophantic focus results from this. Thus we return to the traditional orientation of logic conceived of as theory of judgment and, in particular, as theory of predicative judgment. "With this supposed as such, the mere correlate of the 'supposing' or 'opining' (often spoken

of as the opinion, δόξα), we have now laid hold of what is called the judgment (apophansis) in traditional logic and is the theme of apophantic logic" (126). We can say that, as science of *science,* logic has an ontological focus and that, as *science* of science, it has an apophantic focus. As science of the second degree it forms judgments about judgments. Thus the province of judgments becomes a proper thematic field. And this thematic field is the field *emphasized* by logic, for the fact of being a science of the second degree is for it the characteristic fact. For science the object would be the immediate theme and the judgment the intermediate theme. Logic, on the contrary, directs itself only mediately toward the object, toward the existent itself, and it directs itself immediately toward judgments "as suppositions of something existent." [6] Apophantics and ontology are hence two different *thematic* focuses of one and the same science. As *Erfahrung und Urteil* says in very condensed terms,

> . . . the difficult problems concerning the relationship between formal apophantics and formal ontology, i.e., their belongingness together and indeed their inner unity in the face of which their separation proves to be precursory, [rests] upon differences of *attitude* only rather than upon differences in their *fields.*[7]

This venture into the intentionality which governs scientific judging is typical of a phenomenological examination which is not content with "positive" investigations, i.e., investigations exclusively directed toward the objective data, as the sciences are; and Division B, where this examination is presented, rightly calls itself a *phenomenological* clarification of the two-fold character of formal logic as formal apophantics and formal ontology. But there is no reason to believe that simply by following this subjective direction of examination we have reached the level of transcendental research. The cognizing subjectivity to which Husserl refers remains a "natural" subjectivity since it is as yet not separated from the presuppositions attaching to the natural attitude; only the transcendental reduction will reveal these presuppositions. The uncovering of them will be the task of Part II of *Formal and Transcendental Logic.* For the moment there is the question of explicating the genuine

6. *FTL,* Chap. 5, p. 130.
7. *Erf. u. Urt.,* p. 2.

sense of the sciences and logic within the natural attitude, which is the attitude of science. Division B of Part I offers us an intentional epistemology and not a transcendental phenomenology. This is why Husserl, taking the cognition of Nature as the example of scientific cognition, says that "of course one must not fall back on the Nature already given by sheer experience before all thinking" (118). Here there is no question of parenthesizing the productions of science. To be sure, we say that Nature is *in itself*, that it exists *before* our act of judgment. But we can qualify it by our act of judgment. All that we *know* about it we have from our activity of judging. What is more,

> only if we go on synthetically to make our experiencing itself and its productions a theme of judgment, can we have original knowledge of the fact that this (harmoniously flowing) experiencing already bears "implicitly" in itself, "before" our thinking . . . , the being-sense of Nature, as the same sense that thinking explicates (119).

To be sure, one can say that what is implicit was already there prior to its being explicated, but one only *knows* that it is there when it has been explicated. The sense of the judgment cannot be determined by an experience of Nature which is not involved in the activity of judgment. Nature as form-of-scientific-judgment will have, to be sure, under it Nature as form-of-experience, but Husserl says in an astonishing formulation: "[T]he under-it is at the same time an in-it" (118). The notion of Nature prior to any act of judging is a meaningless notion if one does not conceive it beginning from the predicative sphere, and "by the judger, qua judger, only that Nature is accepted which is categorially formed in the judging" (118).

Let us come back to this *criticism* which every scientific cognition must undergo. It ends at the "truth" or the "falsehood" of judgments. From this the *critical* concept of truth is determined. The true judgment is the correct judgment, the *verified* judgment, the judgment verified by means of adequation to the things themselves. But "by virtue of its original (present or past) adjustment to the itself-given actuality, we have then the concept of *actuality*, as the second concept of truth" (127). Husserl soon specifies, in order to avoid every naïvely realistic interpretation, that "naturally the actual

[*das Wirkliche*] in the sense of the real [*des Realen*] is merely a particular case under this broadest, analytico-formal, concept of *actuality*" (127) and that the denomination "actuality" is appropriate not only to states-of-affairs but also to properties, relations, wholes, and so on. The notion correlative to the notion of truth, i.e., the notion of evidence, hence has a twofold sense: the sense of property which the judgment as meaning has about being *fitted* to an actuality which corresponds to it, and the sense of original possession of the true or actual being itself. Evidence, in the first case, is the original consciousness of the correctness of the judgement. This is the evidence pertaining to the critical focus. Certainly criticism wants to attain true being and lead to evidence as possession of the things themselves, but it is continually traversed by evidence as consciousness of correctness. Prior to *Formal and Transcendental Logic* Husserl had not studied critical consciousness in its own right.[8] The value of these critical concepts of truth and evidence arises from the encounter between the method of intentional analysis and a specifically scientific theme. This encounter takes place in *Formal and Transcendental Logic;* the *Prolegomena* had not yet found the phenomenological way, and the *Ideen,* which was in possession of the methods of intentional analysis, was not concentrated upon logic, upon the science of science, as *Formal and Transcendental Logic* is. Now science is cognition which has become genuine through criticism. To express it in a term dear to Husserl, we can say that this concept of critical truth is a concept "native" to the scientific sphere. "The peculiar formal stamp of the intentionality ruling throughout the unity of scientific living and the formations it produces determines the particular stamp of *scientific reason,* as a reason that actualizes 'genuine' cognition by an unremittingly concomitant criticism of cognition" (128). One could think that here we are concerned with the same problems as those of the beginning of the Third Cartesian Meditation, where it is said emphatically: "Reason refers to possibilities of verification."[9] Actually, in the Third Medita-

8. Although the Sixth Investigation (§ 39, "Evidenz und Wahrheit," *Log. Unt.*, Vol. II, Pt. II, pp. 122 ff.) expressly distinguishes, among other senses of "truth," truth as correctness of judgment, this concept is not studied there.

9. *CM*, p. 57.

tion, "constitutional" problems are set aside; there we are already on the plane of transcendental phenomenology. Here, on the contrary, as we have just said, we remain on the level of the scientific attitude, hence in the natural attitude. But there is a *parallelism* here between the procedure of the *Cartesian Meditations* and that of *Formal and Transcendental Logic*. This parallelism is often reflected in language by a community of expression: "By *epoché* we effect a reduction to our pure meaning (cogito) and to the meant, purely as meant," it is said in the Third Meditation.[10] We will go so far as to say that the epoché is a *transcendental conversion of the criticism* of science, for in the criticism of science we begin by abstracting from the reference of "meanings" to the objects which they mean; in the epoché we abstain from making a judgment about the existence or inexistence of a world. By this we do not mean to deprive transcendental phenomenology of its original signification and to lower transcendental investigations to the level of a simple phenomenological epistemology. In fact, one can apply to the parallelism between transcendental phenomenology and phenomenological epistemology what Husserl says in the "Nachwort"[11] about the parallelism between transcendental phenomenology and phenomenological psychology. The passage from phenomenological psychology to transcendental phenomenology points back to a change of attitude. Husserl challenges those who, minimizing the importance of a change of attitude, deny the novel emergence that transcendental philosophy represents. He says that the latter is a "nuance" in relation to phenomenological psychology. But he soon adds that this nuance has a "decisive significance for all genuine philosophy." The Second Cartesian Meditation states in a similar vein: "We have here one of those seemingly trivial nuances that make a decisive difference between right and wrong paths of philosophy."[12]

Remark.—Predicative activities produce objectivities of a sort altogether different from the objectivities pregiven to this activity. Husserl calls them *categorial* objectivities because they are born from κατηγορεῖν. What distinguishes them from the other objectivities is just that they are engendered by an

10. *Ibid.*, p. 56.
11. "Nachwort," p. 557.
12. *CM*, p. 32.

activity and are not pregiven to that activity. As *Erfahrung und Urteil* says, "the κατηγορεῖν is an activity that is to be characterized, in contrast to receptivity, as a *creative spontaneity* through which objects are first *produced*." [13] Here in Chapter 4 of *Formal and Transcendental Logic* this opposition is not studied, for in this chapter we remain in the categorial sphere, where *Formal and Transcendental Logic* has been situated from the start. *Erfahrung und Urteil* systematically insists on this opposition between categorial activity and receptivity since, from the fact of its genetic orientation, *Erfahrung und Urteil* must ascend from structures of receptivity to predicative structures and undertake the differentiation of these two types of structures. The *Cartesian Meditations* puts it similarly:

> Here the radical difference between objectivities that are real (in a broad sense) and categorial objectivities also presents itself. The latter point back to an origin from *"operations,"* from a step-by-step generative-constructive activity of the ego: the former, to an origin as effects of a merely passive (in any case, not an ⟨actively⟩ generative) synthesis. [14]

In this regard Roman Ingarden makes the following objections in his Remarks *(Bemerkungen)* [appended to the German edition of the *Cartesian Meditations*]:

> I completely agree to the distinction between the "operations" that lead to real objectivities and those that lead to "categorial" objects. But can it actually be asserted that the synthetic operations that lead to real objects are of a *purely passive* nature or that the corresponding synthesis is of such a nature? That seems to me to be incorrect even in the case of the operations that lead to perceptually given intuited things; and to a higher degree in the case of numerous cognitive operations that, in scientific work, lead to the construction of the objectivities of physics, which after all are said to be "real." Does the activity or passivity of the synthesis have any great significance here? [15]

Allowing ourselves to remark upon these "Remarks," we observe first that Husserl reserves the term "operation" *(Operation)* for the syntheses which lead to categorial objectivities,

13. *Erf. u. Urt.*, p. 233.
14. *CM*, p. 51.
15. *Cartesianische Meditationen*, Appendix, p. 214 [translated by Dorion Cairns].

whereas he speaks simply of the "performances" *(Leistungen)* of purely passive syntheses. The word "operation" has the emphatic sense given it by the mathematician. Husserl employs this word when he wants to indicate an activity which *engenders* results. The distinction between activity and passivity here has the signification of a separation between, on the one hand, a "constitution" in which "objects" are engendered and which is necessary if these objects are to have an "existence" and even in order for this to be a question, and, on the other hand, a "preconstitution" in which the real objects are grasped in a purely passive manner. But this does not mean that the real objects cannot occasion predicative activities; and, in particular, ⟨this does mean that⟩ categorial activity has done its work in the operations, which, by means of scientific elaboration, lead to the construction of the objectivities of physics.

Let us take an example of categorial objectivity: The state-of-affairs S is p. We see that the objectivity S is p is not an objectivity of the same nature as the substrate-object designated by S; it bears the mark of predication. Yet, in its way, it is an object which can be conceived in its unity and its identity. We can substantivize it, saying, *"The fact that S is p"* and take it as substrate for a new judgment. Here we come back to "nominalization," which Husserl refers to so often. But, as he remarks in *Erfahrung und Urteil*,[16] the nominalization of a state-of-affairs is in principle different from the nominalization of, e.g., a quality ("the green of this tree is beautiful"). In the sphere of receptivity one can find a "pre-form" which corresponds to this nominalized quality. In a purely receptive explication one can grasp *separately* a moment of the object, which, however, is not independent. On the other hand, when one substantivizes a state-of-affairs, and when one takes it for the substrate of a new judgment, one can find nothing analogous to the level of predication in the lower level. "The object which here becomes the subject of a new judgment is not something that could also be grasped in a simply receptive way."[17] It is an object of a sort entirely different from the

16. *Erf. u. Urt.*, p. 284.
17. *Ibid.* Of course the fact that the *nominalization* of the state-of-affairs does not have its analogue in purely receptive experience does not signify that the state-of-affairs itself does not have its ana-

simple substrate-object; one cannot find an antecedent for it qua single object in the sphere of receptivity, and it appears on the highest level of predicative spontaneity. The set [*ensemble*] is another example of categorial objectivity. It is the result of an operation which gathers objects together into a totality. In the sphere of receptivity we can consider a plurality of objects. The objects are not simply grasped one after another; for when one grasps one object, one still "retains" the preceding object. But one does not grasp this plurality of objects as *one totality*, one does not grasp it as *one* object. The state-of-affairs as well as the set are totalities on a level above that where the substrate-object is grasped as a unity in receptivity. Receptivity does not know objects of the second degree. Hence we now understand much more profoundly Husserl's assimilation of formations such as groups to the formations of judgment. In the act of predication, objects are connected by a form of connexion, the copulative connexion. In the act of colligation, objects are connected by a form of connexion, the conjunctive connexion. These two sorts of connexion once more lead to an object. These are not "sensible" connexions but "syntactical" connexions. This is why Husserl often uses the expression "*syntactical* objectivities" instead of "*categorial* objectivities." In *Erfahrung und Urteil* he specifies in a footnote that "this concept, that is concerned with logical form alone, of syntax and of the syntactical must not be confused with the concepts of syntax and syntactical form as they are used in linguistics." [18] Despite this possibility of confusion, Husserl uses the expressions "syntactical objectivities" and "categorial objectivities" indifferently in all of his works. This is why in *Erfahrung und Urteil (ibid.)* we are told that the usage "syntactical" enables us to speak of "syntactical categories" and that it gives rise to derivations such as "syntagma."

---

logue in this sphere of receptivity. The categorial objectivities are founded in the objects which are grasped by the receptive experience. Thus to the *state-of-affairs (Sachverhalt)* there corresponds in receptivity a *situation (Sachlage)* where the things maintain relations among themselves which will be specifically explicated by the *Sachverhalte*. For example, a pair of two magnitudes a, b forms a certain situation within the sphere of receptivity which at the level of predication will give place to the states-of-affairs: a > b and b < a (cf. *ibid.*, p. 285).

18. *Ibid.*, p. 247, n. 1.

The use of "categorial" alone would not have permitted us this facility in expression.

The categorial or syntactical objectivities are hence, as the *Ideen* says, "objectivities derived from other objectivities by means of 'syntactical forms.' " [19] The acts which constitute them are *founded* acts.[20] One can study these categorial objectivities without referring to the objects which served as foundations for the logical production, that is to say, what Husserl calls the "ultimate substrates." But in what follows we will see definitively that the categorial objectivities must refer us to the ultimate substrates, that is to say, to objects which are no longer of the order of syntactical categories.

> No matter how much the determining may become — now and then at different levels — a determining of nominalized substrates, it pertains ultimately to the lowest and primarily thematic substrates (in the sciences, the objects belonging to their provinces); the determination of these substrates is the aim throughout all intermediary steps (113).

19. *Ideen*, p. 24.
20. Cf. Sixth Investigation, *Log. Unt.*, Vol. II, Pt. II, pp. 145 ff.

5 / Apophantics, as Theory of Senses, and Truth-Logic

CHAPTER 5 IS THE LAST CHAPTER of Part I and will make the final points in the study of formal logic. This chapter is not a simple continuation of the preceding investigations. Taking into account the results of Chapters 2, 3, and 4, it goes back over the results of Chapter 1 in order to clarify them with a *new* light. We can apply to these five chapters composing Part I what Husserl said at the beginning of his research in the *Logische Untersuchungen:*

> Considered in and of itself, the systematic clarification of pure logic, like that of any other discipline, would demand that one follow, step by step, the order of the affairs, the systematic nexus of the science that is to be clarified. In our case, however, the security of the investigation itself requires that, again and again, one interrupt this order. . . . The investigation, as it were, zigzags.[1]

The investigation in *Formal and Transcendental Logic* does indeed zigzag, as can be seen in the numerous recurring advances: a cycle of investigations leads to *results* which enable us to *advance* in the understanding of logic. But, while proceeding in this way, one acquires new results, which lead, in turn, to a more profound analysis than that which was previ-

1. *Log. Unt.,* Vol. II, Pt. I, p. 17.

ously completed. Possessed of these new means of analysis, one is to *go back over* the preceding results, which were only provisional.

Let us retrace briefly the itinerary of the investigation up to Chapter 5. Chapter 1 ended at the separation of apophantic logic into three strata: morphology of judgments, logic of non-contradiction, and truth-logic. Chapter 2 introduced an extension of logic which the first chapter did not consider and which was elicited by emphasis on the affinity between logic and formal mathematics. Thus enlarged, logic includes formal mathematics and becomes *mathesis universalis*. Because formal mathematics is incorporated into logic, it brings new views that can enrich the idea of logic. On the one hand, the various disciplines of formal mathematics are primarily concerned with anything whatever. From this we come to the idea of a formal ontology which would be the apriori science of anything whatever. Such a formal ontology is a science correlative to apophantics. On the other hand, formal mathematics teaches a degree of formalization never previously reached. Formalization does not simply touch upon the elements of propositions (the "cores of stuff" being replaced by these variables), and it does not merely touch upon the laws which govern the forms of propositions. Formalization is accomplished on the level of *totalities* which are theories. Logic is then raised above itself, so to speak, in order to become the theory of the forms of theories and is no longer merely the theory of the formations which arise *within* theories (Chapter 3). Once this highest level is reached — hence, once logic is complete — the relationships between ontology and apophantics can be studied in their full breadth. Chapter 4 shows, as we have just seen, that formal ontology and apophantics are actually two thematic orientations toward, or focusings on, one and the same science. Logic's apophantic position results from its orientation toward the *criticism* that every science must undergo. The links between the apophantic attitude and the critical attitude are to be examined more closely, and the problems of the stratification of logic are to be reconsidered in the light of this notion of criticism. This reconsideration is the central theme of Chapter 5.

To criticize judgments is, as we have said, to consider judgments asserted in a "straightforward" fashion as simple

meanings and to thematize them. Then one judges at a second level, and in this judging of the second level the "object" about which one judges is the judgment. The judgment is an "object" distinguished from mere objects by the fact that it is a meaning about objects, that it belongs to the sphere of signification. To take up the critical attitude is "to go over, from the straight-forward stating-and-judging attitude in which we 'have' only the pertinent objects, into the reflective attitude, the attitude in which the corresponding object-meanings and predicatively formed affair-complex-meanings become grasped and posited" (133). Instead of *meaning* ⟨or *opinion*⟩ we can just as well speak of *sense*, Husserl says. Later we will specify the different usages of this word in Husserl's analyses.[2] For the moment it arises as synonym of meaning, more exactly as synonym of *simple meaning,* it being understood that a thematic restriction is indicated here; when we will be oriented toward the judgment *without* being oriented toward the objects about which it judges, we will say that we are considering the judgment qua *sense.* In order to mark the distinction between objects which are senses (or even intended objectivities—*Vermeintheiten* [meantnesses]) and objects which are not intended, Husserl will speak of "regions" within the formal all-embracing region "any objectivity whatever." Objects such as judgments will belong to the *region of sense.* To be sure, these objects refer to other objects, to objects pure and simple. They are, as *Erfahrung und Urteil* says, "senses-of . . ." (*Sinn-von . . .*).[3] They are not objects of the first degree. But, despite this referential quality, they form a *proper* region. In fact one can make them the theme of a study which remains independent of the objects these senses refer to (cf. Chapter 4). Of course they nevertheless merit the title of object, for they are transcendent in relation to the subjective acts which correspond to them. Each of these is a *pole of unity* for the *multiplicity* of categorial acts which relate to it[4] in the same way that every object is a pole of unity for the multiplicity of mental processes relating to it. In *Erfahrung und Urteil* we come upon the distinction between objectivities which are intended objectivities (*Vermeintheiten*) and those which are not. But

2. Cf. *FTL*, pp. 215 f.; *Erf. u. Urt.*, p. 345.
3. *Erf. u. Urt.*, p. 323.
4. *Ibid.*, p. 323.

at present we are involved with the same distinction, that of *Formal and Transcendental Logic* being, so to speak, "rougher." In *Erfahrung und Urteil* the distinction between objectivities which are intended objectivities and those which are not corresponds simply to the distinction between irreal or ideal objectivities and real objectivities. The notion of intended objectivity (*Vermeintheit*) corresponds to the notion of ideal formation (*ideales Gebilde*) employed in *Formal and Transcendental Logic*. An intended objectivity can be Goethe's *Faust,* the constitution of a state, the number π, "S is p," etc. The categorial objectivities are only a special case of these intended objectivities. Nevertheless, in *Formal and Transcendental Logic* the distinction is brought about within the very sphere of the categorial. This is explained by the perspective Husserl adopts in this book, where we are in the categorial sphere from the start. Let us take an example to show more specifically the sense of the distinction used in *Formal and Transcendental Logic*. I can have a "straightforward" attitude and be directed toward the substrate-object S and toward the quality p. I form the judgment *"S is p"; I judge simply.* I can also bring my attention to bear upon the totality S is p qua *totality,* i.e., upon that fact that S is p . . . (*dies, dass* S p *ist . . .*). Then I am no longer focused upon the mere object but upon the object of the second degree, which is the categorial objectivity: S is p. But I can have a third attitude, a reflective attitude, in which I consider the judgment taken in itself, without focusing upon what the simple act of judgment is focused upon, that is to say, the things or the states-of-affairs. I can take the *judgment* as substrate-object of a new judgment and say, for example, "the judgment N is q." In this new attitude the judgment is not considered as a mere categorial objectivity, as would be the case if I said: "the fact that S is p . . . , is a categorial objectivity grasped qua sense." Then I consider the judgment as a *simple sense* without focusing upon the objects which this sense intends, hence without placing myself in the situation of possible adequation. The difficulty lies in the fact that language hides this difference in attitude and in the fact that the word "judgment" applies as much to what is judged in the straightforward judging as to what is judged in the judging of the second degree. When I say that I form the judgment: "This rose is yellow," and when

I say that the judgment "This rose is yellow" is a singular judgment, the same word *judgment* refers to two different themes. I can indicate quite simply that I consider the judgment "S is *p*" as a sense by placing it in quotation marks. But quotation marks are purely relative distinguishing marks, and one must already know the level one is on in order to understand the distinctive sense which the quotation marks imply. It is astonishing that Husserl does not study this use of quotation marks systematically and that he did not resume in a profounder phenomenological sense the scholastic distinction between *suppositio formalis* and *suppositio materialis.*[5] In this respect he would have improved the style of *Formal and Transcendental Logic.*

Possessed of this notion of sense introduced by the thematic limitations implied in the critical attitude, Husserl returns to the stratification of the apophantic. Can apophantics as a whole be called the pure science of "senses"? Actually only the first two strata of apophantics, the morphology of judgments and the logic of non-contradiction, make up a pure systematic theory of the region of sense. For with questions relating to truth one goes beyond the sphere of sense to introduce questions of adequation.

Thus the separation between the logic of non-contradiction and the logic of truth introduced by Chapter 1 takes on a new importance from the fact that it enables us to delimit the sphere of sense with thematic purity. To be sure, the logic of truth also considers judgments as senses, but then only insofar as they are senses-of. . . . Only the logic of non-contradiction abstracts from their referential character. Chapter 1 did not yet consider analytics as having achieved to the status of *mathesis universalis*, and hence, where traditional logic is concerned, it did not establish the separation between the logic of non-contradiction and the logic of truth. Husserl is now going to show that this distinction continues to be valuable for the theory of multiplicity and that one can use it to distinguish a pure *mathesis* of non-contradiction from a *mathesis* of possible truth. In fact, the theory of multiplicity can be developed entirely without reference to concretely actual particular multiplicities. "The

5. It should be noted that Husserl does devote several pages to *suppositio materialis* in the Fourth Investigation (*Log. Unt.,* Vol. II, Pt. I, pp. 322–26).

mathematician as such need not be at all concerned with the fact that there actually are multiplicities in concrete 'actuality' "(138). The mathematical intentionality, taken in itself, does not have the "imperious motives" of interesting itself in questions of the possible actuality of the multiplicities that it constructs.

The fact of considering logic in the enlarged form of *mathesis universalis* not only brings an *extension* of the validity of the tripartition effected upon simple traditional logic. The theory of multiplicity also teaches a purity in the reduction of the material, a purity which traditional logic is not in a position to show us and which, in truth, it is not among its ultimate intentions to show us. In fact, logic, by incorporating formal mathematics, introduces an intentionality which in a certain way—which we shall specify—is foreign to it: "For a (consciously or unconsciously) 'pure' formal mathematics, there can be no cognitional considerations other than those of 'non-contradiction'" (140). Meanwhile, logic "still intends to relate to possible provinces and possible cognition of them, possible systematic theories" (139); and this when it intends to be mere formal logic. In an essential way, the "formal" of formal mathematics can be considered in its own right. The "formal" of formal logic has adequation as its *goal*. From this it must not be hastily concluded that logic must side-step mathematics for fear of alienation. Rather, by looking toward mathematics, it can arrive at a new level of problems which cannot be reached within the narrow perspective of traditional logic. The logician need only integrate the logical project of adequation into pure formal mathematics in order to be able to consider it as an enlarged *logic*. "Here lies," Husserl says, "the sole legitimate distinction between formal logic and mere formal mathematics" (141). There is latent irony here toward the "philosophers." Let us follow Husserl's thinking through to the end: the philosophers who ordinarily think that the logician has nothing to teach the mathematician are only prejudiced. The irreducible difference which they see between logic and mathematics has no basis. Logic must be a "mathematics," a mathematics inbued with the logical interest. The "formal" of formal mathematics and the "formal" of formal logic point back to two different *intentionalities* within the heart of one science, *mathesis universalis*.

On the level of *mathesis universalis* one can truly understand the intention of a theory of pure apophantic senses. With
the doctrine of multiplicity, having broken all ties with the
material, we reach an *experience* of the formal; we are involved there with an exercise in the abstract which has its
own legitimacy, while, on the level of traditional logic, the
separation between the logic of non-contradiction and the logic
of truth is more artificial. The traditional logic which does not
find an intention within itself that focuses it solely on the
problems of non-contradiction is just the traditional logic which
does not benefit from the intentionality of formal mathematics.

One might think that there is a contradiction between the
results of the investigations of Chapter 5 and the preceding
results, for formal mathematics was presented to us as something able to suggest the idea of a formal ontology, but now it
is teaching us what a theory of *pure* apophantic senses is. But
we are able to formulate such an objection because we retain
habits of thinking which lead us to think that disciplines can
be distinguished only by their provinces. Here, on the contrary,
a diversification in thematic interest at the heart of a single
province is operative.

Husserl will return in a specific manner to the relationship
between formal apophantics and formal ontology which pure
apophantics has now studied in its own right. As we have said,
from the moment we inquire after the specifically logical
interest of the *mathesis,* we go beyond the pure sphere of sense
and reach a *mathesis* of possible truth, which thus brings
under consideration the possibility of adequation to possible
things. "In this manner the whole mathematical system of logic
becomes related to any possible objectivity whatever" (143).
"As soon as we . . . [raise] questions of possible correctness,
we stand within logic proper; and in it the whole mathematics
of judgments as senses forthwith takes on a formal-ontological
significance — but still we must not, without more ado, pronounce it formal ontology" (144). Actually we are situated
well within the perspective of possible adequation, but it
is always judgments which are considered as the exclusive
themes. Hence we are still within the framework of the *apophantic.*

The fact that what are grasped as exclusive themes are
judgments derives from the *critical* orientation of logic. Up un-

til now, however, criticism has not been considered except in its initial stage of examining meanings considered for themselves. In the last analysis, all criticism aims at the return to the things themselves, which alone can authenticate meanings and transform them into certainties. In the sciences, "the repeated focusings on judgments are only a *means* serving the primary interest, the interest in the affairs themselves and how they are in truth: so the focusing on judgments is likewise only a means in the case of that logic which does not lose sight of its calling as a theory of science" (145). The initial stage of criticism is a necessary stage, and it properly belongs to logic to be its instrument. From this derives the apophantic focusing of logic. But its profound intention is to be "the science of the possible categorial forms in which substrate-objectivities can truly exist" (145). From this derives its ontological focus. What makes formal logic an apophantics is at first its *function* as science of science; it is its *vocation* as science of science that leads to the thematic shift that makes it an ontology. Now we understand how Husserl's two affirmations can be reconciled: That the "central and privileged" theme of logic is the apophansis and "according to its final sense such a logic is therefore not a pure apophantic logic but a formal-ontological logic" (145).

The specificity of Husserl's examination of logic already appears distinctly at the end of Part I. Defender of pure logic, Husserl nevertheless stands apart from the partisans of pure logic who have gone before him. Kant certainly indicated the separation between pure logic and applied logic with an exemplary firmness. In the *Prolegomena* Husserl claims the allegiance of Kant on this point against the empiricists, who maintained that they had given logic a psychological foundation. But he does not fail to point out that Kant adhered to Aristotelian logic without question. It must be recognized that a reading of Kant's *Logic* brings before us no view that even anticipates a reform of traditional logic. Herbart and Lotze did not succeed in clarifying the idea of pure logic, for they did not know how to delimit this science, and they did not see its links with pure mathematics. To work in logic without an interest in mathematics is a prejudicial defect as far as Husserl

is concerned. It is significant that the only logicians referred to by Husserl in Part I of *Formal and Transcendental Logic* are mathematical logicians such as Leibniz and Bolzano. These logicians at least bring to their conceptions a mathematical rigor without which a logical theory cannot claim a sure Objectivity. Logic has much to learn from the "mathematical preciseness in distinction" and from the "mathematical exactness of the theories" that one finds, for example, in Bolzano's *Wissenschaftslehre*.[6] Yet Husserl does not find predelineated investigations in this work, but only stimuli for thinking. Actually, Bolzano lacked the key for understanding the internal unity of logic and mathematics, i.e., the idea of formal mathematics. In a time which did not prepare him for such intuitions, Leibniz had brilliant insights about the universal mathematics of quality. By his *Ars combinatoria* we can consider him, Husserl says, as the "spiritual father of the *Mannigfaltigkeitslehre* [theory of multiplicity]."[7] In fact we must hold Leibniz to be a "modern" logician, and we understand that Husserl felt himself closest to him, as is affirmed in the *Prolegomena*.[8] But perhaps exactly because Leibniz was too much in advance of his time, his novel logical ideas did not hold sway and hence were forgotten.

However things may stand with the implantation of mathematical views into logic, the constitution of mathematized formal logic must be completed with a philosophical clarification of its problems. And only a philosophical vocation can accomplish this. Mathematical exactness often has as its counterpart a certain aridity which scorns philosophical discussions. But the philosopher can well rail against the somewhat unpolished simplicity of the logical argumentation of the mathematician. The position of the philosopher is no more enviable than that of the mathematician, for the philosopher, if he gets beyond the superficial, brings to the work his thirst for profundity concerning problems which are not those required by the essence of logic, even mathematized logic. We understand, for example, that Husserl could in no way be receptive to a logic à la Hegel, witness to which are a few

6. Cf. *Prolegomena*, p. 226.
7. *Ibid.*, p. 222.
8. *Ibid.*, p. 219.

disdainful allusions to the Hegelian philosophy as more *Weltanschauung* than strict philosophy.[9]

Thus the unity which Husserl establishes between the mathematical spirit of strictness and the interests of philosophy leaves a unique mark on Husserl's logical considerations. But since one can point out that this rare conjunction was actualized in the beginning of the twentieth century with investigations into the foundations of mathematics, one can then wonder quite seriously about the fact that Husserl refers only very rarely to the works of Hilbert and his school. Thinking of these works and of all the attempts at the axiomatization of the theory of sets, Husserl, in 1929, did not feel obliged to revise his judgment in the *Prolegomena* that "these questions can perhaps be evaded by the investigator who, in his delimited field, builds theory upon theory, as does the mathematician, without having to trouble himself very much about the questions of principles." [10] One cannot discount the fact that the "foundational problems" of mathematics have led to a revision of the fundamental concepts of logic and mathematics and to an explicitation of principles. But actually a reading of Chapters 4 and 5 of Part I of *Formal and Transcendental Logic* convinces us that, even before the transcendental questions are raised, Husserl's problem-set develops on a level more profound than that of ⟨the usual⟩ axiomatic investigations. In truth, these axiomatic investigations avoid the problems of evidence which form the center of interest of *Formal and Transcendental Logic*. It can be said that an objective deepening of the problems of mathematics appeared with axiomatic thinking. The technique of theory also has its depths. But it leaves the philosophical questions open, even though the cognition of this technique enables the philosopher to pose his questions in the appropriate manner.

On the other hand, from the purely philosophical point of view, the method of intentional analysis, which the investigations of this first part have already exposed, gives the phenomenological examination an original style which Part II will bring more fully to light.

9. Cf. *ibid.*, p. 226; cf. also "Philosophy as Rigorous Science," pp. 77 f.

10. *Prolegomena*, p. 227.

Part II
From Formal
to Transcendental Logic

1 / Psychologism and the
Laying of a Transcendental
Foundation for Logic

As we have just seen, the analyses of Part I have enabled Husserl to "explicate" the genuine sense of traditional formal logic. As a result of this explication of its sense, logic was brought to a clear view of its goals. This led to the essential delimitation of its province, to the baring of its internal hierarchical structure, to the profound understanding of the correlation between its set of apophantic themes and its set of ontological themes. Hence one can say with Husserl: "It might now appear that, as philosophers, we were through with this logic and could leave its theoretical development to the mathematicians, who are already working on it anyhow, untroubled by the requirements of philosophic cognition" (149). If there can still be logical tasks, they would appear to be of the sort that lead us *beyond the formal*—tasks which, in addition, impress themselves upon our desire for cognition. The form is thought spontaneously as an empty framework which *should* be filled out if cognition is to be reached. Hence the analytico-formal theory of science calls for a *material* theory of science. But then a question arises. The analytico-formal theory of science is an apriori universal theory: it transforms the "cognition-materials," the "cores," into arbitrary cores; "this theory was to deal with the (in the broadest sense) 'formal' Apriori pertaining to all sciences as

such: that which embraces them all with apriori universality" (149). In passing from the formal to the material theory of science, must we abandon the original idea by which logic is conceived as universal theory of science? "If we let fullness flow back into these cores, which have been kept emptily universal" (150), can we arrive at a material theory of science which is also *universal*? In order to safeguard universality, it is not a question of finding the concrete singularity of cognition-materials; rather it is a question of determining a "synthetic" Apriori, a material Apriori which is a feature of the cores. Husserl is not very explicit about this material Apriori:

> Is not every existent — thought of concretely as materially determined and determinable — essentially an existent in a universe of being, a "world"? Is not every possible existent (as this word "essentially" indicates) something that belongs to its possible universe of being; accordingly, is not every material Apriori something that belongs to a universal Apriori, namely the Apriori that predelineates the apriori material form [*die apriorische sachhaltige Form*] for a possible universe of the existent? (150).

If Husserl does not specify how this idea of a *material ontology* is to be developed, it is because, contrary to appearances, the moment has not come for entering upon that task. "For it is not the case that we were actually through with formal analytics — we, not as mathematical technicians, but as philosophical logicians and therefore as seriously intent on doing justice to the final idea of an analytico-formal theory of science" (150). Actually, in the "Preparatory Considerations" Husserl has put forward a twofold requirement for logical researches. The objective themes should be followed up with a subjective set of themes. The subjective themes were touched upon in Part I. But there the sense of this set of subjective themes is not grounded in a genuine clarification. In fact the intentional analyses of Chapters 4 and 5 of Part I involve subjective activities only insofar as these activities are simple correlates of the objects of thinking they deal with. The subjectivity one would then recognize would be, for example, the judging as correlate of the judgment, the deducing as correlate of the deduction. The study of this subjectivity could hardly lead to what Husserl calls an analytic "technology." And if one can speak of criticism in this case, it is the analytical criticism of cognition, that is to say, a criticism "re-

lating to the ideal cognitional results (those belonging to the 'theory') and, on the subjective side, relating to what is ideal in a correlative sense, namely the acting (concluding, proving) that corresponds to these idealities" (170). But every science has another sphere of criticism which concerns, not objective results and the processes for reaching these results, but rather the constituting subjectivity itself. Only then can one speak of the properly subjective orientation of the themes of logic. "Here," Husserl says,

> the regard is directed to judging as a function [*Leistung*] of consciousness in which the constructs arise with all of their claim to be the expression of cognition. Traditional logic did not place the problems presented by judging in the center of its considerations, where they necessarily belonged, but believed that they could be turned over to psychology.[1]

Such a criticism has not yet been undertaken. With this criticism we have to do with

> criticism of the constitutive sources from which the positional sense and the legitimacy of cognition originate; accordingly criticism of the effective performances that remain hidden during the inquiring and theorizing directed straightforwardly to the province. This is the criticism of "reason" (taken either psychologically or transcendentally); or, contrasting it with analytic criticism of cognition, we may say it is *transcendental* criticism of cognition. What we have said holds good for logic as well as for every other science (171).

Without this transcendental criticism oriented toward subjectivity, one cannot hope to lay a foundation for logic in its genuineness. The analyses of Part II of *Formal and Transcendental Logic* will be devoted to bringing to light the sense and *legitimacy* of this set of subjectively oriented themes. But here, Husserl says, "stands the bogy of psychologism" (151). Coming from the one who fought against psychologism in the *Prolegomena*, the irony of this expression can be surprising. Actually, as we will see, Husserl always completely assumes the anti-psychologistic position of the *Prolegomena*. But he reacts against those symbolic logicians who, in their fear of the psychologistic danger, see manifestations of psy-

1. *Erf. u. Urt.*, p. 9.

chologism even where it does not arise. If the upholders of psychologism have had their fill of pure logic, the symbolic logicians [*logicistes*], on their part, deny all investigations directed into subjectivity, for, just like the maintainers of psychologism, they are victims of a confusion which leads them to take any investigation oriented toward subjectivity for a psychological investigation. A convinced "antipsychologizer," Husserl will have to defend himself against the accusation of the symbolic logicians, who saw in the investigations of Volume II of the *Logische Untersuchungen*—investigations directed into "phenomenological" subjectivity—transgressions against pure logic and interpreted the new direction of the works after the *Prolegomena* as a relapse into psychologism. It was just this misunderstanding of the new dimension of the investigations, introduced in the second volume of the *Logische Untersuchungen* and subsequent works, that permitted this reproach to take root. The goal of the struggle of the *Prolegomena* against psychologism was, as *Formal and Transcendental Logic* puts it, "the supremely important one of making the specific *province* of analytic logic visible in its purity and ideal peculiarity, freeing it from the psychologizing confusions and misinterpretations in which it had remained enmeshed from the beginning" (172). Hence the *Prolegomena* was a necessary defense of *pure* logic. But if one vindicates for pure logic its *own* right to be, that is to say, if one radically separates it from psychology, is it then still necessary to conceive of it as an autonomous science which is ultimately sufficient unto itself and whose destiny would be independent of a *transcendental criticism* of cognition? For Husserl one cannot *separate* objective science from such a criticism of cognition. This includes pure analytic logic, just as it includes every other objective science. The defense of pure logic *does not exclude* subjective investigations; let us say, more specifically, that it does not exclude the initiation of a criticism oriented toward constituting subjectivity. It is even the case that, by backing up pure logic with a "subjective" logic, one will be in a position fully to understand the genuine sense of logic. The transcendental criticism of cognition has a *logical function*, and, by misunderstanding this function, one can interpret the adherence to the transcendental criticism of cognition as a relapse into psychol-

ogism. The specific plan of *Formal and Transcendental Logic* is precisely that of reaching a logic which transcends objective logic by integrating it into a logic able to attain a full understanding of itself. "Our chief purpose is to show that a logic directed straightforwardly to its proper thematic sphere, and active exclusively in cognizing that, remains stuck fast in a naïveté which shuts it off from the philosophic merit of radical self-understanding and fundamental self-justification" (153). By limiting itself to the consideration of objective logic, the *Prolegomena* is hence tainted by the naïveté which *Formal and Transcendental Logic* denounces. But on the objective plane where it is situated, its criticism of psychologism is a healthy criticism that one must pass through in order to disenfranchise the psychologistic falsifications of objective logic. *Formal and Transcendental Logic* will hence be able legitimately to resume the struggle against psychologism developed in the *Prolegomena*, but by radicalizing it, that is to say, by placing it in the horizon of a doubly oriented logic. This is a new horizon which makes it possible to *extend* the bearing of this criticism and to *overcome* the problems.

Formal and Transcendental Logic is thus going to present an "extreme generalization" of the idea of psychologism presented in the *Prolegomena:* "We intend . . . to give the problem [of psychologism] a purer form and also set it in more general contexts, which will provide a transition to the clarification of the necessary sense of a 'two-sidedly' inquiring logic, one that is, in the genuine sense, philosophic" (153). But the psychologism to which the *Prolegomena* refers is a psychologism taken in an entirely determinate sense, which is not the only possible one: "It is noteworthy," Husserl remarks,

> that readers regarded the *"Prolegomena zur reinen Logik"* as an unqualified overcoming of psychologism and failed to take notice that nowhere in that volume was psychologism pure and simple (as universal epistemological aberration) the theme. Rather the discussion concerned a psychologism with a quite particular sense, namely the psychologizing of the irreal significational formations that are the theme of logic. The obscurity still generally prevalent today concerning the problem of a universal epistemological psychologism, an obscurity that affects the fundamental sense of the whole of transcendental philosophy (including so-called "theory of knowledge") is something that, at the time, I

myself had not entirely overcome; though precisely the "phenomenological" investigations in the second volume, so far as they
paved the way to a transcendental phenomenology, opened up at
the same time the necessary avenues to the setting and the radical overcoming of the problem of transcendental psychologism
(152).

Chapter 6 of this second part of *Formal and Transcendental
Logic* will take up the general problem of psychologism, viz.,
the problem of transcendental psychologism which is characterized by the confusion of pure psychology with transcendental phenomenology. For the time being, while giving it
an extremely general form, Husserl still remains with the *particular* problem of the *logical* psychologism dealt with in the
Prolegomena.

In the *Prolegomena,* after juxtaposing the psychologistic
and logicistic arguments, Husserl distinguishes the prejudice
of psychologism: What logic is concerned with, i.e., judgments,
deductions, demonstrations, etc., are nothing other than psychic
phenomena. This is the key prejudice to such a degree that in an
entirely natural fashion psychologism arrives at the conclusion
that judgments, deductions, demonstrations, etc., belong, like
all other psychic phenomena, to the province of psychology.
To such a thesis the logicists reply that the proper domain
of logic is constituted by judgments, deductions, and demonstrations qua objective formations and not as the psychic
processes in which these formations are formed. One must not
confuse the judgment and the judging, the deduction and the
deducing, the demonstration and the demonstrating. One of
the principal arguments developed by the *Prolegomena* for
the logicist refutation of the psychologistic thesis is that if
one thus accepts a dependency of logic on psychology, then
one must do so just as much where mathematics is concerned
and say that mathematics is also a branch of psychology. In
effect, numbers—multiplications, for example—also refer back
to psychic acts—the act of counting, the act of multiplying.
And yet nobody would think of making mathematics depend on
psychology; and in this the interpretation of the laws of mathematics as psychic laws is recognized as a "false μετάβασις."
"But," as he says in the *Prolegomena,* "there was also something else that necessarily made us doubtful here: the natural

kinship between purely logical and arithmetical doctrines, which had often led even to the assertion of their theoretical unity." [2] We have seen that this "natural" kinship was late in being recognized. But we should not believe that, once this kinship had been established and properly utilized in the elaboration of mathematical logic, the psychologistic interpretations would be eliminated. As we have seen,[3] misunderstandings of the nature of the ideal *objects* presented by the logical formations, which is like that of mathematical formations, would subsist and thus offer purchase for psychologistic interpretations.

Against the psychologistic thesis, the *Prolegomena* sets the argument that "the province of research belonging to pure logic, analogously to the one belonging to pure mathematics, is ideal," [4] which is to say, a province where one never deals with an object grasped in its singularity but rather with "ideal *species*." But the *Prolegomena* does not succeed, as does *Formal and Transcendental Logic,* in completely distinguishing the universal objective law which governs this ideality. What psychologism in essence suffers from is a failure to understand the *ideal object.* Psychologism by nature is empiricist, and all empiricism is a misunderstanding of ideality as such; for what empiricism cannot reduce to real Objectivity it relegates to the province of psychic activities. It does not recognize the special status of ideal objects. They are not objects of the external world, i.e., "real" objects. Rather they are, in their way, "objects" which are transcendent to the psychic activities in which they are formed. With logical formations we are dealing with ideal objects. Like all ideal objects (of which they are a particular case), they "float obscurely between subjectivity and Objectivity" (82). On the one hand, they are given exclusively from within, "exclusively by means of spontaneous activities and

2. *Prolegomena,* p. 168. It is also necessary to state that most of the adversaries of psychologism did not recognize this kinship. The logicists thought they could give a foundation to the separation between logic and psychology by means of the normative character of logic, which they considered to be one of its essential characteristics. This conception prevented them from seeing the essentially theoretical status of logic and hence its kinship with mathematics (cf. *Prolegomena,* p. 157).

3. Cf. *supra,* pp. 30 f.

4. *Prolegomena,* p. 169 (title of §46).

in them" (81). The logical formation "is nothing alien to the psychic, nothing like a physical process, a physical formation accruing in physical action" (153). From this derives the psychologistic assimilation of judgmental formations to the phenomena of internal experience. "On the other hand, . . . after having in fact been generated they are still taken to be existent; one 'returns to them' as the same formations" (81). In this sense, then, logical formations are "objects." They

> offer themselves, not as Ego-acts do (as transient and merely reiterable), but as *Objects* do; and that signifies: as, so to speak, seizable objectivities, steadfast under observation, always re-identifiable, and accessible to repeated observation, analysis, and description — not much otherwise than objectivities of external experience.[5]

While "the particular formative processes of thinking are temporally outside one another, . . . [and] are individually different and separated" (155), logical formations have, as Husserl puts it in the "Ursprung der Geometrie," a *supertemporal* existence (*überzeitliches Dasein*).[6] Even more precisely, "their supertemporality turns out to be *omnitemporality,* as a correlate of free produceability and reproduceability at all times."[7] Judgments formed in repeated similar acts are judgments which are themselves not similar but identical. These are "numerically the same judgments." I can reproduce the demonstration of the Pythagorean theorem at different moments, I will conclude with the same theorem, and I will say "*the* Pythagorean theorem."

Moreover, the essence of logical formations, like that of all irreal psychic formations, excludes spatial extension. Hence logical formations are not objects in the same way that objects of the external world are objects, i.e., they are not necessarily "located" in space. "Like other products of the mind, they admit, however, of a physical embodiment: in their case, an embodiment by the sensuous verbal signs" (155). Through writing and speaking, the logical formation comes to have a spatiotemporal existence. By such an embodiment we arrive, in the words of the "Ursprung der Geometrie," at "the 'locali-

5. *FTL,* p. 41.
6. "Ursprung der Geometrie," p. 209.
7. *CM,* p. 127.

zation' and 'temporalization' of something that, according to its being-sense, is non-local and non-temporal." [8] But precisely from the fact that, according to its "being-sense," the logical formation (like every irreal formation) is nonlocal and nontemporal, the spatiotemporal existence which it acquires is only a "secondary" existence. "The [written or spoken] sensuous utterances, like all bodily processes, like everything embodied in bodies, have spatio-temporal individuation in the world. But the spiritual formation itself, 'the ideal Objectivity,' the 'sense' *of* the sensuous utterances, is not spatio-temporally individuated." [9] In *Erfahrung und Urteil* Husserl is able precisely to define ideality by this impossibility of its being spatio-temporally individuated:

> We designate as "real" in the specific sense *all* those determinations of something that is "real" in the broader sense of the word, *that have the sense of being essentially individuated by their place in space-time.* We designate as *"irreal"* on the other hand *any determination that can present itself in different realities as* — not just quite like but — *identical even though, through its presenting itself in space-time, it is founded in something specifically real.*[10]

This is true of logical formations and equally applies to all cultural objectivities *(Kulturgegenständlichkeiten)*. Goethe's *Faust* has certainly been reproduced in a great number of copies in many different editions. We say that we are dealing with the *same* book, meaning by "book" not the material object in which the material signs are imprinted but the spiritual sense itself — the work. "The work of art, the spiritual formation as such, is determined by this spiritual sense which, although 'embodied' [*verkörpert*] in the real world, is not individuated by this embodiment." [11] In sum, "every kind of irreality . . . has manners of possible participation in reality. Yet this in no way alters the essential separation between the real and the irreal" (155).

8. "Ursprung der Geometrie," p. 210.
9. *Ibid.*
10. *Erf. u. Urt.*, p. 319.
11. *Ibid.*, p. 320. We have seen in the "Preparatory Considerations" of *Formal and Transcendental Logic* that thought is embodied (*verleiblicht*) by means of language. But this embodiment of language was itself spiritual. Then language is introduced by its ideality. Even

Thus far, by distinguishing the ideality of all psychic formations, *Formal and Transcendental Logic* has only reinforced the antipsychologistic criticism in the *Prolegomena* by remaining within the orientation of its investigations. Now, *Formal and Transcendental Logic* is going to reach a deeper understanding of the objective status pertaining to the ideal formations by turning to the comparative study of the evidences within which the real object and the ideal formations are given, i.e., by initiating investigations focused on subjectivity.

Before turning to this comparative study, Husserl is led to a general characterization of evidence itself. Only after such a digression into the study of evidence for its own sake can we understand how the objectivity of logical formations is specified. In the meantime, no matter how general this characterization of evidence is, it is at present only a mediate theme. One must wait for the fourth and following chapters in order to reach the problems of evidence set up by the constitutive criticism of logic.

Having recourse to the appropriate passages in the *Ideen* and the *Cartesian Meditations,* let us specify the Husserlian conception of evidence.

Evidence is a mode of consciousness in which a thing is " 'itself there,' 'immediately intuited,' *'given originaliter.'* " [12] The thing is given itself and not by means of an image or in an empty meaning. Evidence is "original consciousness" of presence. Hence we understand the sense in which Husserl can say that "all evidence is experience in a maximally broad, and yet essentially unitary, sense." [13] But to say that in evidence one grasps the object "itself" means that the object is grasped as *remaining the same,* as having a permanent *identity.* "The possibility of such original identification belongs, as essential

---

though it can be designated as the body *(Leib)* of thinking, it was itself considered an ideal objectivity. Meanwhile, what is here under consideration is the purely material side of language. The sensible signs of words, the sounds of language, are considered as physical events, as *"körperliche Vorgänge"* ("Ursprung der Geometrie," p. 210). They are individuated as bodies *(Körper)* in the real world. By signs and sounds, the ideal formations are not only *verleiblicht* but also *verkörpert.*

12. *CM,* p. 57.
13. *Ibid.*

correlate, to the sense of every object of experience in the usual and pregnant sense" (156). And this identification is possible only thanks to a synthetic totality of "experiences" and not through one single act of experience.

> Hence it follows without more ado that the particular evidence does not as yet produce for us any abiding being. Everything that exists is "in itself," in a maximally broad sense, and stands in contrast to the accidental being "for me" of the particular acts; likewise every truth is, in this broadest sense, a "truth in itself." This broadest sense of the In-Itself refers us to evidence, not however to a particular evidence as a de facto experience, but rather to certain potentialities, which are grounded in the transcendental Ego and his life: first of all, to the potentiality of the infinity of intendings of every kind that relate to something as identical, but then also to the potentiality of verifying these intendings, consequently to potential evidences which, as de facto experiences, are repeatable in infinitum.[14]

If one can say with the *Prolegomena*[15] that evidence is the *Erlebnis* [living experience] of truth, it must not be forgotten that this *Erlebnis* has a *horizon of potentialities,* potentialities that can be expressed as "I can always reproduce" the first evidence. Taking the example of internal perception, *Formal and Transcendental Logic* shows that it is a fully objectivating performance only if a synthesis of recognition is joined to it. "We accept internal perception as a grasping of an object itself, only because we are tacitly taking into account possible recollection, repeatable at will" (157).

But, as is said in the *Cartesian Meditations,* "in yet another and a much more complicated manner evidences refer us to infinities of evidences relating to the same object." [16] Such is the case for the object of external experience. In it the object is originarily given in a *one-sided* manner. Experience as individual experience cannot give the object in all of its richness. This evidence has a still "unfulfilled" *horizon of anticipations* which are to be fulfilled by other evidences. For example, we anticipate the perception of the other facets of a die only certain of whose facets we presently perceive. Experience as individual evidence is hence imperfect because insufficient. But it is

14. *Ibid.,* pp. 60–61.
15. *Prolegomena,* p. 190.
16. *CM,* p. 61.

perfected in a progression of concordant experiences. Actually, experience taken no longer as individual act but as continuing experience has the form of a synthesis of concordant experiences which verify anticipations. To be sure, it is possible that the anticipation will be, not confirmed, but canceled by a subsequent experience. The progress of experience hence brings confirmation and correction. Then one understands the profound sense of a passing remark in *Formal and Transcendental Logic:* "I do not find that sufficient attention has been paid to the clarification of evidence and of all the pertinent relationships between mere 'intention' and 'fulfillment,' which was first effected in the *Logische Untersuchungen,* II. Teil, and deepened in my *Ideen.*" [17] The individual evidence refers in an intentional manner to other evidences. There is no priviliged instant in which the thing manifests its presence in a total and definitive fashion. Certainly the consciousness of a thing is consciousness of that thing as *one* thing, but "a spatial thing is nothing other than an intentional unity that, of essential necessity, can be given only as the unity of such manners of appearance [of the thing]." [18] The "experience" is actuality. But one must separate the actuality from its context of potentialities and anticipations, a context which can be progressively explicated only in the development of the experience itself. As always, the *concretum* studied by phenomenology is not the *singular.*

Such a characterization of evidence results in a *relativization* of the notion of evidence in several respects. In the first place, such a conception of evidence implies the recognition of *degrees* of evidence. Evidence is more or less close to perfection. Moreover, if a series of originary acts leads us, through synthetic transitions, from evidences to yet other evidences, as is the case with external experience, in this case "no imaginable synthesis of this kind is completed as an adequate evidence: any such synthesis must always involve unfulfilled, expectant and accompanying meanings." [19] Unful-

17. *FTL*, p. 162. The clarification of evidence and the relationships between intention and fulfillment effected by the *Logische Untersuchungen* were deepened in the *Ideen* in particular because the *Ideen* specifically introduced the notion of the horizon of intentionality, which had not appeared in the *Logische Untersuchungen*.

18. *Ideen*, p. 78 [author's addition – Translator].

19. *CM*, pp. 61–62.

filled intentions are always implied in evidence. To be sure, one can *explicate* the horizons of experience, but in this explication the new evidences that come to fulfill the intentions make "new horizons . . . incessantly arise within the old." [20] The absolutely perfect empirical evidence which would give the object in all of its richness and which would be a complete synthesis of possible experiences *is only an "idea."* Hence we see that the evidence in which the object is itself given in an *originary* manner is still not *adequate* evidence and that, in the particular case of external experience, the adequate evidence is no more than a never achieved ideal of perfection.

But then, the ideal perfection is itself differentiated. There is "another type of perfection" than adequation; this is *apodicticity.*

> It is *absolute indubitability* in a quite definite and peculiar sense, the absolute indubitability that the scientist demands of all "principles"; and its superior value is evinced in his endeavor, where groundings already evident in and by themselves are concerned, to ground them further and at a higher level by going back to principles, and thereby to obtain for them the highest dignity, that of apodicticity.[21]

Types of perfection is a surprising expression. But if there are types of perfection of evidence it is because there are *types of evidence.* Evidence can be characterized in a general way as the giving of the things themselves. But the things are given in different manners according to the provinces to which they belong.

> Category of objectivity and category of evidence are perfect correlates. To every fundamental species of objectivities—as intentional unities maintainable throughout an intentional synthesis and, ultimately, as unities belonging to a possible "experience"—a fundamental species of "experience," of evidence, corresponds, and likewise a fundamental species of intentionally indicated evidential style in the possible enhancement of the perfection of the having of an objectivity itself (161).

In particular, it is external experience upon which the science of Nature *must* rely

> because external experience is precisely that mode of the having of something itself which pertains to natural Objects. . . . And

20. *Ibid.*, p. 64.
21. *Ibid.*, p. 15.

again, only because imperfect experience is still experience, still a consciousness that is a having of something itself [*Bewusstsein der Selbsthabe*], can experience adjust itself to experience and correct itself by experience (161).

External experience, however imperfect, is not for that reason reduced in value, especially, as we have already pointed out, when it is conceived in its progression, which is a factor in the process of perfection.

Just this misunderstanding of diversity in the structure of evidences is what Husserl decries in the current interpretation of evidence.[22] Husserl reproaches other theories of evidence for conceiving evidence exclusively as apodictic evidence. This reduction of evidence to an ideal type of perfect evidence is haunted, he says, by an absurdity; for having established the totality of evidence according to an absolute criterion of truth, one has recourse to a *"feeling"* of evidence. "Thus it happens that evidence is usually conceived as an absolute apodicticity, an absolute security against deceptions—an apodicticity quite incomprehensibly ascribed to a single mental process torn from the concrete, essentially unitary, context of subjective mental living" (157). The *Ideen* already insisted upon the fact that "one notes then forthwith that the tacit presupposition of the feeling-theory of evidence . . . [wherein] . . . one speaks of an 'evidence-feeling,' which as a mystic index of the true [*Index veri*] confers on the judgment a feeling-color, . . . is fundamentally erroneous." [23]

22. *Erf. u. Urt.*, p. 12: "We therefore designate as evident a consciousness of any sort that, with regard to its object, is characterized as giving it-itself, without inquiry whether this giving of it-itself is adequate or not. In so doing we deviate from the customary use of the word *Evidenz* [evidence], which as a rule is employed in cases that, correctly described, are such adequate givenness and, on the other side, apodictic insight. Such a manner of givenness too is characterized as a giving of things themselves, namely idealities, universal truths. But each sort of objects has its sort of giving of things themselves (= evidence); and not for every sort of objects—for example: not for spatial physical objects of external perception—is an apodictic evidence possible. Nevertheless they too have their sort of original giving of themselves and, with that, their sort of evidence."

23. *Ideen*, pp. 40 and 39; cf. p. 300: "Evidence is indeed not some index or other of consciousness which, being attached to a judgment . . . , calls to us like a mystic voice from a better world: Here is truth!; as though such a voice has something to say to us free spirits and did not have to show its titles of legitimacy."

But if Husserl denounces the reduction of all evidence to apodictic evidence, he none the less recognizes the place of apodictic evidence. And we think it impossible to interpret Husserl's thought as Mr. Merleau-Ponty does, in the Preface of his *Phenomenology of Perception,* when he declares: "There is no apodeictic self-evidence, the *Formale und transzendentale Logik* (p. 142 [= English trans., pp. 158 f.]) says in effect." [24] On the contrary, the notion of apodictic evidence is brought to light everywhere in Husserl's works, from the earliest to the latest. And it goes without saying that since the principal theme of Husserl's researches is the problem-set of logic and science, apodictic evidence plays a role of the first order. In the *Cartesian Meditations,* which appeared in the same year as *Formal and Transcendental Logic,* when Husserl studies evidence in its relationships with the idea of genuine science, he emphasizes "the highest dignity of apodicticity." The very notion of apodicticity is what gives meaning to the word *Einsicht,*[25] which comes up so often in Husserl's work, particularly in *Formal and Transcendental Logic.* The *Ideen*[26] explicitly proposes reserving the word *Einsicht* for apodictic evidence, reserving the word *Evidenz* for the supreme concept which embraces in its signification the assertoric seeing as well as the apodictic seeing.

In sum, while safeguarding the dignity of apodictic evidence, Husserl views evidence as the general form par excellence of the intentionality in which the object is present to consciousness as the object "itself," as the object grasped "in person" *(selbst),* this general form being differentiated according to the various structures to which the various types of objects correspond.

Then a new task arises. On the one hand, it is necessary to study the universal intentional function of evidence, for in

24. English translation by Colin Smith (London, 1962), p. xvi, n. 2.

25. [Husserl's term *Einsicht* is usually translated by the author as *évidence rationelle,* though it is sometimes rendered by *évidence apodictique.* Here she refers to an "indication given by Husserl at the beginning of *Formal and Transcendental Logic* (p. 16): *vernünftiges, nämlich einsichtiges oder auf einsichtige Wahrheit gerichtetes Denken,*" which Cairns renders: "the quality of insight, or thinking directed to a truth given in insight." (Note modified by Translator.)]

26. *Ideen,* p. 286.

evidence consciousness *renders the things present*. What is more, this function of evidence has its effect upon the unlimited multiplicity of possible modes of consciousness of things. We could say, forcing the expressions of Husserl, who speaks of "a pointedness toward 'reason' " and "a pervasive tendency toward it" (160), that there is in us a *will* to render the things present to us, a will to verify that the things are just what we think they are, a will to be correct. In a word, a will to justify permeates the whole life of consciousness. Thus, thanks to evidence, Husserl can say that "the whole life of consciousness has an all-pervasive teleological structure" (160).

On the other hand, one must study the various modes of the originality of evidence and the diverse provinces of objects. Besides the primitive mode of the giving of the thing, which is perception, one must study, for example, primitive modes such as remembering, etc. Apodictic evidence no longer being the measure of all evidence, the various evidences must be descriptively distinguished. The problem of evidence must be considered precisely as a problem, and one should not think that one knows, at the outset, what evidence is.[27]

But to maintain, as Husserl does, that evidence is the intentional action of the giving of the things themselves *(Selbstgebung)*, is this not to contrast a new "theory" to the traditional theories and to subject the descriptive examination of the different types of evidence to a *petitio principii*? Husserl protests, against such an objection:

> We are not opposing our universal characterization of evidence to the usual one as though ours were a new "theory," an attractive interpretation. . . . Rather we are presenting it as an evidence attained at a higher level, by the phenomenological explication of any experience and of any actually exercised "insight" (something that others, without reason, have separated quite essentially from what are usually called experiences). This higher evidence, in turn, can be itself explicated and understood in respect of its effect only by means of an evidence belonging to a third level; and so *in infinitum*. Only in seeing can I bring out what is truly present in a seeing; I must make a seeing explication of the proper essence of seeing (158–59).

Such a reply gives rise to an objection as grave as that which

27. *Erf. u. Urt.*, pp. 9–10.

it would answer. The return *in infinitum* is the Achilles' heel of a philosophy which continually places the demand for justification on the first level. But the moment has not yet come when Husserl's philosophy must suffer this trial.

Now that we have specified the Husserlian conception of evidence, let us return to the main theme of this chapter, i.e., the comparison of the evidence of ideal objects and the evidence of real objects. The identity which, as we have seen, confers the character of object upon the real object is grasped in just as immediate a manner in the case of the ideal object. On many occasions Husserl insists upon the *gain* that an ideal formation represents, e.g., a judgment, an acquisition to which one can return at any moment. Once a judgment has been made, it is our possession *(Besitz)*.

But, as we have seen, an important reservation limits the analogy between the evidence of ideal objects and the evidence of real objects. In contradistinction to a real object, an ideal object "is not individuated in consequence of a temporality belonging to it originally" (156). And if one is able to speak of a reference of the ideal objects to space and time, it is a reference "external to the essence" or even, in the words of the "Ursprung der Geometrie," a "secondary" reference. This difference in temporal viewpoint leads to another difference:

> The modification of itself-giving as perception and recollection plays very different rôles for real and ideal objectivities respectively. . . . Merely because of an essentially possible alteration of attitude or focus, any clear explicit recollection of an ideal *species* changes into a perception of it—something naturally impossible in the case of temporally individuated objects (158).

However it may be with these differences, the possibility of identifying an ideal object is "actually . . . like that of an 'experience'" (156). One has before one the object—for example, the judgment "itself," "in person"—grasped as an object that remains identical. To be sure, what constitutes the identity of the objects of external experience is more readily accessible. For the datum of external experience has a transcendence which cannot be separated from the immanent mental processes of consciousness. It is first grasped as a pole of identity appearing in the multiplicities of mental processes. Yet

a transcendence is also implied by the objective sense of the ideal objects insofar as these objects stand in contrast to the consciousness of them. "If, in spite of this, we still separate immanent from transcendent objects, that can involve a division only within this broadest concept of transcendence" (166). Hence we see that experience, in the broad sense "experience," retains the essential character of experience in the usual sense: the appearing of something numerically identical in numerous processes of consciousness, of something transcendent, which is constituted in the immanent sphere of consciousness. The object, be it real or ideal, is a transcendent *pole of identity* in relation to the particular mental processes in which it appears.[28] To be sure, this pole of identity is initially given in an indeterminate manner. It is determined bit by bit during the course of a synthetic succession of concordant experiences.

In this respect, Husserl speaks of the "explication" *(Auslegung)* of these determinations. This term *Auslegung* can lead to misunderstandings. It is not necessary to believe that there is a sense to the object which is already there, entirely preformed, which only needs to be uncovered and explicated in a way that is, so to speak, external. Actually, the object which is a transcendent pole of identity is at the same time a pole of identity *immanent* to the particular mental processes. And, "such an affair as an object . . . draws the ontic sense peculiar to it . . . originally from the mental processes of experience alone. . . . Experience is the primal instituting of the being-for-us of objects" (164) which correspond to it.

Husserl's researches now for the first time reach the problems of "constitution." "An evidential giving of something itself must be characterized as a process of constitution, a process whereby the object of experience arises" (164–65). Hence one must be on guard against a twofold misunderstanding con-

28. Husserl specifies the sense in which the rapprochement he brings about between the ideal objects and the real objects is to be understood. Ideal objects and real objects are for the same reasons transcendent objects in contrast to the immanent sphere of mental processes. They can be treated in the same way as substrates for possible predications. But Husserl still does not forget that real objects have a privilege in existence over ideal objects, and from this point of view they are not to be placed on the same plane: "In respect of its being, reality has precedence to every irreality whatsoever, since all irrealities relate back essentially to an actual or possible reality" (169).

cerning the "being-sense" of the object. Where it is a question of the ideal object, there is a tendency to deny its transcendence and not to see that "even fictions have their type of being." Where it is a question of the real object, there is a tendency not to see that its transcendence acquires its sense only in the "constructive life" of experience and that from this fact one can speak in a certain sense of its immanence. If one calls "transcendent" that which by its identity and its unity is opposed to the multiplicity of mental processes of experience,[29] one can then say that every object, be it real or ideal, is at once immanent and transcendent.

Hence Husserl can legitimately affirm that he has arrived at an ultimate generalization of the criticism of logical psychologism, since he has shown, in a reflective examination, that ideal objects, among them logical formations, are "objects" and that they must not be psychologized, i.e., their essence as objects must not be denied for the sake of subjective mental processes. He adds that such a psychologization is "the fundamental characteristic of every bad 'idealism' *(lucus a non lucendo!)* like Berkeley's and Hume's" (170). Such a critique of the "bad" idealisms must be followed through to the end, never losing sight of the fact that empiricism and psychologism go hand in hand. In the *Ideen,* after noting that "we have the extraordinarily widespread inclination in our times to *psychologize the eidetic.* To it many who call themselves idealists also are subject," Husserl adds: "indeed all empiricistic conceptions have a strong effect upon the idealistic camp." [30] If one thinks of the Berkeleian idealism, one must, in our opinion, denounce, as Husserl does, the paradoxical collusion of idealism with empiricism. The Husserlian "refutation of idealism" which we find in this chapter of *Formal and Transcendental Logic* is based on that criticism. We will see below the sense in which transcendental phenomenology is an idealism. For the moment let us keep in mind that Husserl does vindicate the appellation *idealism*[31] for his philosophy and notice that he deliberately overlooks the Kantian transcendentalism and proclaims

29. The qualifier *immanent,* in the strict sense, is uniquely appropriate to mental processes of experience themselves.
30. *Ideen,* p. 116.
31. *FTL,* p. 170.

the "phenomenological idealism" to be a new idealism, fundamentally different from idealism in the usual sense. Yet we can justify the absence of reference to Kantianism at this point, for only later did Husserl envisage a historico-critical examination. At present he is merely interested in showing that the phenomenological idealism can receive its precise sense from the criticism of this psychologism which develops from the idealistic attitude of a Berkeley.

Psychologistic idealism is essentially simplification and reductionism. Against this, the phenomenological idealism recognizes, as we have just seen, that there are types of evidence, of "experience," and that each type has its own legitimacy. The various types of evidence, of "experience," correspond to the various provinces of cognition and above all to the various regions of existents. Moreover, each province can be studied according to different thematic perspectives: to each straightforward cognition of the province there is added a criticism of the cognition of the province. We have seen that this criticism can be quite simply an analytic criticism of cognition. But there is a third thematic sphere — the transcendental criticism that transcends every set of psychological problems.

Transcendental logic is destined to come to such a transcendental criticism. Formal logic, even expanded into *mathesis universalis*, can only be an analytic criticism of cognition, a criticism of theories and of ideal processes which result in these theories. Only a transcendental criticism can truly set up a *universal* theory of science, for it is the criticism of the intentional life that itself "constitutes" provinces and theories. Thus we are to reach the transcendental by passing through the examination of logical requirements. Hence the itinerary of *Formal and Transcendental Logic* is essentially conditioned by what the essential possibility of genuine science implies. But that is no reason for a failure to recognize the fact that the simple "analytic" criticism remains indispensable to every science, which explains why the problems of the *Prolegomena* are not denied by *Formal and Transcendental Logic*. The logical analytic, grasped in its purity (this task of reducing the analytic to purity occupied Part I), is necessarily the first stage of logic. This logic "alone is now delimited for us cer-

tainly" (174). It is the one which the Husserlian investigation has reached, the themes of transcendental constitution not yet being brought up, except as requirements to be met.

Logic conceived not simply as analytic theory of science but as universal theory of science is hence called upon to be the ultimate justifying discipline for the steps of science. But it is itself a science which, like every science, must receive its justification. If the particular sciences can have logic specifically for the tasks of justification, logic itself has no other recourse than itself, for it must be in a position to justify its own concepts and its own theories.

Properly speaking, this problem of self-reference had already arisen on the level of analytic criticism, hence on the level of formal logic. It seems that logic is inevitably caught up in a circle. Every logician is aware of this objection, which, it is claimed, blocks his first steps. Such an objection misunderstands the very movement of logic by which a naïve use of concepts can reach a new plane where a strict procedure is set up for validating these very concepts. At bottom, what is involved is not a circle but a helical movement. Moreover, the rigorous steps of logic have a deductive style that enables the logician to posit in good conscience principles of deduction which he does not have to prove. Hence it appears that logic has what it takes to satisfy the demand for a *tabula rasa*, a demand which is in actuality wrongly presented. But this "criticism" of science — which criticism is formal logic — remains an "objective" science, and, as the *Ideen* shows, it too falls before the phenomenological reduction.[32] With the coming of transcendental logic, formal logic can be relieved

---

32. Cf. *Ideen* (§ 59: "The Transcendence of the Eidetic. Exclusion of Pure Logic as *mathesis universalis*"), pp. 111–13. In this section the affirmation of the exclusion of pure logic as *mathesis universalis* is not made without prior scruple. Here in its broadest lines is Husserl's argument: "Every researcher must, above all, be able to call freely upon formal logic (or formal ontology). For, no matter what he explores, they are objects, and what holds good formaliter for objects universally (for all properties, all syntactically formed affair-complexes, and the like) concerns him equally. No matter how he frames concepts and propositions, draws conclusions, and so forth, what formal logic ascertains with formal universality concerning such significations and genera of significations concerns him too, and every other special researcher, in the same manner. Hence it concerns likewise the phenomenologist. Every pure mental process is

of the task of ultimate justification. We will then see how, on the level of transcendental logic, the difficulties of the self-reference of a theory in which the deductive style does not reign are presented. But if one can clarify the relationships between phenomenology and objective logic, it seems that one still encounters a fundamental obscurity where the relationships between transcendental logic and phenomenology are concerned, i.e., where they both appear as the ultimate justifying disciplines. But first let us examine the steps of transcendental logic.

---

subordinate to the logically broadest sense of object. Therefore, it seems, we cannot exclude formal logic and formal ontology. . . . But, if we consider the matter more closely, we find that, under certain presuppositions, there arises a possibility of 'parenthesizing' formal logic and, with it, all the disciplines of formal *mathesis* (algebra, theory of numbers, theory of multiplicities, and so forth). If it is presupposed, namely, that phenomenology's investigation of pure consciousness sets for itself, and has set for itself, only tasks of descriptive analysis, which can be solved in pure intuition, then the theory-forms of the mathematical disciplines and all their mediate theorems can be of no use to it. . . . Now phenomenology is in fact a *purely descriptive discipline,* exploring the field of transcendentally pure consciousness *in pure intuition.* . . . Therefore we can include formal logic and the whole *mathesis* universally in the expressly exclusive *epoché.*" In the period of the *Ideen* Husserl had not shown, as he would in Part II of *Formal and Transcendental Logic,* the implicitly "mundane" *(weltlich)* character of formal logic. Logic, even in its most purely formal aspect, still presupposes the existence of the real world (cf. Chapter 5). By this fact it must hence be put out of play by the phenomenological reduction.

2 / Initial Questions of Transcendental Logic: Problems Concerning Fundamental Concepts

WITH CHAPTER 2 WE TAKE UP the problems of transcendental logic. Transcendental logic will have as its first task the submission of the straightforward evidence in which the logical formations are "given" to a "thematic reflection." This thematic reflection will make it possible to go beyond the "naïveté" with which straightforward activity is performed. This activity is rightly to be governed by method and thus to profit from methodological lucidity, but it remains quite hidden so long as the reflective regard does not take it as a theme. It remains "anonymous." Husserl uses the tern *anonymous* when he wants to reveal a conscious activity absorbed in its accomplishments, invisible on its noetic side. Now every activity is intention and actualization. Evidence has to be examined for "what it was aiming at and what it acquired" (177). Then one is led to an intentional analysis which can be termed genetic, even though Husserl does not expressly employ that word here. This intentional analysis is actually a search for the original and follows the way taken by the intention. To be specific, in naïve activity the intentional aimings can shift. There can be unnoticed "shiftings" in sense. Then it is necessary, after the fact, to search for the original in this activity. But this "after the fact" should not lead us to forget, as we are going to see, that this search for the original is a "constitutional" investigation

in the full sense, an investigation that informs and grounds what it clarifies.

Hence one must become aware of these shiftings in sense. Husserl specifies that these shiftings in sense do not derive from equivocations that pertain to the life of signification and that the examination of language would reveal: "Rather it is a matter of internal shiftings of intentionality and its product, shiftings that are tied together, and demanded, by essential interconnexions" (177). From this derives the necessity for the reflective examination of intentional aimings.

As an example of such a reflective examination, Husserl cites the investigations of Part I that conclude in the stratification of logic. Hence it seems that after the fact he elevates the subjective investigations of Part I to the status of transcendental research. To be sure, these investigations were to some extent directed into transcendental and not psychological consciousness. It was by distinguishing three sorts of attitudes in the justificatory attitude, three sorts of evidences, that Husserl was able to account for the three sorts of judgments at work in formal logic. Nevertheless, can we say that those investigations bear the mark of transcendentalism? Actually, phenomenological investigations themselves universally fall under the purview of a phenomenological examination and should be judged in their intention. *On the level of Part I*, the demonstration of the stratification of logic, or, equivalently, the clarification of its fundamental concepts, is an investigation beyond which there is nothing more to study. Such a clarification is thought of as coming to an end. As Husserl says in Chapter 1 of Part II, it seems that, once the investigations of Part I are carried out—after the clarification of the fundamental concepts of formal logic and analogous clarifications, such as that of the correlative senses of apophantics and formal ontology— we are done with formal logic and have nothing more to learn. But *in the present part,* on the contrary, these clarifications are taken up again as the point of departure for the problems of transcendental logic; they are thought of as the beginning, yet they are only a beginning, "the beginning of beginnings," as Husserl says. In fact, we are going to see that the criticism they inaugurate is, in itself, only an incomplete criticism which calls for an even more profound criticism.

Hence let us regrasp the results of Part I's researches under

the new perspective of transcendental logic. The natural starting point for this set of transcendental problems consists in
demanding a thematic reflection upon straightforward evidence and hence a clarification of logical formations, the fundamental concepts above all. Part I has shown us that there are
three species of judgmental concepts correlative to the evidences, each of which corresponds to one of the three levels of
logic: the "clear" judgment (the concept of judgment pertaining to truth-logic), the "distinct" judgment (the concept of
judgment pertaining to the logic of non-contradiction), and
judgment in the broad sense (the concept of judgment pertaining to morphology and for which abstraction is made from differences in confusion, distinctness, and clarity). Part II regrasps
this differentiation of concepts of judgment by showing that
it is a shifting in concepts which correspond to a shifting *in
intentionality itself.* "Here it is a matter of a shifting . . . that
went on in the logician's thinking, not for accidental but for
essential reasons" (178). From one concept of judgment to
another there is no simple *change* of sense, but instead the
change in sense is both "*shifting* of sense" and "*coincidence*
of sense.*" It is a coincidence of sense, for, despite what the new
concept of judgment introduces with regard to that of the preceding level, the lower-level concept is ready for identification
with that of the higher level. Beyond the intentional study of
this very remarkable "change" in the sense of the judgmental
concept, one can discern the outlines of an intentional study
of the very notion of stratification. At the same time there is a
dependence and an independence of levels within the hierarchical structure, for the intention which permeates these
levels changes while retaining a unity that firmly binds the
levels together. Emergence and identification are grasped
simultaneously in a unity of thinking.

If one speaks of equivocation in the use of the term judgment, one must quickly add that this equivocation is "for essential reasons" that derive from the fact of the diversity of
concepts of judgment. But this necessity should not lead the
logician simply to accept the equivocation. *To overcome* the
equivocation in a *fundamental* fashion through distinguishing
the three fundamental concepts of judgment is an absolute
necessity for the logic which would be genuinely established.
The "straightforward" thinking of the logician recognizes only

one thematic unity within which the structural distinctions are hidden. The logician should subject this naïve thinking to a criticism, since "for him there must be no naïve, instinctive, hidden doing, because, on the contrary, he must be able to render an account for every doing and its effect" (179–80).

The fundamental concepts which were simply "given" in straightforward evidence are then created in their genuineness by this clarification. But one can go so far as to say that to create the fundamental concepts in their genuineness is simply to create them, for, unless it achieves genuineness, a science cannot be said to truly exist. The very idea of science restricts the idea of genuineness. Critical reflection on the naïve method is hence not passive meditation on naïve method. Rather it is the "teleological fashioning" of this method, the "active fulfillment" of the anticipations of "straightforward" cognition. The intentional analysis of fundamental concepts thus leads to the *constitutional* clarification of these concepts. Hence we see how different it is from a simple psychological analysis, which, concerned with clarity, would examine how these concepts are actually formed. Husserl tells us that "only at the outset is constitutional inquiry such a reflection and progressive uncovering of the method used in fact and 'unconsciously' " (180). To be specific, psychological examination offers a departure point for the *elaboration* of the phenomenological method itself. And viewing things from a higher standpoint, one can affirm that in a general way, as a text written in 1913 puts it, "descriptive psychology offers a starting point for the elaboration of the idea of phenomenology." [1] Husserl adds:

> Such was the way that led me to phenomenology. But on the other hand, a more profound investigation absolutely guarantees that phenomenology as we understand it – i.e., eidetic phenomenology also resting on the transcendental reduction – is absolutely not descriptive psychology, and in strict truth, has absolutely nothing in common with it. [2]

Husserl remarks that understanding the creative function

1. Fragment appearing in French translation in *Etudes philosophiques*, (January–March, 1949), under the title "Rapport entre la phénoménologie et les sciences," p. 5. [In the Husserl Archives this text is M III L I 6. Passages translated from the French. – Translator.]
2. *Ibid.*

of this phenomenological analysis constitutive of fundamental concepts

> already projects a light on the much-discussed problems of the *foundations,* not only of mathematics, but of all other Objective sciences. . . . Everywhere we observe, as in the setting up of other epistemological problems, the repeatedly cited error of accepting the sciences as something that already exists—as though inquiry into foundations signified an ex post facto clarification or, at most, an improvement that would not essentially alter these sciences themselves (181).

Hence the foundation of the sciences has to be a genuine "creation," for, prior to being founded, the sciences surely had an existence; but then they existed only as *theoretical techniques* and not as *genuine* sciences, as sciences in the emphatic sense.

Yet we will also be able to say that this founding action manifest in the constitutional analysis of fundamental concepts projects a light on the very notion of "constitution." One can wonder whether the notion of constitution is inseparable from the notion of activity, since Husserl several times speaks of "passive constitution," and whether it is necessary to bestow a full sense upon the notion of activity in the expression "active constitution." To be sure, one can concede to those who suppress the active character of Husserl's "active constitution" that this is quite different from constitution in the Kantian sense. But the defenders of this thesis are thinking of the notion of activity as it presents itself in the natural attitude, as an activity creating something *ex nihilo,* as the power to bring something into existence. We believe, on the contrary, that in a general way the "constitutional" activity must be analogously conceived as an activity of grounding which brings something, not into existence, but into genuine existence, i.e., into an existence which can be accounted for.

3 / The Idealizing Presuppositions of Logic and the Constitutive Criticism of Them

THE CLARIFICATION OF the fundamental concepts of logic is only a first step in the constitutive criticism. More specifically, this clarification, which thematizes the critical examination of "naïve" logic, i.e., objective logic, straightforward logic (*Logik-geradehin*), *in turn* remains caught up in a naïveté which will have to be overcome by a new criticism. Can a criticism which performs a grounding function continue to retain a degree of naïveté? To raise such a question is to forget the difficulty which subsists even for a consciousness devoted to the tasks of elucidation, the tasks of inquiring into matters of course. Actually, the critical clarification of fundamental concepts is guided by idealizing presuppositions which a more profound criticism must bring to light.

Husserl is first going to consider the pure mathematical analytic, that is to say, the logic of consequence, and to take as his theme the constitutional criticism of its "presuppositions"— first of all, the presupposition of the ideal identity of the judgment.

The ideal identity of the judgment is not a question for the analytic. In what sense can one say that the affirmation of this ideal identity is a "presupposition"? Husserl himself, at the level of the investigation he conducted in order to authenticate logic, did not cease affirming that the judgment is an ideal

objectivity, which, like any object, has the characteristics of identity and permanence. Once one has formed a judgment, that judgment is an "enduring possession" *(bleibender Besitz)*, an "acquisition" *(Erwerb)*. It pertains to our disposition at all times *(jederzeit verfügbar)*. One can refer to it as to any object which remains self-identical. But if, when he affirms purely and simply the ideal identity of the judgment, Husserl has already gone beyond the level of a straightforward logic, of a logic having an exclusively objective focus, if he is engaged in "intentional" analyses, at least he has not yet reached the level of transcendental inquiry. At present it is a question of knowing what *guarantees* this identity; and to know this, we must do without the implicit presuppositions implied by the "natural" attitude. Chapter 1 of Part II emphasizes the ideal identity of judgments by referring to the evidences in which judgments are given.

> As a mental occurrence, the intentionality of the judging varies: but, where we speak nevertheless of the same judgment, there is maintained an intentional unity, directedness to one and the same judgment, which becomes itself-given in evidence as the same — the same that was at first a confused meaning or opinion and then became distinct (184–85).

But such a reference to evidence is not an absolute guarantee, because the identity of the judgment is evinced only when the evidence is still "living." While the processes are being performed which render distinct the judgment which was a confused meaning initially, the judgment is given as an intentional unity in an original fashion. But in the progress of thinking, when we return to this unitary judgment, we are once more aware of it through the intermediary of a recollection, a recollection which Husserl emphasizes is in no way intuitive. "Recollection, succeeding as actual intuition proper, would indeed be restitution of each single moment or step of the original process. But, even if that takes place, even if a new evidence is thus brought about, is it sure that this evidence is restitution of the earlier evidence?" (185). Now logic relates to the judgment as to an identical unity beyond the actual evidence in which it is given as such. To affirm such an identity is hence to let oneself be guided by a *presupposition*. Can this presupposition receive a certification of its success? It should be under-

stood that by its success one must not think of the success of praxis, of purely empirical success. But it is a more normative success, which nevertheless cannot authenticate this presupposition. Actually, Husserl tells us that

> even if the method used naïvely to acquire these ideal identities . . . does perform what is demanded of it, and the presupposition made by logic has accordingly an original legitimacy, still we cannot *legitimately* accept that presumed legitimacy, as long as the method – being used naïvely – remains anonymous, and its intentional performance has not been made a theme and clarified (187).

Actually, the judgment as an identical and permanent unity has an identity which *transcends* the living evidence in which it is given. When it brings to evidence this ideal being of judgments, it gives itself over to a presupposition. But this presupposition conditions the possibility of genuine science. Genuine science cannot exist without this ideal being of judgments. Yet, while responding to the role that a normative science of science must have, logic does not fully assume this role inasmuch as it does not consciously thematize its intentional performance. By satisfying an original demand, it none the less bears the mark of naïveté. Only by thinking of the ideal being of judgments as an actual fundamental norm with full awareness, hence only by uncovering the presupposition that it makes, can logic truly assume its normative function. Thenceforth the logical investigations assume a resolutely subjective focus, and their methodical action is no longer "anonymous." Immediately the method becomes conscious of its intentional and creative doing, which is creative insofar as it brings the "existing" sciences into genuine existence. But in a recurring way this new awareness of method has within it the problems of the fundamental concepts of logic. Like all logical significations, the fundamental logical concepts have this ideal identity. The first step of the critical investigations hence receives a deepening from the investigations which follow it.

As Husserl himself recognizes at the end of his Introduction, Part II "suggests more than it carries through to a finish." [1] It indicates the types of problems which are subject to transcendental reflection. It does not follow through on each problem with a complete and systematic analysis, as did Part I, which

1. *FTL*, p. 17.

only had to clarify the traditional conception of formal logic. Thus, having uncovered an idealizing presupposition of the analytic in the example of the ideal identity of the judgment, Husserl goes on to study the other idealizations which play a role in the analytic. He is content to indicate the idealization "and so forth," which has as subjective correlate "one can always again." It is an idealization since one cannot *in fact* carry through a reiteration indefinitely. This idealization plays a major role in the logic of consequence as well as in morphology. In morphology the laws of the connexion of concepts and judgments are characterized by their unlimited possibility of reiteration. Actually, on this level of logic, no demand for analytic coherence restricts the freedom of operative constructions. At the higher logical level one enters the province of infinite mathematical constructions, such as the infinite construction of the series of wholes. Husserl tells us that this fundamental form "and so forth" has never been brought to the fore by logicians. Yet we must indicate investigations contemporary with those of Husserl which question the mathematical existents which infinite processes imply.[2] For the intuitionist school, what is uniquely given to us intuitively are the infinite discrete totalities such as the series of wholes. As Oskar Becker says:

> According to the intuitionist conception infinity is only accessible under the form of the series which does not *be* but which instead *becomes*. The only species of infinity which is legitimately acceptable is hence potential infinity. The prototype of such a series is the series of natural numbers; all other infinite formations must be understood beginning from this series.[3]

As Brouwer said in a course taught at the Sorbonne (December 13, 1949):

> Intuitionist mathematics constitutes an activity of the human mind which finds its origin in the perception of time. This perception of time can be described as the decomposition of an event into

2. The first writings of Brouwer, leader of the intuitionist school, date from 1908.
3. Oskar Becker, "Mathematische Existenz, Untersuchungen zur Logik und Ontologie mathematischer Phänomene," *Jahrbuch für Philosophie und phänomenologische Forschung*, VIII (1927), 447–48 [translation by Dorion Cairns].

two distinct and qualitatively different things, one of which dis-
appears before the other. When the bi-unity born from this is
emptied of all qualitative character, a bare form remains, a substratum: this is the "basal" intuition of mathematics.[4]

Beginning from this fundamental intuition, intuitionism retains from mathematics only what can actually be constructed
in accordance with a law of construction which one is in a position to indicate. A mathematical entity is said to "exist" only if
it rests upon a fundamental intuition or if one can furnish the
law of construction by which it is engendered. It might be
thought that Husserl tends in the same direction as intuitionism when he affirms: "Obviously we have here a repetition of
the problem concerning subjective constitutive origins: as the
hidden method of constructions which is to be uncovered and
reshaped as a norm, the method by which 'and so forth,' in
various senses, and infinities as categorial formations of a new
sort become evident" (189). But Husserl never — either here or
anywhere else in this book — alludes to intuitionism. Interpreting Husserl's silence on this point, we think that he remains
an orthodox mathematician who is obliged to consider intuitionist mathematics as a mathematics on the *fringe* of classical
mathematics. One can rightly object that in wanting to
"ground" mathematics through a fundamental reform, intuitionism only succeeded in setting up a new mathematics alongside classical mathematics. The intuitionist conceptions, while
giving themselves over to a sort of intentional inquiry, concluded in such an amputation of traditional mathematics that
they cannot claim to institute a grounding sense-investigation
for mathematics. Husserl, on the contrary, is unwilling to
sacrifice any part of classical mathematics. Once one has a
clear awareness of the presupposition of, for example, the "and
so forth" qua presupposition, it is not a question of refusing or
according legitimacy to it uniquely in certain cases favored by
a fundamental intuition; it is rather a question of accepting it
with a new awareness: it must be assumed qua norm. With the
reiterative construction to which the *new normative form* is
given, the "and so forth" becomes evident in various senses.
The assumed idealization gives full power to virtual constructions.[5]

4. [Our translation.]
5. If one takes into consideration classical modern logic, one can

Husserl next goes into subjective problems which concern the "principles" of logic. For the moment he conducts his inquiry exclusively within the framework of the logic of consequence. When he speaks of a law of construction, it is hence a question of the *analytic* law of contradiction and not of the law of truth-logic, which was traditionally in view when the principle of contradiction was spoken of. Early in §20 (Part I) it was shown precisely how truth-logic's law of contradiction has an *analogue* in the sphere of simple consequence. At present Husserl is concerned with transferring this *analytic* law of contradiction from the objective problem-set to the subjective problem-set: "Every contradictory judgment is 'excluded' by the judgment that it contradicts. Every judgment that is an analytic consequence of another is 'included' in it" (189). This has as its subjective expression: "Of two judgments that (immediately or mediately) contradict one another, only one can be accepted by any judger whatever in a proper or distinct unitary judging" (190)—acceptance here meaning, to be sure, not truth, but simple "distinctness" in judging.[6] The objective statement of the law of contradiction is a statement concerning ideal mathematical "existence" (in the sense in which mathematicians ordinarily speak of existence, i.e., remaining on the level of the logic of non-contradiction). Hence it is a statement about the compossibility of "distinct" judgments. But only in turning toward a subjective study can one discover the corresponding apriori structure of evidence, the consciousness of

---

also view Husserl's judgment as hasty. If not in a universal manner, at least in significant cases, the "and so forth" has become a problem for the logician. In particular the logical study of the property of recurrence of the series of wholes brings about a veritable *thematization* of the "and so forth." But one must recognize that the investigations of modern logic have an orientation entirely different from that of Husserl. They tend toward a purely objective rigor. And they remain absolutely uninvolved in "intentional" analysis.

6. We should note that § 20 states the analytic law of contradiction in a form which is not pure. Subjective expressions alternate with the objective expressions: two contradictory judgments cannot both be animated by the evidence of distinction, for they do not both have "mathematical existence." The moment has not yet come for opposing the two focusings, objective and subjective. It is exclusively a question of showing the transition from the traditional principles of logic to their analogues in the logic of consequence.

"not being able to do otherwise." It does not matter who cannot do otherwise than deny the conjunction of two contradictory judgments. One can be deceived in regarding as "trivial" the affirmations to which the subjective inquiry leads. A simple indication by Husserl gives us the feeling that such an inquiry can be fruitful:

> All the subjective structures have an *Apriori pertaining to their functions*. . . . [T]his Apriori must be consciously fashioned, to become the originarily clear method for a radically legitimized theory of forms and a full analytics legitimately grounded in such a theory—an analytics for which there can be no paradoxes and the legitimate applicational sense of which must be beyond question (191).

In fact, an intentional analysis which goes back to the original can deliver us from paradoxes. If we live in the intention, we see that the results in which the intention is objectivated have various intentional charges which place them on different levels or in different orientations. But to such a "solution" of paradoxes, logicians can always reply that precisely by restricting themselves to the purely objective field they set their task of resolving the paradoxes that appear in this objective field.

What are the problems that arise for the subjective inquiry when it turns to the logic of truth? As we have already noted, the passage from "pure" *mathesis universalis*[7] to truth-logic is not a passage from one theory to a new theory. Rather, *mathesis universalis* is enriched with some fundamental concepts and some propositions relative to these concepts. Actually, the logic of truth is *mathesis universalis* animated by a new interest which thematizes possible truth as well as coherence. *Mathesis universalis* assumes the specific function of a *logic* of *cognition*. There is then a *conversion* of the pure analytic into a true theory of science. But there is no reason to forget that the logic of truth continues to be *formal* logic. Hence it seems that one encounters the same type of problem that was encountered on the preceding level. Yet, as we are going to see, the logic of truth is more concerned with problems and diffi-

7. We recall that what Husserl calls a "pure" *mathesis universalis* (*die "pure"* mathesis universalis) is a *mathesis universalis* conceived on the plane of the logic of consequence. Cf. supra, p. 14.

culties which are of a new type and which, as Husserl says, "reach much further" (192). More specifically, the way to the logic of truth *reveals* the presuppositions which already have their role in pure *mathesis universalis*, though a limited examination of this mathematical analysis fails to bring this out. We shall discover once more an example of that recurring understanding which is symptomatic of phenomenological research.

Let us grasp the principle of contradiction again, this time in its traditional statement, which expresses the general impossibility that contradictory judgments are true (or false) at the same time. In its subjective expression this principle says that when a judgment can be animated by adequation to the things, its contradictory opposite is not only excluded a priori as a judgment (something which relies on the demand for noncontradiction) but cannot itself also be led a priori to such an adequation. To this principle is to be added the principle of excluded middle, which decrees from the objective point of view "the general impossibility of contradictory judgments being true (or false) together" (193) and from the subjective point of view that "every judgment necessarily admits of being brought to an adequation" (194). The subjective statement leads us to a cognition supplementary to those that correspond to the correlative translation of the objective statement. It not only tells us *when* a judgment can be brought to adequation — either positive or negative — but even that *every* judgment *can* in principle be brought to (positive or negative) adequation. In the subjective statement we see the connexion between excluded middle and the problems of decision, which we will soon be going into. The objective statement takes into account a given situation only, while the subjective statement indicates that we can always put ourselves in that situation. It goes without saying that this possibility is in principle an idealization, for it is rare that one *in fact* arrives at clear judgments (whether in a positive or a negative manner).

But there are other idealizing presuppositions which, thus far, the analysis has not systematically distinguished. A judgment is not sometimes true or sometimes false; it is true or false *once for all*. The traditional statement of the principles of logic lets this "once for all" (194) escape unseen. If it remains implicit in the statement of the principle of identity as in the two other principles, the "once for all" still makes up an

integral part of the profound signification of this principle. When a judgment is true, it is true once for all, and this can be the expression of the principle of identity.

But why does Husserl say that this "once for all" is a "subjective locution, which does not belong in the purely objective principles" (194)? Is not the expression "once for all" the mark of an objective permanence which transcends the temporalized mental processes manifested by subjectivity? Actually, the "once for all" is a decree of the subjectivity which frees itself from the temporal condition of subjective mental processes. We say further that "true once for all" is connected to true "for everyone" *(für Jedermann)*. It is not that the "true once for all" would be the *ratio essendi* of the "true for everyone," while the "true for everyone" would be the *ratio cognoscendi* of the "true once for all," but that the signification "true once for all" supports the signification "true for everyone." To say that the judgment is an ideal unity which remains identical is to say simultaneously that, as someone in general, I can refer to that unity at any time. This is also to say that *anyone* can refer to it at any time. The identity of the true judgment hence refers back ultimately to the universal intersubjective evidence of this identity. This is the first time that Husserl alludes to the problems of intersubjectivity. But, he says, "already in pure mathematical analytics we could have related the identity of judgment-senses to 'everyone'" (194). The judgment which is simple meaning is also, *as such*, actually a stable unity to which everyone can refer. My meaning is not only *my* meaning but *one* meaning that anyone can have. But the ideal unity which is the judgment, the judgment that has undergone the test of contact with the things, bears witness in an unimpeachable way to the Objectivity recognizible by everyone, since it is an Objectivity to which everyone is forced to agree.

The notion of objective truth, of truth "in itself," [8] remains to be examined. If a study of judgment can be developed apart from the concern for truth, at least the logician who becomes interested in cognition, hence the true logician, considers the

---

8. Before studying the notion of truth-in-itself, Husserl goes back very briefly to formulate the subjective statement of *modus ponens* and *modus tollens*, first as principles of the logic of consequence and then as principles of truth-logic.

judgment as an *assertion to be verified.*[9] After undergoing criticism, every judgment must become true or false. Every judgment can be "decided." Husserl uses the expressions decision and decidability, which are technical expressions in modern logic. To say that a proposition is "decidable" is to say that one can decide its truth or falsehood. But when one affirms that every judgment is decidable, one actually depends upon an idealizing presupposition. For if judgments are decidable *in themselves,* many are not *in fact* decidable. We can very easily have judgments whose truth or falsehood we are in no position to pronounce judgment upon. We can ascertain our own impotence in this regard and say that, up until now, we have not been able to find a demonstration or refutation of such and such a statement. But still we are sure that this statement is true or false. "In itself" this is decided. "A fundamental conviction already awaits the logician and logic in the state of positivity, the unspoken conviction that guides every scientist in his province: his settled belief in truth-in-itself and falsity-in-itself. . . . In itself every judgment is decided" (197). By passing from objective logic to subjective logic, the logician converts a presupposition unformulated as such into a fundamental norm. He becomes aware of the hiatus which exists between the *in fact* and the *in-itself.* While naïve consciousness naturally affirms truth-in-itself, reflective consciousness is a consciousness of astonishment before the marvelous dogmatism of this idealization.

> All this imputes an astonishing Apriori to every subject of possible judging and therefore to every actual or conceivable human being—astonishing: for how can we know a priori that courses of thinking with certain final results "exist in themselves"; paths that can be, but never have been, trod; actions of thinking having unknown subjective forms but that can be, though they never have been, carried out? (198).

But Husserl does not avail himself of this astonishment to bring this presupposition truly into question. The normative consciousness immediately introduces a functional guarantee. "The possibility of sciences depends entirely on this certainty that their provinces exist in truth, and that, concerning their provinces, theoretical truths-in-themselves exist, as actualiza-

9. Cf. Part I, Chapters 4 and 5.

ble by following explorable and gradually actualizable ways of cognition" (199). There is an evidence of the presupposition of truth-in-itself. Beginning from particular cases, taken as examples, in which the decision is manifest, apodictically we grasp through an essential universalization the impossibility of its being otherwise.[10] If such presuppositions are subjected to criticism, it is because they are questioned about their own sense and "bearing." But in a significant formula concerning his actual reflection, Husserl will say: "We do not intend to give up any of these truisms; they surely rank as evidences" (199). Now it happens that this presupposition—that every judgment can be decided—not only has been questioned but has been disqualified by modern logic. The works of Gödel, to which we have alluded,[11] have shown that in any system sufficiently formalized to contain arithmetic and for which there is a finite number of axioms, there are propositions that cannot be decided (in particular the proposition which affirms the non-contradiction of this system). Now there is a *problem* of decision: in a given formalized system, *can* one find a general method which permits one, in a finite number of steps, to decide the truth or falsity of every proposition of this system? This problem has already been examined for many systems; and in many cases the problem of decision is insoluble. Thus, sometimes one arrives at methods of decision and at other times one arrives at the knowledge that this problem is insoluble. Must we interpret this "insolubility" as what has not been solved *in fact*? No, for it is a matter of a fundamental impossibility which pertains neither to the insufficiency of our knowledge nor to the imperfection of our methods but rather to the very contexture of certain deductive systems. The problem of decision and the problem of completeness go hand in hand. Hence it is not astonishing that here with the notion of decidability, as before with the notion of nomology,[12] we find Husserl's reflection running onto the same reef: an Apriori of reflection loses its value through the results of the technique of modern logic.[13] Nevertheless it must be noted that propositions "which cannot be decided" are quite few in number. The

10. Cf., *infra,* our study of essential variation.
11. Cf. *supra,* pp. 52 f.
12. Cf. Part I, Chapter 3.
13. In another direction of investigation, intuitionism denounces

scientist and even the logician continue in a practical manner to be guided by the presupposition of the truth-in-itself and the falsity-in-itself of statements — propositions which cannot be decided being relegated to a teratology in the demonstration.

At the conclusion of this chapter Husserl announces new problems which enlarge and deepen the present problem-set of "truth-in-itself." It is a question of grounding the sense of "truth-in-itself," on the one hand by clarifying the relations of "true once for all" with "true for everyone," and on the other hand by referring to the concrete infrastructure of the ultimate substrates of the judgment. In the *Prolegomena* the absolutistic conception of "truths-in-themselves" remains under the influence of traditional logic, which thinks of truth-in-itself as having as objective correlate "an absolute being, to which the relation to the cognizing subjectivity and its actual or possible subjective 'appearance' is non-essential" (201). The notion of truth-in-itself is now integrated into an intentional theory of judgment.

---

the "irresponsible" application of the principle of excluded middle. For intuitionism, one cannot say of every statement whether it is true or false. One can only say that it is non-contradictory or false. Assuming the demand of intuitionism, that no mathematical existence be accepted except that which can actually be constructed, one cannot conclude automatically from the non-contradictoriness of a statement its mathematical truth. Thus one can only say: such and such a theorem is true or false if one possesses the algorithm leading — at the end of a perhaps long, yet still finite, period of time — to the solution of the question. Now this is not always the case. Hence it is seen that the unconditional application of excluded middle is of a piece with intuitionist demands concerning demonstration.

4 / Evidential Criticism of Logical Principles Carried Back to Evidential Criticism of Experience

HUSSERL BEGINS THE INTENTIONAL THEORY of judgment by returning from the judgment to the substrates of the judgment, to the objects about which one judges. In the first place it must be noted that within the framework of the purely formal analytic the notion of substrate is an entirely *relative* notion. If we remain within this framework, we cannot ultimately distinguish what relates to the form and what relates to the substrate. Certainly we can say that S in the categorial judgment S is *p* symbolically represents a substrate. But from the fact of the purely formal project of the analytic, the substrate is thought of as something-in-general, as anything-whatever. This indeterminateness in which the substrates are left keeps open the possibility that the S itself can *in turn* have a syntactical organization, that it can be specified as "S' which is *a*" or as "S' which is in relation with Q," etc. "S or *p* . . . signify nothing other than empty spaces to be filled in without restriction." [1] The pure analytic is unable to say whether or not substrates are ultimate substrates, or "cores," i.e., stuffs *(Stoffe)* that enter into the syntactical organization without having yet received a syntactical form. As a matter of fact, the pure analytic *does not care.* Husserl affirms, without for the moment explaining himself, that it is "quite the contrary for truth-logic:

1. *Erf. u. Urt.,* p. 19.

because ultimate substrate-objects are individuals, about which very much can be said in formal truth, and back to which all truth ultimately relates" (203). As cores which no longer contain syntaxes, the ultimate substrates can actually be only "individuals." As *Erfahrung und Urteil* remarks explicitly,

> For any universality and any plurality, even the most primitive, point back to some act in which several individuals are taken together and therefore to some more or less primitive logical activity in which the individuals thus brought together are categorially formed in some way, in which they receive some universal form.[2]

But how is the reference of a *formal* logic of truth to individual objects to be understood? In this connexion, how can the formal of the pure analytic and the formal of truth-logic be differentiated? As we have just said, the pure logic of consequence, qua formal mathematics, considered as pure analytic independent of the logical function of cognition, does not raise the question of the reduction of judgments to ultimate judgments, which are syntactical constructions formed with ultimate cores. To say that every judgment ultimately leads us to ultimate substrates which no longer contain syntaxes is already, by taking up new interests, to go beyond formal mathematics. But to say this is not yet to place oneself on the level of the logic of truth, for one is still on the level of distinctness and is not raising questions of adequation. On the contrary, the logic of truth, which, as we have seen, is fundamentally interested in problems of adequation, has a right to speak of individual objects and not only of ultimate substrates. And, "to the reduction of judgments to ultimate judgments with an ultimate sense, there corresponds a reduction of truths: of the truths belonging to a higher level to those belonging on the lowest level, that is: to truths that relate . . . directly to individual objects in their object-spheres . . ." (204). But how can a truth-logic which holds to its purely formal project affirm that "*every* conceivable judgment ultimately . . . has relation to individual objects" (204)? Such an affirmation can be completely justified only if it can be shown that universal judgments which say nothing about individual objects can still be ultimately related to individual objects. The possibility of this reduction is quite evident if one considers the universal judg-

2. *Ibid.*, p. 20.

ments which have to do with the material. One can always go back from the universal to the particular in a finite number of steps. But where one deals with universal judgments, such as those encountered in formal mathematics, reduction, if it does lead to the particular, leads to what can be called the abstract particular, to the anything-whatever. Under this anything-whatever, one can think of *any* arbitrarily chosen object whatsoever, which in turn can have an analytico-formal ground. The judgments of formal mathematics thus seem to constitute an obstacle to the envisaged universality of the reduction. But Husserl remarks that "with all its freedom in the reiterative forming of forms, and with all its reflexive relatedness to its own scientific character, formal logic still intends . . . not to remain a playing with empty thoughts . . ." (205). It intends to retain the possibility of application to material elements, to *"Sachhaltigkeiten."* Hence, through the possibility of their application, analytico-formal judgments also have a reference to individual objects. One cannot object to this that the resort to the possibility of application is a digression which dilutes the basic force of the argument, for, as the very title of § 40 states, the relation to a possible application is implied by the *logical* sense of the formal *mathesis*. The first part (particularly § § 40 and 52) has shown that there are two ways in which to conceive of a *mathesis pura*. Alongside the "mathematics of the mathematicians," which is uniquely a mathematics of non-contradiction, an analytics in the narrow sense, there is mathematics as it concerns the logician. The logician "cannot accept a mathematics conceived κατὰ μηδεμίαν συμπλοκήν, a mathematics that tears itself away from the idea of possible application."[3] For him the *mathesis pura* must be guided by a cognitive interest; it must be a logical *mathesis pura* which, without betraying its formal character, constantly has in view a possible application. Hence all judgments can be traced back to ultimate judgments bearing upon individual objects. These judgments are "ultimate," since they are the termini of the reductions. But *in themselves* they are *first*, since they designate an origin back to which all judgments can be brought.

Correlatively, the evidence "first-in-itself" is the evidence in which the individual is given, i.e., experience. Husserl specifies that this is experience "in the first and most em-

3. *FTL*, p. 109.

phatic sense." Actually, the concept of experience encountered up until now is a broad concept, applying just as well to the giving of numbers, the giving of judgments, etc., as to the giving of a particular object, provided that this giving is the giving of an object "itself," "in person." The concept of experience in the broad sense therefore respects the character of presence of the object without, however, retaining the direct reference to the individual which specifies experience in the emphatic sense. But this concept of experience in the emphatic sense, so far as it enters into the expression "judgments of experience" is taken here in a sense we can term as broad;[4] and from a certain point of view it is even broader than the one which Husserl has used thus far. Hence experience is understood not only as the giving of the individual itself in the mode of simple certainty; we must also take account of the modifications of this certainty (presumption, probability, etc.) and even of the neutrality modification.[5] This extension is justified by the fact that the notion of experience thus understood comes to be registered in judgments which by the same token are *original* in relation to universal judgments. But, among these original judgments, those that involve experience in the mode of simple certainty of existence retain a significant role. They are, so to speak, the most original among the original judgments.

Once this point is made, how are the tasks of a theory of

4. This same usage of the concept of experience is found in *Erfahrung und Urteil*, pp. 21 and 23.

5. Cf., *Ideen*, § 109: "It [namely: the neutrality-modification] does not cancel, does not 'do' anything [*Sie 'leistet' nichts*]; it is a consciousness that is the reverse of every doing [*das bewusstseinsmassige Gegenstück alles Leistens*]: its *neutralization*. It is included in every abstaining from doing, every putting out of action, every parenthesizing, every 'leaving undecided' and now having as 'undecided,' every phantasying of doing or merely thinking of what is done, without 'joining in doing' [*sich 'in' das 'Leisten' 'hineindenken,' ohne 'mitzutun'*]. . . . For each of the expressions just now assembled to indicate in a preliminary manner [this modification] contains in its sense a surplus. In each case an arbitrary doing is also designated; whereas it is not intended to be at all a matter of such a doing. We therefore eliminate it. . . . If we thus exclude from leaving undecided everything volitional, if however we also do not understand the matter as something doubtful or hypothetical there remains a certain having of something left undecided or, better yet, a having of something standing there, which we are

judgment presented? To be sure, it is a matter of an *intentional* theory of judgment and not what is ordinarily called a theory of judgment. Actually, theories of judgment exclude from themselves any subjectively focused investigation, which they leave for a properly psychological inquiry. The Fourth Investigation has already shown that the main fault of theories of judgment lies in their failure to distinguish the various *radically* distinct strata in the problem-set of logic.[6] It is the return to the intending, as we have already seen, that permits a deeper understanding of the stratification of logic. Only after he has separated judgment from judging and has understood the essence of intentionality as constitutive performance (and hence has grasped the ideality of the judgment) can the logician *ground* this stratification by following the shifts of intention. Hence his first task is to finish the phenomenological clarifications which make it possible to unravel the various intentional relations. The first part of *Formal and Transcendental Logic* is devoted to this task, and the beginning of the second part enlarges it to the fullest extent by revealing its transcendental dimension. Let us look, then, at the task which falls to a transcendental theory of judgment.

There exists another sort of intentional relation whose clarification calls not only for an attempt at distinctness but even for *reductive* deliberations like those which Husserl has just begun. These reductive deliberations "uncover the hidden intentional implications included in judging and in judgment itself as the product of judging. Judgments as senses accordingly have a sense-genesis" (184). Here we are engaged in a new type of investigation characteristic of Husserlian phe-

---

not conscious of 'actually' as standing there. The positional character has become powerless. The believing is now no longer seriously a believing, the supposing no longer seriously a supposing, the denying no longer seriously a denying, or the like. There is a 'neutralized' believing, supposing, denying, and the like, whose correlates repeat those of the unmodified mental processes, but in a modified manner: the existent pure and simple, the possibly, probably, questionably existent, likewise the non-existent and each of the other negata and affirmata, is there as an object of consciousness [*bewusstseinsmassig da*], not however in the manner proper to the actual but rather as 'something merely thought,' as 'a mere thought'" (pp. 222–23). For the relations between the neutrality modification and phantasy, cf. *Ideen*, § § 111 and 112.

6. *Log. Unt.*, Vol. II, Pt. I, p. 342; cf. also *Ideen*, p. 264.

nomenology. Its importance cannot be overemphasized. If the very notion of genetic analysis is introduced late in Husserl's writings (not until these sections of *Formal and Transcendental Logic* can one find a systematic usage of this notion), the first analyses in the genetic style date from the years 1910–13. And, in our opinion, these genetic analyses are what give to Husserl's thought its horizon of originality. The importance of the *Selbst da* ["itself there"] within Husserlian phenomenology should not mislead us. It is quite true that the phenomenologist, disdaining theories which draw a screen between him and the things he is concerned with, must concentrate on the things as they are themselves. But he cannot be content to consider them qua intentional unities – completed, finished, "constituted." To be specific, he must not forget that intentionality is productive, "constituting," intentionality, and he must question the constitution of these finished unities. Intentional analysis must not remain static analysis; if it is to be a thoroughgoing phenomenological analysis, it must become genetic analysis. As Father van Bréda says, "the inventory of what is now presentiated is only a starting point and nothing more; phenomenology must recover the processes by which what is presently offered to it is constituted in consciousness." [7] But it is not a matter of rediscovering the psychological formation of the intentional unities or of retracing their historical evolution. In a word, there is no question of setting up a genetic epistemology in the sense of Piaget. We shall see how genetic analyses avoid considering inductive empirical processes in the example of the judgment. As it is put in *Erfahrung und Urteil*, whose project is precisely the investigation of the "genealogy" of logic, "this clarification of origins . . . has as its theme neither a problem of the 'history of logic' in the usual sense nor a problem of genetic psychology";[8] it is rather a matter of rediscovering the hidden essential grounds from which traditional logic springs.

If we take judgments simply as senses, we already see what the return to the origin means. Thus all nominalization refers back to a more original form. For example, the nominalized predicate *the red* refers back to the original predicate *red.*

7. Lecture at the Collège philosophique, Tuesday, 21 February 1956 [our translation].
8. *Erf. u. Urt.*, p. 1.

As we have already indicated, no chronological character need be attached to the notion of origin. It can happen that I conceive of "the red" before conceiving of "red." It can happen that I continue to use the signification "the red" which presents itself to me in some context of thinking. But, independent of all the empirical steps of my thinking processes, the signification "the red" contains in itself the possibility of a return to the signification "red." Hence in the sense that is *open to all* there is always implied an original sense that is *hidden*.

Thus far we have limited ourselves to syntactical implications. We shall find more profoundly, however, a genesis which concerns the cores and which points back to experience. Hence let us place ourselves once more in the perspective of the adequation of judgments to the things of which they speak. We have just seen that a reduction leads us from true judgments of the higher level down to true judgments *directly* relating to the individual objects, and we have seen that the individual objects are given through experience. The judgments *first in themselves* are then judgments of experience. These are the most immediate judgments of the categorial form, where one has the evidence which procures the presence of the things "themselves." The judgment of experience is the *original*, and the theory of the evidence of the judgment of experience is the theory of the judgment "first in itself." The ranking of judgments from the point of view of this genesis thus has a guiding principle entirely different from that of the stratification brought about in Part I from a purely static point of view. In intentional genesis the nonevident judgment points back to the evident judgment (in the sense of the evidence of clarity) and still more originally to the judgment of experience.

The basic level of the categorial, the judgment of experience, contains in itself "immediately" the source of experience. Hence we should place ourselves there in order to know what experience is. But we should not lose sight of the conditions under which this explication of experience is accomplished. On the one hand, the experience presents itself as inserted into the categorial. Let us recall what Husserl says in Part I: "Nature as judgment-formation [*Urteilsgestalt*] . . . will of course have under it Nature as an experience-formation [*Erfahrungsgestalt*] . . . : But the under-it is at the same time

an in-it." [9] This is the case to such an extent that experience and the relation to the categorial "are interwoven in the task of clearing up the lowest level of judging." [10] On the other hand, there is something that numerous expositions of Husserlian phenomenology have tended to forget: "this explication of experience, as the activity that precedes the specifically categorial activities and takes on shape in them, must be restricted to a 'formal' universality . . . a universality that is 'formal' in the sense that, on the subjective side, it is the correlate of the sense in which analytics is formal." [11]

By placing ourselves on the lowest level of the judgment, which is the judgment of experience, we come to discover that what one would believe to be pertinent to the predicative sphere, i.e., certainty and its modalities, intention and fulfillment, etc., is already pertinent to the intentionality of experience. Husserl's remarks on this point come quite abruptly: "Thus one comes," he says, "from the experiential judgment . . . to experience and to the motive for that broadening of the concept of judgment already indicated by Hume's concept of *belief*" (210). We have here the first systematic exposition involving genetic phenomenological analysis. Hence it is not surprising that this new type of investigation is not examined fundamentally and that one does not yet see very well all the conclusions that can be drawn from it. The limitation of *Erfahrung und Urteil* to the genetic theory of judgment will authorize a more detailed discussion of these problems. Hence we are going to refer to that discussion in order to understand the bearing of such a return to experience.

The decisive and fundamental remark which will serve to legitimize the enlargement of the concept of judgment indicates that, when one turns toward the datum in experience, one has already performed an *activity*. Perceptual consideration *(die betrachtende Wahrnehmung)* is already an active behaving which must be distinguished from a simple receiving [*pâtir*]. There is a believing in the existence (*Seinsglauben*) of the pregiven which is entirely passive. In this case there is "the mere 'stimulus,' the barking of a dog, for example, that comes from something in the surrounding world," which we

9. *FTL*, p. 118.
10. *Ibid.*, p. 221.
11. *Ibid.*, p. 212.

hear "without our paying the least attention to it." [12] But from the time we pay attention to it, from the time we take it as an object of interest, there is an activity—an activity of a lower level, to be sure, but an activity all the same. In a general way, "each time it is a question of attention, there is already such a lower-level activity." [13] There is, then, an *antepredicative* activity, and the antepredicative and the pregiven must be distinguished. Under these conditions it is understandable that one can extend the concept of judging to include this antepredicative activity and not reserve it exclusively for the predicative judging, as traditional logic always does. In *Formal and Transcendental Logic*, Husserl even speaks of the syntactical that is encountered within the antepredicative sphere: "even this founding experience has its style of syntactical performances" (212), and he notes that this broadened concept of the categorial was not even foreseen in the Sixth Investigation, which introduced the concept of the categorial, having in view only the syntactical [*le syntaxique*] which is found in the predicative judgment.[14] If the predicative activity of judging alone creates objects of cognition in the emphatic sense, nevertheless the objectivation which takes place in perception must be included among the activities of the ego. These activities of the ego, whether on the lower or the higher level, have their modes of clarity and confusion in a similar fashion. Hence one is able to accept the concept of judging [*jugement*] in a sense so broad that it designates the totality of objectivating acts of the ego.

In *Erfahrung und Urteil*[15] it is said that judgment taken in this extremely broad sense must not be confused with the pas-

12. *Erf. u. Urt.*, p. 61.
13. *Ibid.*, p. 62.
14. *FTL*, p. 212, n. 2. These "syntactical" performances are, to be sure, still exempt from all grammatical and conceptual formation. On all of these questions cf. *Erfahrung und Urteil*, "Part I: Ante-Predicative Experience." In particular, the different perceptual levels are distinguished: (1) mere grasping and mere consideration (*schlichte Erfassung und Betrachtung*), (2) explicitating consideration (*explizierende Betrachtung*) of the object, and (3) a level where interest is turned, no longer toward the object itself, but toward the objects around it. Then one is no longer concerned with "internal" determinations but with "relative" determinations which explicate what the object *is* in relation to other objects.
15. *Erf. u. Urt.*, p. 63.

sive *belief* of Hume, and yet we have just seen in *Formal and Transcendental Logic* that this concept of judgment "is indicated by Hume's concept of *belief.*" But actually there is no conflict between the intentions of these two texts, for in *Formal and Transcendental Logic,* soon after assimilating this new concept of judgment to the Humean concept of *belief,* Husserl expresses a basic reservation concerning the concept of *belief*: "Historically, to be sure, the apprehension of this broadest concept remains crude, even countersensical" (210). What he objects to in the Humean concept is that it is taken as simple datum of internal sensibility that does not greatly differ from a datum of external sensibility. He denies passivity to "belief" while retaining the original extension bestowed upon it by Hume. We have just seen that what motivates the broadening of the concept of judgment in Husserl is the fact that the antepredicative is already in the sphere of activity. Hence we see how Husserl is led to speak of the absurdity of Hume's concept. In sum, *Erfahrung und Urteil* refuses to accept the concept of "belief" in its historical sense, which it *did* take on with Hume; *Formal and Transcendental Logic* accepts it as it *could have been* taken over by a philosopher avoiding every naturalization of psychical problems.

At the beginning of Chapter 4 Husserl asserts that every conceivable judgment ultimately has relation to an individual object and that consequently it has "relation to a real universe, a 'world' or a world-province, 'for which it holds good' " (204). But now he does not examine this notion of world that the judgment points back to. Here again *Erfahrung und Urteil* allows us to clarify the rather compressed text of *Formal and Transcendental Logic.* Numerous remarks in *Formal and Transcendental Logic* allow us to understand that everything which is grasped by experience has an open *horizon* of experiences. We can say, in the language of *Erfahrung und Urteil,*[16] that every experience of an individual thing has its *internal* horizon. Actually, as the Second Cartesian Meditation puts it (§ 20), there is always a *something-more* to be grasped which exceeds what is in fact grasped at a particular moment of experience. But, in addition, each individual object has its *external* horizon of co-objects *(Mitobjekte)* (horizon in a second sense, which relates to the internal horizon). Prior to every experien-

16. *Ibid.,* p. 28.

tial grasping, we are affected not by an isolated object but by an entire horizon of data. To be sure, we do not immediately turn an active regard toward this horizon; still, however, we can do so at any moment, depending on our interest. There is, so to speak, a marginal and virtual grasping which we can actualize at any time. This horizon, internal and external, forms the *world* of experience, and this world of experience is the basis upon which all cognitive activity is founded.

But what is this world of experience, this world in which we live our everyday lives? A fragmentary or selective reading of *Erfahrung und Urteil* could lead one to believe that it is enough to open one's eyes and live in order to find this world of experience: "Return to the world of experience is *return to the 'life-world,'* i.e., the world in which we have always lived." [17] But the world in which we live has always been given as impregnated with logical achievements. The life-world in its original purity, prior to all cognitional activity, is not the living world [*le monde vécu*]. The world of life is the world in which we live; but it is not the world which we live. This is why the return to the life-world cannot be carried out through a genetic *psychological* inquiry. Such a psychological inquiry leads us to mental processes "just as they are, viz., as experiences of the world, of a world . . . upon which modern science has already carried out its work of exact determination." [18] We believe that we grasp the life-world *as such* because the teachings of science have become so familiar to us that they seem *natural* in every sense of the word. It seems to go without saying that the infinite totality of all that can exist in itself is a rational totality which can be completely mastered by a universal science. But in fact the exact natural sciences, i.e., mathematical physics, have covered the life-world, the world of experience grasped in its immediacy, with *idealizations*. Using an image from the *Krisis*, repeated in *Erfahrung und Urteil*, we can say that they have covered the life-world with a "garment of ideas." [19] To return to the original, to pure experience,

17. *Ibid.*, p. 38.
18. *Ibid.*, p. 46.
19. Cf. *Krisis:* Galileo, the founder of modern physics, performed "the substitution of the mathematically constructed world of idealities for the uniquely actual world, the one that is actually given perceptually, the always experienced and experienceable world — our everyday life-world" (p. 49). "The garment of ideas, 'mathematics and

would be to strip the world of these idealizations, with which it has been clothed by science. This is a difficult task, for the performances of science, the logical activities, are *sedimented* and cannot be exposed by hasty original investigations. Hence one must return all the way to the original according to the sedimented historicity of the activities of cognition, whether these be activities of explication, unification, disjunction, relation, deduction, induction, etc. Only after getting around these sedimentations can we then reach the "pure Nature common to all." As *Erfahrung und Urteil* states explicitly, "this 'pure Nature, common to all.' . . . For the concretely existing world, that is an abstraction." [20] This is an abstraction

---

mathematical natural science' or, instead of that, the garment of symbols, of symbolico-mathematical theories, comprises everything that, as 'Objectively actual and true Nature,' takes the place or disguises the life-world for scientists and likewise for educated laymen. Because of the garment of ideas we take as true being that which is a method" (p. 52).

One can wonder about the fact that we are more inclined to refer to *Erfahrung und Urteil,* which was not written by Husserl, than to *Krisis,* which was not only written by Husserl himself but also one part of which he let be published. If we find in *Krisis* broad indications of a philosophical faith which still does not harm the nuances of thought, at least we can regret on several occasions certain concessions to the tastes of the day, to the philosophies of existence. Reading *Krisis* in a more circumspect manner than the other works of Husserl, we do not mean simply to set aside with an arbitrary gesture the Husserlian texts which could undermine our "interpretations." Actually, we believe it impossible to separate the reading of *Krisis* from the consideration of the contemporary philosophical situation. It seems to us that Husserl yielded to the temptation of responding to the trials which a philosophy currently undergoes in setting a value on the rational activity of philosophy apart from existence. He wanted to show that his philosophy was also capable of accounting for existence, of true being, just like the philosophies which consider existence as the one magical pole of reflection. Let us return instead to the Husserlian itineraries that are guided by a stern method and by the absolute preoccupation with remaining oneself.

20. *Erf. u. Urt.,* p. 57. *Erfahrung und Urteil* even says (pp. 239–240): "When we separate two levels of interest and, corresponding to these, two levels of objectivating productivity, viz., the productivity belonging to *receptive experience* on the one hand and the productivity of *predicative spontaneity* on the other, this separation of levels should not be construed as if the differing productivities were somehow separate from one another. On the contrary, the levels, which for purposes of analysis must here be treated separately and recognized

in the sense that one must exclude (*ausschalten*) all of the idealizations which impregnate the concretely existing world. This is enough to indicate that an existentialism cannot legitimately avail itself of Husserl's return to the life-world.

In resorting to *Erfahrung und Urteil* we have gone far beyond what is explicit in *Formal and Transcendental Logic*. Yet we believe that such a digression is justified. In fact, not only does *Erfahrung und Urteil* bring to *Formal and Transcendental Logic* a development and a deepening which make us better able to evaluate the investigation of origins, but, in addition, a comparison of the two books provides assurance that what is often called the later philosophy of Husserl does not undermine the teachings of *Formal and Transcendental Logic*. In fact, even in *Erfahrung und Urteil*, where the guiding theme is a genealogy of logic going back to the sources of antepredicative evidence, there is no deprecation of categorial activity for the sake of the sphere of receptivity — there is no "denial of science." The return to the original is not inspired by a nostalgia for sources, by a slothful primitivism. It proceeds from the will to grasp in its purity the necessary basis upon which the activity of cognition can be established in full clarity. Abolishing the idealizations of science is the only means of calling attention to them as such and hence of fully understanding them. Then one can give its full sense to the affirmation of Husserl which we have previously quoted: "we mean to neglect nothing which is a matter of course." The naïve obliviousness of the scientist who idealizes without knowing it[21] is succeeded by a new consciousness that gives

---

as belonging genetically to different levels of objectivation, are *in fact usually closely intertwined with one another*. That receptivity precedes predicative spontaneity does not mean that the former is in fact something independent — as if it were always necessary to run through a chain of receptive experiences before there could be any awakening of genuine cognitive interest. . . . In such a case, the predicative forming and cognizing goes from the outset hand in hand with receptive grasping, and what from a genetic point of view is to be separated as belonging to different levels is then in fact inseparably intertwined into the concretion of one consciousness."

21. Cf. *Krisis*, p. 52: "Because of the disguising garment of ideas, the proper sense of the method, the formulae, the theories, could not become understood and, what with the naïve origin of the method, had never been understood."

idealizations a positive character. "Since the logician be-lieves that the originariness of experience can at any time be generated without further ado and does not ask back beyond this superimposition of idealizations upon the world of origi-nary experience, he also measures cognition by this ideal of exactness, i.e., by *epistémé*, as the ideal of exact, 'objective' knowing." [22] Accepting the search for the original, the logician will simultaneously re-evaluate science and experience in the pure state. Experience in its purity is not experience as we live it, shot through with poorly recognized cognitional products. This is only a tissue of opinions *(Meinungen)* upon which cog-nition has done its work, but these opinions have not passed through the sieve of cognitional criticism. It is truly an experi-ence which can be reached only through a genetic *reduction,* in which the presence of the object presents itself [*s'offre*] in an unchallengeable manner, prior to all cognitional activity, and upon which all cognition is to be established. It is a prim-itive δόξα which has the privilege of being original. But to recognize this privilege

> involves not the least deprecation of exact cognition or of the apo-dictic evidence of the logician himself. It is but an elucidation of the way by which such higher-level evidence may be obtained and an elucidation of the hidden presuppositions, upon which it rests, that determine and limit its sense. The content of such evidence is not thereby placed in question. On the contrary, the point is that cognition terminates in it; the path of cognition rises necessarily from doxa to epistémé — yet, in our enthusiasm for the ultimate goal we should forget neither the origin nor the lower levels in their own right.[23]

Then we understand Husserl's regret that the term *archae-ology* had already been taken by an existing science.[24] If it is true that "all sedimentation is, in a certain manner, a 'for-getting,'" [25] phenomenology is to be an archaeology which brings us into the presence of the original; it is to give us an

22. *Erf. u. Urt.,* p. 44.
23. *Ibid.,* pp. 44–45.
24. Eugen Fink, "Das Problem der Phänomenologie Edmund Hus-serls," *Revue internationale de philosophie,* No. 2 (January, 1939), p. 246.
25. "Ursprung der Geometrie," p. 212.

alert recollection of origins ⟨when we are engaged⟩ in exercises of cognition far from these origins.

But, assuming that the "origin" of these judgments is experience, how is the remembering of the origin to be recorded in a purely formal logic? Up to a certain point Husserl has already replied to this question by showing that experience is the horizon of possible application for *every* conceivable judgment. And specifically, as *Erfahrung und Urteil* emphasizes,

> the return to objective, prepredicative evidence receives its import and its full significance only when it is recognized that this relationship of founding concerns not only judgments made on the grounds of experience but any possible evident predicative judgment whatever and therefore concerns also the judgments of the logician himself and their apodictic evidence which nevertheless claim to be valid "in themselves" irrespective of their possible application to any definite realm of substrates.[26]

But this reference to the founding experience which genetic analysis discloses to us could be conceived of as a simple preface rather than an integral part of the formal theory of judgment. This is not the case. For Husserl, formal logic must have a theory of experience in continuity with it. Resistance to such a conception stems from the tendency to consider formal logic only in its objective focus, as a deductive system of statements taken as completed unities studied from a purely static point of view. But from the moment one turns to subjective logic and its "criticism of cognition," investigations of origins become the integrating part of logic. For, as we are going to see, they contribute to grounding the legitimate *sense* of the apriori logics — something which a direct examination of statements can never reveal. To be sure, it remains the case that the theory of judgment has to do with laws which are reached by universalizations of two quite different types: alongside the universalizations that remain in contact with the material, there are the formalizing universalizations that know no cores other than indeterminate substrates. And Husserl can say that, contrary to the evidence of laws introducing a material Apriori,

> the evidence of laws pertaining to the analytic Apriori needs not such intuitions of determinate individuals. It needs only some ex-

26. *Erf. u. Urt.*, p. 13.

amples or other of categorialia; even categorialia having indeter-
minately universal cores will do (as when propositions about numbers serve as examples). They may indeed point back intentionally
to something individual; but they need not be further examined
nor explicated in this respect (213).

Hence there is an *obligation* to respect the independence of
formalizing universalizations in relation to experience, an
obligation not to become involved in "a materially filled sense"
(213), even if one transcends the exclusively objective problems and goes into the problems of evidence. But all this applies only so long as one stays at the static point of view. And
static analyses are still naïve analyses. The sense of the analytic laws, and above all the principles of logic, cannot be
explicated totally unless one goes back to the origins of the
formation of this sense. What must be thoroughly understood
is that, though they reveal the naïveté of the static analyses,
the genetic analyses still do not supplant the static analyses
nor undermine their teachings. The conscience of the logician
is a twofold conscience: on the one hand he must accept a
rigor in formalization which abstains from recourse to materially determinate examples, which "empties" (*entleert*)
the individual of its material content, in order to reach the
anything-whatever. But at the same time he must search out
the hidden presuppositions behind the "naïve" evidence of the
logical principles and thus rediscover the bare foundation of
experience. In doing this he does not betray the legitimate
sense of formal logic, which claims to be *formal ontology* —
which claims to apply to every conceivable existent.

Hence let us follow the genetic criticism of the principles of
logic through to the end. Let us inquire into their sense. The principles of logic apply universally to every conceivable judgment.
But what is to be understood by "every conceivable judgment"?
If we let ourselves be guided exclusively by what the stratification of logic developed in Part I teaches, we can say that, from
the moment when a unity of significations is governed by the
laws of the connexion of syntactical categories which the morphology sets forth, it can be given the name judgment. If thus we
avoid nonsense (*Unsinn*), the heteroclite mass of significations
to which one cannot give the name judgment because it does
not follow even the simple laws of grammar, it seems that we

can say nevertheless that we have to operate with no other restriction on the concept of judgment. And yet the proposition
which *goes without saying* — i.e., that every judgment possible
with respect to the laws of morphology can be considered a judgment, properly so called — harbors a *presupposition*. And if this
presupposition is not indicated as such by the logician, it is because he concentrates on syntax and neglects genetic considerations. Actually, we have seen that "the possibility of properly
effectuating the possibility of a judgment . . . is rooted not only
in the syntactical forms but also in the syntactical stuffs." [27]
When one says that the principles of logic apply to every conceivable judgment, it must be added: to every conceivable judgment which is not senseless *as to content*. Take an example
given by Husserl of a judgment senseless as to content: "The
sum of the angles of a triangle is equal to the color red." Such
a "judgment" cannot have the principle of excluded middle applied to it; one cannot even apply to it the analogous principle
of a simple logic of consequence. This judgment cannot be confronted with the questions: Is it contradictory or not? Is it true
or false? These questions simply *do not reach it*. This is the
sense in which Husserl's statement must be understood, that
such a judgment is "exalted above harmoniousness and contradiction in its 'senselessness' " (216), exalted above (*erhaben
über*) non-contradiction and contradiction, above truth and
falsehood. Actually there is no need to see a spatial metaphor
in this expression, which would indicate a stratification. One
cannot say bluntly that a sphere higher than those of non-contradiction and truth is designated in this way. Besides, on two

27. *FTL*, p. 217. Appendix I will show the deeper reason for Husserl's calling the stuffs of judgment *syntactical* stuffs. Actually, the
difference between syntactical forms and stuffs is more relative than
a superficial distinction would lead one to believe. One cannot simply
set the syntactical forms and stuffs apart. Only a meticulous phenomenological analysis can let us progressively establish this classification.
The term syntactical stuff emphasizes the fact that we are considering
still unformed stuffs which the simple dismemberment of the proposition presents us with. For example, in the proposition: *the roof is
red*, the stuff: *the roof* is taken with its syntactical function, i.e., with
its functional form as subject. The term core, on the contrary, will
be reserved for the stuffs obtained by a more advanced and considered dismemberment, abstraction being made of their syntactical form.

occasions when Husserl uses this expression *above*, he corrects it with a significant *so to speak*.[28]

Hence we come to a notion of nonsense entirely different from the one studied by the first stratum of logic, by morphology. Adhering to Husserl's terms, one could confuse the two sets of problems. In *Formal and Transcendental Logic* Husserl writes, "The single propositional elements are not senseless; they are good honest senses. But the whole presents no unitarily concordant sense. *It is not a whole that is itself sense*," [29] and one can read this passage as an echo of several sentences in the *Logishe Untersuchungen*:

> The word *Unsinn* [nonsense] is to be understood here . . . strictly and properly. A mass of words like *king but or similar and* is not understandable unitarily; each word by itself has a sense, but the composition has none.[30]

> If we say, on the other hand, *a round or, a man and is,* and the like, there exist no significations at all which would correspond to these combinations as their expressed sense. The words arranged together excite, in us, it is true, the indirect objectivation of a *certain* unitary signification expressed by them; but we have at the same time the apodictic evidence that such a signification cannot exist, that signification-parts of such sorts, connected in such a manner, are incompatible in a unitary signification.[31]

But the term *sense* is taken differently in the context of the Fourth Investigation on pure grammar (or in the first part of *Formal and Transcendental Logic*) from the way it is taken in the context of the genetic analyses with which we are currently occupied. As Husserl recalls in the present chapter, the distinction effected in the *Logische Untersuchungen*[32] between the quality and the matter of the judgment clarifies the concept of sense just introduced. Let us be specific. On the one hand, the judgment can be considered as the sense of a statement (integral statement, *voller Urteilsatz*[33]), account being taken of the thetic quality in which it is posited. If I say, "S *is p*" and "*it is possible that S be p*," I assert two different judgments; I can say that

28. *Ibid.,* pp. 216 and 221.
29. *Ibid.,* p. 216.
30. *Log. Unt.,* Vol II, Pt. I, Fourth Investigation, p. 334.
31. *Ibid.,* p. 326.
32. *Ibid.,* Fifth Investigation, pp. 426 ff.
33. *Erf. u. Urt.,* p. 345.

I am dealing with two *different* "senses." On the other hand, one can understand by the term sense the matter of the judgment, the content, which remains identical through the possible variation of the different thetic modalities. In this second usage, I will say that I am dealing with the same sense when I assert *"S is p"* and *"it is possible that S be p."* In the first usage, we consider the sense as state-of-affairs, in the second as categorial meaning.[34] But a new specification arises. If the notion of sense introduced by Husserl in these genetic analyses of *Formal and Transcendental Logic* corresponds to the second usage we have just indicated, the first usage must be assimilated to the grammatical notion of sense belonging to morphology. The latter notion is the sense as it is understood on the second stratum of logic, where it is the opposite of *Widersinn* (countersense), not of *Unsinn* (nonsense).[35] In this usage the "sense" is the *intended judgment as intended,* and the thetic character of the judgment forms part of the sense. As it is still said in *Erfahrung und Urteil,*[36] the thetic character is a structure of the noema itself. In sum, we can distinguish three notions of sense. If we

34. To be sure, S *is* p can itself be taken in these two ways, depending on whether one considers the meaning "S *is* p" or the content S is p of the statement, i.e., the state-of-affairs or affair-complex. On the other hand, a new complication appears with the fact that one can consider the state-of-affairs at different levels of categorial organization. For example, where the judgment *It is possible that S be p* is concerned, one can consider that the state-of-affairs is S *is* p and that the state-of-affairs is posited with the modality of possibility. But placing oneself at a higher level, one can also consider *It is possible that S be p* as the affair-complex; then one considers the *fact* that it is possible that S be p. Before having introduced the distinction between the two usages of "sense" which we are examining, Husserl showed this duality of standpoints in Chapter 4 of Part I, a chapter where he distinguishes between focusing on objects and focusing on syntactical operations. In the first case that we have indicated, the state-of-affairs S *is* p receives from without a functional form that can vary (for example: It is possible that S be p, It is sure that S is p, S which is q is p) in the syntactical activities, which, so to speak, gain ground and surround the affair-complex, this functional form not being accounted for in the state-of-affairs itself. On the contrary, in the second case, the functional form *It is possible that* constitutes an integral part of the state-of-affairs, for *It is possible that S be p* is then a state-of-affairs "of the higher level," which is not the state-of-affairs S *is* p.
35. Cf. *supra*, p. 7.
36. *Erf. u. Urt.*, p. 345.

pay attention to the syntactical forms, we first consider the purely grammatical sense proper to morphology. A statement must have a unitary grammatical intelligibility. If this unity is lacking, we are dealing with a pure nonsense, such as *a man and since*. Next, the notion of sense is grasped on the level of the logic of consequence, which is governed by the concept of "distinct" judgment. To the concept of "distinct" judgment there stands in contrast the countersense *all A's are B's, among which some are not B's*. But such an analysis omits the conditions for the possibility of the judgment which are *more fundamental,* the conditions of agreement among the *cores of stuff.* Thus we come to the third notion of sense, which is based on the possible unity of the content of the judgment. The "concept of the distinct judgment . . . is in need of a supplementary essential determination and a correspondingly deeper clarification. The unitary effectibility of the judgment-content *is prior to . . .* the effectibility of the judgment itself" (217).

The genetic analysis is then going to show that the stuffs presented in the unity of a judgment must *have something to do with one another.* Actually, we have seen that the genetically most original mode of judgment is the evident judgment and, more profoundly, the judgment founded upon experience. To be sure, there can be discordances in experience, but that which brings about a contradiction still has a "community of essence" (218) with what it contradicts. Since the original intentionality is a founding intentionality, what was just said about original judgments transfers to all possible judgments, and one can say that *it is experience — the universal basis of all possible judging — which brings about the material homogeneity of the cores of all possible judgments.* If it can be said that the cores *should* not be brought into the considerations of objective formal logic, it must be added quickly that subjective logic is to discover, by means of its genetic analyses, a hidden presupposition of objective logic, a presupposition that is related to these cores: the cores which form the stuffs of every judgment cannot be variable in a totally free manner, for they "have 'something to do with each other' materially" (219). That presupposition then tacitly brings in a restriction of the concept of judgment, for the judgment with which logic is concerned is not just the judgment which respects the rules of morphology but is also the judgment which ad-

ditionally respects the rules of the material homogeneity of the cores.

Formal universalization, *in its functioning*, hence need not be concerned with core-stuffs. But if one wants to clarify its evidence entirely, one must refer to the conditions of agreement in stuff among the cores. This is the case to such an extent that Husserl can pose the question of the relationships of dependence of the cores, not only with respect to the universal pertaining to the material, but even with respect to the formal universal.[37] And he will be able to conclude that "in the evidence of formal universalization, the cores are not wholly irrelevant" (214).

Thus we come to the end of the "criticism" of the principles of logic by uncovering the most profoundly hidden presupposition. "If logical principles were to relate to judgments universally, they would not be tenable, certainly not the law of excluded middle. For all judgments that are 'senseless' in respect of content violate this law" (220). The principles of logic are valid in an unconditioned manner only if one means by judgment the judgment whose cores have a harmony of stuffs. An awareness of this presupposition is the key to understanding the true sense of the logical principles, and we have reached this awareness only by recourse to the intentional genesis of the judgment.

If we must recognize that the intentional theory of judgment has met the requirements of the task demanded of it in the perfecting of the criticism of the principles of logic, we are not yet done with this theory. For, by bringing ourselves into contact with the original, we are led to question once more the notions of truth and evidence.

37. Cf. *FTL*, § 87, p. 212.

5 / The Subjective Grounding of Logic as a Problem Belonging to Transcendental Philosophy

ONCE IT HAS UNCOVERED the presuppositions upon which the logical principles are based, the grounding criticism of logic is obliged to revise the notions of evidence, truth, and true being, which, insofar as these presuppositions remain tacit, are still "naïve" notions.

In the preceding chapter we saw that every judgment points back intentionally to an experience of the individual and more specifically to a "world" of individuals, every existent being implied within a totality, the totality of what can be grasped in experience.[1] This is why *Erfahrung und Urteil*[2] will say that logic is logic in the world *(Welt-Logik)*. To be sure, logic, by the fact of its apriori character, is not concerned with the world in a thematic fashion; however, the world is the horizon of all possible judgmental substrates. Traditional logic does not express the following presupposition as such: on the one hand, it does not clearly see the *universality* of the reference to the world by what is intentionally implied in all judgments, including the judgments which are the results of a formalizing universalization; on the other hand, when it takes the form

1. Or at least what can be grasped within a region of experience. There can be various unitary spheres of experience. On the notion of region cf. *Ideen,* pp. 9 and 19.

2. *Erf. u. Urt.,* pp. 36 and 37.

of a formal ontology, hence when it vindicates the possibility of the application of its truths to every conceivable existent, it does not dream of questioning itself about the existence in-itself of the world, to which it grants a status beforehand. In fact, "it is a [traditional] logic . . . for a real world, thought of as given beforehand" (224). For a real world *(für eine reale Welt)*? Is *the* real world *any* world *whatever*? The existent, as *Erfahrung und Urteil* states briefly, is, "if not the existent of the actually real world, at least the existent of a possible world."[3] In the present chapter of *Formal and Transcendental Logic*, there is a continual shifting of expression from "the actually existent world" to the expression "a possible world." Having said, for example, that "all the judgments, truths, sciences, of which this logic speaks, relate to this existing world" (224), Husserl quickly distinguishes among the sciences those sciences which apply to facts and which hence concern the *de facto* existence of the world and the sciences which concern the being of a possible world. And it is the latter apriori sciences which logic has in view. Actually, the relationship of an empirical science to the existent world and the relationship of an apriori science to a possible world are different in principle when one studies them in a "straightforward" fashion, i.e. as facts. But with regard to "critical" inquiry, they are not essentially different; for the presupposition of a possible world has the same critical importance as the presupposition of the real world. From this critical point of view, what matters in the relationship to the existent world is that this is a relationship to that which has the *essential* form of a world. Then we foresee the importance of the investigation of essences for constitutive phenomenological investigations, an importance which will not be expressly emphasized by Husserl until the next chapter.[4] For now, in a passing remark, Husserl says simply that the apriori sciences "concern what is necessarily valid when the matter-of-fact world is freely varied in phantasy— necessarily valid as an essential form of any world whatever, and *therefore of this given world*" (224). While studying this method of variation more closely,[5] we will see that the fact has no privilege among the variants which the imagination

3. *Ibid.*, p. 36.
4. *FTL*, § 98.
5. Cf. *infra*, pp. 174 f.

freely forms in order to reach that fact's essence, for the facts are to be treated as "possibilities among other possibilities." [6] Thus something which could appear as an uncertainty in expression is justified. But Husserl does not stop there. He refers to the psychological sense, hence to the "mundane" *(weltlich)* sense that traditional logic gives to every subjective investigation, for logic "engaged in investigations directed to the subjective . . . took these as psychological in the usual sense: investigations concerning the objectivating and thinking life and the evidential consciousness of human beings in the world . . . " (224 f.). To us this argument seems to make the Husserlian demonstration deviate, since recourse to psychological considerations was rejected as violating the purity of the project of logic by the logicistic current of traditional logic. Nevertheless, there is an ample amount of demonstration, which Husserl also seems to be aware of:

> In any case, the already-given actual world is always there, in the background—though it sufficed us, after all, that the relation of logic to an apriori-possible world, no matter how that relation came into logic, signifies a presupposition, and one with no less importance to the critic than the presupposition of the de facto world (225).

The presupposition of the being-in-itself of the world is accompanied by the presupposition of the possibility-in-itself of coming to know this world in an absolute manner. In the preceding chapter, following the exposition of *Erfahrung und Urteil*, we have already emphasized that the world can be *mastered* by the exact methods of natural science.[7] Undoubtedly, we can only actualize this ideal in an imperfect fashion and through successive approximations. But still we believe, so to speak, in the actuality of this ideal. In advance we are convinced that the objects of our experience are in themselves determinate and that science has the task of absolutely knowing these determinations of an absolute true being. The "Objectivity" of science lies in this. "Just as the realities belonging to the world are what they are, in and of themselves, so also they are substrates for truths that are valid in themselves—'truths in themselves,' as we said with Bolzano" (225). Thus the notion

6. *Erf. u. Urt.*, p. 423.
7. *Ibid.*, p. 40.

of "truth-in-itself" is understood by reference to the unquestionable belief in the being-in-itself of the world. Moreover, it must be noted that these absolute truths are grasped in absolute evidences. The truth is true once for all and for everyone — *ein für allemal und für jedermann*. Absolute being, absolute truth, absolute evidence — these notions dominate traditional logic and present no problems for it.

From the fact of its naïve presupposition of the being-in-itself of the world, logic finds its place among the "positive" sciences for which the being of the world in effect raises no problems. Logic can break with the naïve objectivism of the positive sciences only after this presupposition is unmasked. Now this presupposition can only be unmasked by means of a *radical* criticism of cognition. Husserl recognizes Descartes as the one who was first to engage in such a criticism of cognition whereby not only *epistémé* but even the lowest level of all objective cognition, i.e., sensuous experience and correlatively the world itself, are placed in doubt. But Descartes, Husserl says, did not remain loyal to the radicalism of his devotion. An entire heritage of "prejudices" weighed upon the new way of philosophizing which he inaugurated. In the first place, he presupposed the validity of logic; and yet, as we have just seen, logic implies belief in the existence of that world which Descartes proposed to doubt. To be sure, Husserl does recognize that the Cartesian *epoché*[8] "has, in fact, a hitherto unheard of radicalness, for it expressly includes the acceptance [*Geltung*] of all hitherto accepted *sciences* — even mathematics, which lays claim to apodictic evidentness. . . ."[9] But Husserl's reproach bears more specifically on the fact that

8. For the difference which Husserl establishes between the phenomenological epoché and the Cartesian doubt cf. *Ideen*, § 31: "*In the attempt to doubt* that accompanies a thesis (which, as we presuppose, is certain and continued) the 'disconnection' is brought about in and with an antithetical modification, namely the 'trial' [*Ansatz*] of non-being, which is therefore part of the substratum of the attempt to doubt. In Descartes this part is so predominant that one can say his attempt to doubt universally is properly an attempt to negate universally" (p. 55). The Husserlian epoché, by contrast, is "a certain suspension of judgment which involves itself in a persuasion of the truth which remains unshaken, even unshakable, if it is evident" (p. 56). For the phenomenological epoché, cf. *Ideen*, §§ 31 and 32, and *Cartesian Meditations*, §§ 8 and 15.

9. *Krisis*, p. 27.

after having found the ego as the only absolutely indubitable existent, Descartes infers from it to the existence of God and in short to all the rest of the world by operating with logical *deductions*,[10] a logic which has not been examined as to its presuppositions. Descartes's undertaking suffers from the difficulty of all theories of cognition which do not examine the autonomy of logic. Not only does that not become a question for them, but in these theories the criticism of cognition is carried out with the modes of logical deduction that actually cannot be grounded except through that criticism.

Moreover, this first reproach is connected to another reproach which will complete its sense. One can say that Descartes was the founder of transcendental philosophy since he discovered "the great reversal that, if made in the right manner, leads to transcendental subjectivity." [11] But he "misses the proper transcendental sense of the ego he has discovered" (228), since "for Descartes, an absolute evidence makes sure of the ego . . . as a first, indubitably existing, bit of the world" (227). The *mens sive animus sive intellectus* is still, actually, a *human*

10. In exact terms, Husserl says that Descartes is "expressly or implicitly using the mathematics of probability, which is itself a part of logic, and perhaps using the rest of ancient formal logic" (228). If we can acquiesce in Husserl's judgment that Descartes "projects hypotheses and probability inferences" (228) from the cogito, it must be recalled, at least where properly formal logic is concerned, that Descartes rejects formal logic and its syllogisms lest our reason remain "idle" and "not trouble to consider the inference in an evident and attentive manner" (Rule X). As to the root of the issue, we cannot examine it, assuming that Husserl's objection ultimately points back to the great problem of the foundation of the Cartesian notion of evidence. Note that in every case Husserl decries only Descartes's deductive argumentation beginning from the *cogito* and that he does not claim that the *cogito ergo sum* would be a syllogistic deduction — an objection which Descartes answered, saying, "When we apperceive that we are things that think, this is a first notion which derives from no syllogism; and when someone says: I think, hence I am, or I exist, he does not conclude his existence from his thinking as by the force of some sort of syllogism but as a thing itself known; he sees it through a simple inspection of the mind" (*Secondes réponses, Pléiade*, 2d ed., pp. 375–76) [our translation]. Hence where the *cogito* itself is concerned, Husserl does not differ fundamentally from Descartes. Actually for Husserl there is a transcendental "experience" of the ego. And in this experience the ego reaches himself [*s'atteint*] in an original manner.

11. *CM*, p. 18.

ego, a natural reality, while the *ego* to which the transcendental phenomenological reduction leads us is a *pure ego*. One does not reach the *pure ego* simply by abstracting from physical reality and restricting oneself to the *pure* data of internal experience. Psychic life itself must also fall before the epoché, for it is still a natural reality or, as *Formal and Transcendental Logic* puts it, a "sense-moment pertaining to externality" in opposition to "the pure internality" (230) of the *ego*. Having in view the transcendental purity of the reduction, Husserl denounces in Descartes the "psychologistic falsification" of the pure ego and the fateful character of the substitution of the specifically psychic self in place of the ego, of psychological immanence in the place of egological immanence, of the evidence of "internal" psychic perception or of "self-perception" in the place of the egological self-perception.[12] There is in this, according to Husserl, a *"realistic* error" which thoroughly falsifies Descartes's transcendentalism. It must be admitted that this "error" is in fact quite natural, for it has its source in that second naïveté, we could say, which leaves us satisfied when we have reached a purified reality through the spiritual discipline [*ascèse*] of a philosophical reflection. In particular it must be remembered that the reader of the *Ideen* can often believe (and in this he is supported by Husserl's manner of expression) that he has reached the end of the transcendental reduction when actually the reduction is still in the service, not of transcendental phenomenology, but of a phenomenological psychology.[13] If one goes no further than Chapter 2 of Part II of the *Ideen*, entitled "Consciousness and Reality," one can believe that the transcendental reduction is fully understood when Husserl tells us that ". . . consciousness has in itself a being of its own which, in its own absolute essence, is not touched by the phenomenological exclusion. Therefore it remains as a 'phenomenological residuum,' as an essentially unique region of being, which can indeed become the field of a new science, phenomenology." [14] But, to cite *Krisis*, "the

12. Cf. *Krisis*, § § 18 and 19.

13. Meaning to overcome the misunderstandings which the *Ideen* can occasion, Husserl himself, in the "Nachwort," recognizes the difficulties presented by this difference between transcendental phenomenology and phenomenological psychology (cf. p. 554 in particular).

14. *Ideen*, p. 59.

ego *is not a residuum of the world.*" [15] The transcendental *ego* is what *remains* when all that is "mundane" is *excluded*, even though this reductive operation is the way which leads us to the discovery of the transcendental *ego.* The transcendental *ego* is not pure immanence separated from the transcendencies. It is that *within* which all transcendencies can have their *sense* and their *being-status.* But, on the other hand, it is still not necessary to interpret this relationship of the transcendencies to the transcendental as a relationship of *inclusion.* As it is remarked in the First Cartesian Meditation, "just as the reduced ego is not a piece of the world, so, conversely, neither the world nor any worldly Object is a piece of my Ego, to be found in my conscious life as a really inherent part [*als reeller Teil*][16] of it." [17] In the immanence of the *ego,* transcendencies retain their sense as transcendencies.

Thus by understanding the heterogeneity, both epistemological and ontological, of the transcendental and the transcendent, one is protected from the two extremes of absurdity which are transcendent realism and "dogmatic" idealism. On the one hand, it is necessary not to make of the *ego,* as Descartes did, "the point of departure for inferences according to the principle of causality." [18] If one can say, as Husserl repeats on several occasions,[19] that the transcendental ego *precedes,* from the point of view of cognition, the being of the world, it is not necessary to take this "precedes" in the sense of a priority of one reality over another reality. It is not necessary to understand the transcendental *ego* as a reality beginning from which one can *deduce* another reality. Hence we now see the whole bearing of the preceding reproach which Husserl directed at Descartes for operating deductively from his discovery of the *ego.* The *ego* is not a "premise" [20] for objective cognition. Between the transcendental ego and objective existence there is a *grounding of the transcendental order* which can be expressed by saying that all existence derives its *sense* and *status* from the transcendental *ego* and by saying that

15. *Krisis,* p. 81.
16. Husserl always uses the term *reell* to characterize immanence. *Reell* is hence contrasted to *real,* which characterizes reality.
17. *CM,* p. 26.
18. *Ibid.,* p. 24.
19. *Ibid.,* p. 27; *FTL,* p. 227.
20. *CM,* p. 26.

this *ego* is a "constituting" subjectivity. But, on the other hand, while thus connecting it to the *ego,* it is not necessary to dissipate the transcendent as such and fall into a dogmatic idealism. It must be shown how what unfolds in the immanence of my consciousness can acquire an objective significance. This will be the main task of Part II, Chapter 6, of *Formal and Transcendental Logic.* In this difficult task Husserl will in no way be assisted by the *Meditations* of Descartes, since he will refuse the call of the divine veracity which is the means for resolving the Cartesian problem of Objectivity. But before undertaking this task, it must be emphasized that there is a problem in the very setting-up of this task. *From the first,* nothing assures us that we can encounter again within the immanence of the *ego* something which has an objective signification. The hypothesis according to which an *external* real world is to be reached by taking the being of the *ego* as a base is a hypothesis which attracts the realist as a matter of course. But

> is not this *outside,* is not the possible sense of a transcendent reality and that of an Apriori belonging to a transcendent reality and including the forms (space, time, and causality) that permit inferences, the problem? Is not the problem how, in the immanence of the *ego,* this outside can take on and confirm that sense of transcendence which we have, and use, naïvely-straightforwardly?[21]

The danger of realism is hence more pressing than the danger of idealism since its *prejudicial* manner bars us from access to the clear awareness of the problems as such. And this is undoubtedly because the hypothesis of realism has its base in an

> almost ineradicable naïveté [which] is also what brought it to pass that, for centuries, almost no one objected to the "obviousness" of the possibility of inferences from the ego and his cogitative life to an "outside" and that strictly no one asked himself the question whether, with reference to this egological sphere of being, an "outside" could have any sense whatever—which, to be sure, makes this ego a paradox and the greatest of all enigmas.[22]

This "realistic hypothesis" was so present in Descartes's mind that, despite his demand for rationalism, he set up his goal

21. *FTL,* p. 230.
22. *Krisis,* p. 82.

beforehand: to find in a manner that is certain the cognition of an external world having an existence in itself. And Descartes was so eager to reach his goal that he did not "take the time" to examine that transcendental *ego* which for him was no more than a step on the path which had to lead to his destination. Husserl, on the contrary, means to inquire into the transcendental experience by means of which "the ego can explicate himself ad infinitum and systematically." [23] The Second Cartesian Meditation will have the specific task of laying open "the infinite field of transcendental experience." [24] *Formal and Transcendental Logic* will not be able to explicate this infinite field of experience since the essential task of this book is the grounding of logic. But it must be kept in mind that the grounding of logic leads us directly to the transcendental problem-set *in its full breadth,* for it is the whole real world which is placed in question when the radical grounding of logic is envisaged. Hence logic cannot be separated from a *transcendental* theory of cognition which gives it its ground.

23. *CM,* p. 31.
24. *Ibid.*

6 / Transcendental Phenomenology and Intentional Psychology. The Problem of Transcendental Psychologism

WE HAVE JUST SEEN that, to be a radical criticism, the criticism of logic must encompass the most universal transcendental problem-set. Now, therefore, it is a question of clarifying this problem-set, a question of grasping its sense and bearing.

For the reflective consciousness which practices the phenomenological epoché, there is no longer a world existing *in itself* or a science valid *in itself*. This does not mean that the world and science disappear from its field of experience. It does, however, signify that what has existence and validity has existence and validity only *for* consciousness. And there is no restriction to be placed upon this truly universal affirmation: *Every* existent is "constituted" in subjectivity. But it is not necessary to understand constitution as a *creation* of beings. To say that every existent is constituted in subjectivity means that it has its sense and being-status there. It does not mean that subjectivity forges it.[1] Then we must recall a term which we have encountered many times already in the first part of *Formal and Transcendental Logic*, the term *Seinssinn* (being-sense), an untranslatable term unless one is resigned, as we are, to an enigmatic translation, the awkwardness

1. *FTL*, p. 251.

of which is entirely foreign to our language.[2] In our opinion, this notion is a fundamental notion in the sense that it allows us to specify the Husserlian idealism. Constituting subjectivity is what confers upon being its *being-sense*.

To be sure, the world continues to be *transcendent* in relation to the *cogitationes* and the *ego*. But this transcendence has no sense "other than that of an *intentional* unity making its appearance in the subjectivity itself of consciousness" (236). Actually,

> it must not be overlooked that epoché with respect to all worldly being does not at all change the fact that the manifold *cogitationes* relating to what is worldly bear this relation *within themselves*, that, e.g., the perception of this table still is, as it was before, precisely a perception of this table. In this manner, without exception, every conscious process is, in itself, consciousness *of* such and such, regardless of what the rightful actuality-status of this objective such-and-such may be, and regardless of the circumstance that I, as standing in the transcendental attitude, abstain from acceptance of this object as well as from all my other natural acceptances.[3]

Hence transcendence subsists for the consciousness which strictly observes the transcendental reduction, but this transcendence is not an alien something which intrudes upon consciousness. Transcendence has its sense only from constituting intentionality.

If one wants to understand the sense of transcendence and also of all that one can do, will, or think of it, one must inquire into this constituting intentionality. One must systematically *explicate* intentionality itself, the actions of which intermingle within the life of consciousness, the consciousness of the "meditating ego." Later we will specify the methodological significance of this uncovering of intentionality. For now let us recall only that Husserl avoids the itinerary of Descartes's *Meditations* by engaging in this examination of intentional life. Husserl, like Descartes, recognizes the apodictic evidence of the *cogito ergo sum* — the first foundation of cognition. But,

2. [The author's French is *sens-d'être*, and since "being-sense" or "existence-sense" may seem to many as enigmatic in English as *sens-d'être* does to the author in French, this sentence is allowed to stand. — Translator's note.]

3. *CM*, p. 33.

as we have already emphasized, Husserl reproaches Descartes for not having undertaken the systematic examination of the pure *ego* in his "haste" to ground objectivism and the exact sciences.

In a few pages Husserl is going to rough out the basic lines of this examination of intentionality, which was carried out in some detail a few months later in the redaction of the *Cartesian Meditations*. Given the similarity between the problems and methods of the *Cartesian Meditations* and those of the present chapter of *Formal and Transcendental Logic*, we can make use of the meditations in explicating the often allusive text of *Formal and Transcendental Logic*.

In transcendental reflection the world exists as it is *for* consciousness; to be more precise, for *my* consciousness, for me, the meditating subject. But in any inquiry into the consciousness I have of the world, it must be recognized immediately that the world is thought of as *the* world of *all of us*. It is thought of as the *objective* world, i.e., as the world valid once for all and for everyone. Hence there is an *intersubjective* constitution of the world. We have already encountered this "definition" of Objectivity on the level of science and predicative truth. But this is already valid for the world of experience prior to predicative explications. "The world itself, according to its sense, is the one identical world, to which *all of us* necessarily have experiential access" (236). Now when I say that I have consciousness of the world as the one identical world which everyone can experience, I do not "go out" of myself. It is *for me* that the world is *the world for all of us*.

Not only the world of things, but also others exist *for me* in the same way. It is in my *ego* that the *alter ego* as such has his sense and his status. It is for me that the *alter ego* has that sense whereby for him I am an *alter ego* just as he is alter ego for me. Thus the consciousness that I have of the *alter ego* includes the consciousness of the *reciprocity* of the relations between him and me. Hence, all that exists has existence only for me; all that exists is "constituted" in me. In this way we come to a transcendental idealism whose problem is to show how these transcendencies which are present in the *immanence* of my *cogitationes* can take on an *objective* significance. This is what Husserl often calls the *"enigma"* of the transcendental problem-set.

But for an enigma, this set of transcendental problems, thus presented, is less simplistic than it seems. It is not the case that, on the one hand, there is I, and, on the other hand, facing me, separated from me, there is the world (the beings and things). I am myself "in" the world, I make up part of the world as a psychophysical being. Hence the transcendental problem-set must already have its role within the relationships between me and me—between me, transcendental *ego*, and me, psychophysical being. My transcendental *ego* is not identical with me as "real" being. And yet I say "me" twice, once in the natural attitude, when I find myself as man, and once in the transcendental attitude, when I find myself as transcendental *ego*. Moreover, this problem of the constitution of my psychophysical self by my transcendental *ego* has repercussions for the problem of the constitution of the other. For the other is constituted by my *ego* with a sense which first refers to me specifically as a psychophysical being. And in order to see the whole complexity of this problem, it must be added that the constitution of the other is in principle different from that of my own psychophysical being, since I do not grasp the other in the original manner in which I grasp myself.

Here Husserl does not consider the problem of the constitution of the psychophysical ego for its own sake. It appears only insofar as it is implied in the problem of the constitution of the other. Actually, this second problem is what *Formal and Transcendental Logic* has ultimately in view for this chapter, for now the criticism of logic has led us to a transcendental theory of cognition which, as we are going to specify, is itself grounded in a transcendental theory of the experience of the other.

How is this problem of the constitution of the other presented? Husserl introduces this set of problems in the following manner:

If it is certain to me and, thanks to transcendental clarification, already understandable that my psyche is a self-Objectivation of my transcendental *ego*, then the other psyche also points back to a transcendental *ego*, but, in this case, another's, as the *ego* that someone else, for his part, starting from the world given him beforehand in his experience and going back to ask about the ultimate constitutive life, would have to grasp in his "phenomenological

reduction." Consequently the problem of "others" takes also the following form:

To understand how my transcendental *ego*, the primitive basis for everything that I accept as existent, can constitute within himself another transcendental *ego*, and then too an open plurality of such egos—"other" *egos*, absolutely inaccessible to my *ego* in their original being, and yet cognizable (for me) as existing and as being thus and so.[4]

This setting-up of the problem is less a point of departure than an anticipation of the development which this problem will undergo in the successive stages of its explication. Actually, how can I infer it from my transcendental experience that the psyche of the other also points back to a transcendental *ego*? Hence let us follow through to the end the progressive explication of the constitution of the other.

Let us start from the transcendental *ego*[5] reached by means of the reduction. We have already said that for me as *ego* the world has the sense of *objective* world, i.e., existing for everyone—*für Jedermann*. The constitution of the objective world by my *ego* hence presupposes the constitution of a sense "everyone," by which it is not then necessary to understand "every man," i.e., every psychophysical being which pertains to the objective world, which would therefore presuppose the constitution of the world. At this lower constitutive echelon, the other is not yet a man in the objective world. Now the other as other points back to me. We have just seen that he refers

4. *FTL*, pp. 239–40.
5. To be sure, only the self as transcendental *ego* can ask transcendental questions. As a natural man I cannot present the problem of the objective signification of what is lived through within my consciousness as evidence. As a natural man, "can I ask seriously and transcendentally how I get outside my island of consciousness . . .? When I apperceive myself as a natural man, I have already apperceived the spatial world and construed myself as in space, where I already have an Outside Me. Therefore the validity of the world-apperception has already been presupposed, has already entered into the sense assumed in asking the question—whereas the answer alone ought to show the rightness of accepting anything Objectively valid. Manifestly the conscious execution of phenomenological reduction is needed, in order to attain that Ego and conscious life by which transcendental questions, as questions about the possibility of transcendental knowledge, can be asked" (*CM*, p. 83).

back to me not as a transcendental *ego* but as a psychophysical self. This psychophysical self of mine can no longer be, at this constitutive level, a self existing in the objective world. My psychophysical self then pertains to an "intrinsically first Nature" which is not yet objective Nature. And there we are led to the true *point of departure* from which one can find the way to the solution of the transcendental "enigma." With this intrinsically first Nature, Husserl says, one has a "first, not yet intersubjective Objectivity [which] is constituted in my ego as, in a signal sense, my own, since as yet it contains nothing other than my Ego's own – that is: nothing that by a constitutional involvement of other Egos, would go beyond the sphere of actually direct, actually original, experience" (241). And without further explanation Husserl adds that

> it is clear that this sphere, the sphere of my transcendental *ego's* primordial ownness, must contain the motivational foundation for the constitution of those transcendencies that are genuine, that go beyond it, and originate first of all as "others" (other psychophysical beings and other transcendental *egos*), the transcendencies that, thus mediated, make possible the constitution of an Objective world in the everyday sense: a world of the "non-Ego," of what is other than my Ego's own. All Objectivity, in this sense, is related back constitutionally to the first affair that is other than my Ego's own, the other-than-my-Ego's-own in the form, someone "else" – that is to say: the non-Ego in the form "another Ego." [6]

We can refer to the Fifth Cartesian Meditation in order to explicate this scheme of the constitution of the other. To reach this transcendental sphere, which pertains properly to the *ego,* Husserl will go to a new epoché, this time *within transcendental experience itself.* There is no question of parenthesizing the being-status of the other, as was the case in the epoché which enabled us to reach transcendental being. The new epoché is an *abstractive* epoché which reduces my transcendental being to my *own* transcendental being. In this epoché "we disregard all constitutional effects of intentionality relating immediately or mediately to other subjectivity." [7] "Mediately" applies to the case where I consider myself as an actuality existing in the objective world, the objective world whose possibility of existence for me has the constitution of

6. *FTL,* p. 241.
7. *CM,* p. 93.

the other as a condition. But, it should be noted, when I have circumscribed within the horizon of my transcendental experience what is properly my own *(das Mir-Eigene)*, "we retain a unitarily coherent stratum of the phenomenon world," [8] a stratum which has a *concrete unity;* this is why Husserl can say in the same sentence that, by means of an *abstraction* concerning that which transcendental constitution presents me with as alien to myself, I reach my *concrete* transcendental self.[9] *Despite* the abstraction which eliminates from the phenomenon[10] "world" all that is not an exclusive property of the self, "we can go on continuously in our experiencing intuition" while remaining exclusively in this stratum of "pertinence" (to the ego). . . . "From the phenomenon world, from the world appearing with an Objective sense, a substratum becomes separated, as the 'Nature' included in my ownness." [11] This "Nature included in my ownness" is what *Formal and Transcendental Logic* indicates with the expression "intrinsically first Nature," a Nature which does not yet have the Objectivity of the Nature studied by the natural sciences. It is a " 'mere Nature,' that has lost that 'by everyone.' " [12]

Among the material bodies of this "primordial" Nature I find my own body, which stands out from the other bodies by the fact that it is not only a body *(Körper)* but an animate organism *(Leib)*, that it is a psychophysical unity, and that this unity is governed by me as pole of my various mental processes. Then we arrive at

> a sequence of evidences that yet, in their sequence, seem paradoxical. The psychic life of my Ego (this "psychophysical" Ego), including my whole world-experiencing life and therefore including my actual and possible experience *of* what is other, is wholly unaffected by screening off what is other.[13]

We see that the fact of intentionality resists even this second epoché performed within transcendental experience. The emphasis on intentionality is one of the most popularized aspects

8. *Ibid.*
9. *Ibid.*
10. In the transcendental attitude the world is no longer for me a world existing in itself; it is "phenomenon" only.
11. *CM*, p. 96.
12. *Ibid.*
13. *Ibid.*, p. 98.

of Husserl's philosophy. But, the more one repeats that every consciousness is consciousness *of*, the more one is limited to referring to intentionality as it is encountered in the natural attitude. Now what is in fact significant about Husserl's intentionality—for the philosopher who does not limit himself to interest in a purely psychological description—is that intentionality subsists in the transcendental attitude when, thanks to the second epoché, one has reached the furthest limit to which the phenomenological reduction can be carried. Then the fact of intentionality imposes its solution to the transcendental problem: "consequently there belongs within my psychic being the whole constitution of the world existing for me." [14] And we can say that the fundamental Husserlian evidence is not *ego cogito* but *ego-cogito-cogitatum*. Then we understand the whole bearing of the affirmation in *Formal and Transcendental Logic*[15] according to which the world which is always there for me is a "fact of consciousness" (*Bewusstseinstatsache*), a fact of consciousness not only for the self in the natural attitude but also for the transcendental self, which in addition is for the transcendental self "reduced" to its own sphere. In order to answer the transcendental questions, it is enough that the *cogitationes* of this transcendental self, considered as much in its potential as in its actual experiences, and so, too, in its *habitualities*, be progressively explicated. We will indicate only a few important points in this progressive explication.

The explication of the actual or potential experience of the *ego* reduced to its sphere of ownness hence reveals not only this experience but, in addition, a "universe" of transcendent objects which "pertain" to this sphere. These "objects" are constituted as spatial unities and are transcendent with respect to the stream of mental life. But here there is only a question of a "multiplicity of objects of possible experience—this experience being purely *my own* life, and what is experienced in this experience being nothing more than a synthetic unity inseparable from this life and its potentialities." [16] The world "reduced" to what pertains to me reveals itself as an "immanent transcendence." Yet this world does not present itself

14. *Ibid.*
15. *FTL*, p. 242.
16. *CM*, p. 104.

only as a purely meant *(vermeint)* world; its being is *confirmed* in me by concordant experiences. Then it must be understood how the immanent transcendence can take on the sense of objective transcendence, of transcendence properly so called.

A more extensive explication of transcendental experience will bring us to this transcendence, which in the order of constitution comes next after the primordial transcendence. The first step in the constitution of the objective world is the constitution of the other. The first non-ego is the other, but this is an other who has not yet acquired the sense "man in the objective world." Then it is a matter of inquiring into the experience we have of the other and elucidating its type of intentionality. In the experience of the other I can say, as it is often said, that I have the other before me in "flesh and blood" *(leibhaftig)*. Yet the other's own being is not accessible to me in a direct manner. Hence there must be a certain *mediateness* of the intentionality which makes the being of the other accessible in an indirect but veridical manner. Within my perceptual field the other appears to me as a mere body. And this body can only have the sense of organism from an "apperceptive transfer" that starts from my own body. This transfer is founded upon a *resemblance* which in the primordial sphere *associates* this other body with my own. Such a transfer by resemblance is encountered also in all of our everyday experience. In the second appendix of *Formal and Transcendental Logic* Husserl characterizes the founding role of "apperception" for every category of objects. There is apperception or appresentation each time we are in the presence of an object (using the term as broadly as possible), the sense of which we understand in an immediate manner even though it is new to us. This is because we have seen objects having an *analogous* sense, because we find ourselves in an analogous *situation*. This apperception by analogy is not a *reasoning* by analogy since it is specifically the *immediate* way in which we grasp the sense of these "new" objects. The old datum and the new datum are *associated* in a truly fundamental passive synthesis, and Husserl can say that wherever there is an "objective datum" there is this associative, analogical, apperception.[17] But the apperception of the other

17. *Ibid.*, p. 112.

is distinguished from other apperceptions in a remarkable fashion. Although in the case of the experience of the external world the appresented object, the "new" object, *must be able to be the first object* in another experience, which object, as a formerly known object, transmits its sense to the other object, this inversion can never take place in the case of the appresentation of the other. The other can never be given in an original manner; he will always be only an appresented object and will never play the role of an object which founds an appresentation. The other can only be thought as something analogous to what "pertains" to me. From this it is understood that "with the other *Ego,* there is appresented, in an analogizing modification, everything that belongs to his concretion: first *his* primordial world, and then his fully concrete *ego.* In other words, another monad becomes constituted appresentatively in mine." [18] And in carrying the intentional explication of the other further, one would come to the transcendental constitution of the objective world in the usual sense. Actually, as in every associative transfer, there is between my being and the being of the other an assimilation and a mutual adaptation of their significations. Such a transfer is at the same time a "fusion" *(Verschmelzung).* This is of such a nature that there is a necessary and immediate unity of sense between what pertains to me and what is alien to me. And from this fact,

> I can identify a Nature constituted in me with a Nature constituted by someone else (or, stated with the necessary precision, . . . I can identify a Nature constituted in me with one constituted in me *as* a Nature constituted by someone else). This identification is no greater [an] enigma than any other synthetic identification. It is therefore no more mysterious than any [other synthetic identification], by virtue of which, as an identification confined to my own original sphere, no matter what objective unity acquires [its] sense and being for me through the medium of presentations. [19]

Thus, beginning from the other pure selves (not yet having the sense of beings in the world) a community of existing egos "one with another and one for another" is constituted. [20]

18. *Ibid.,* p. 115.
19. *Ibid.,* p. 126.
20. Remaining on the plane of the natural attitude, in Part I ("Pre- ·

It is a community which "(in its communalized intentionality) constitutes the one identical world" in which "all Egos again present themselves, but in an Objectivating apperception with the sense 'men' or 'psychophysical men as worldly Objects' "; then

> the Objective world as an idea — the ideal correlate of an inter-subjective (intersubjectively communalized) experience, which ideally can be and is carried on as constantly harmonious — is essentially related to intersubjectivity (itself constituted as having the ideality of endless openness), whose component particular subjects are equipped with mutually corresponding and harmonious constitutive systems.[21]

After the clarification of the constitution of the objective world as it is grasped by experience pure and simple, other constitutive problems of higher levels present themselves. Among these problems *Formal and Transcendental Logic* refers simply to those relating to its own interests, i.e., to the constitution of the world from the point of view of *theoretical* cognition. One of the most important problems is the clarification of the *idealizations* of science. The phenomenological analyses of *Formal and Transcendental Logic* conclude with these by opening out upon constitutional transcendental analyses. Thanks to these analyses, there is disengaged from the intentional sense of the sciences and logic the fact that the "being-in-itself" and the "truth-in-itself" they speak about are idealizations. Only a return to the constitutive sources allows us to uncover these idealizations as idealizations and "preserves us from any absolutization" of the being of the world and its exact determinations. Only thus are we conscious of the sense of cognition and its "bearing."

Having traced the broad outlines of these constitutional investigations, *Formal and Transcendental Logic* comes to an explicit characterization of the method which has guided these researches. This investigation of the sense of the method

---

paratory Considerations," p. 32) Husserl calls for "a community of scientific investigators" working "for and with one another." Rational intersubjectivity already gives us a first image of transcendental inter-subjectivity.

21. *CM*, pp. 107–8.

permits us to return to certain difficulties which we have provisionally set aside.

The constitutional method is essentially an uncovering of the various intentional actions which intermingle in the life of consciousness. If it can be said that all that exists for consciousness is constituted in consciousness, it must be added hastily that every sort of existent, every sort of "intentional unity," has its own constitution. In this there is a fundamental fact which makes a constitutive analysis having the intentional unity or, more simply, the intentional object as guiding clue possible. In the *Cartesian Meditations*[22] as well as in the present chapter of *Formal and Transcendental Logic*,[23] Husserl warns the reader that he does not use the term *analysis* in the usual sense. Intentional analysis is not a decomposition into parts; it is a revelation of *intentional implications*. It goes beyond the actual mental processes under consideration, since every mental process has a *horizon,* a horizon of *potentialities,* which, taking it purely as an actual mental process, are specifically "implied" in it. For example, the perception of such and such an object has a horizon which embraces other perceptual possibilities. And these perceptual possibilities are *implied* in the sense of the object perceived. Thus a cube is *grasped in advance* as a cube even though all of its facets have not been seen. On the other hand, intentional analysis can consider the object not as a completed unity but as the terminus of a genesis, and it then unfolds how, beginning from a basic sense which derives from a former performance, the present sense of the object is formed. Hence there is implied in the objective sense a "sedimented 'history,' "[24] and intentional analysis becomes a *genetic* analysis.

It is not necessary to believe that this uncovering of intentional implications is a surrender to the contingency of an empirical development. Actually, "in the flux of intentional synthesis . . . an essentially necessary conformity to type prevails,"[25] and the typical essential structures can only be revealed to an examination which inquires into essences — and into essences which, as we are going to see, are separated

22. "§ 20. The Peculiar Nature of Intentional Analysis."
23. *FTL*, p. 245.
24. *Ibid.*, p. 250.
25. *CM*, p. 49.

from all connexion with facts. Very specifically put, every intentional object (taking as example any physical thing) has an essential type (here the type any physical thing whatever). And if one keeps this intentional object quite identical through the variations of the diverse modes of consciousness that one has of it, then one sees that these modes of consciousness, no matter how diverse and undulating they may be, exhibit the same structural type, the type characteristic of the intentionality constitutive of the intentional object considered. In the example we have taken,

> the multiplicity of possible perceptions, memories, and, indeed, intentional processes of whatever sort, that relate, or can relate, "harmoniously" to one and the same physical thing has (in all its tremendous complication) a quite definite *essential style*, which is identical in the case of any physical thing whatever and is particularized only according to the different individual things constituted in different cases.[26]

In a similar fashion one can indicate the type of intentionality which has ideal objects for intentional objects. In a definitive way, all actual or potential modes of consciousness hence fall into determinate and differentiated types. Then one can say that "the whole life of consciousness is governed by a universal constitutional Apriori, embracing all intentionalities" (246). Before showing the importance of this "subjective" Apriori for the orientation of the phenomenological method, we would like—at the risk of digression—to study the method for investigating essences in order to show specifically that the process which is involved has nothing directly or indirectly to do with the process of empirical induction.

Hence let us examine in itself the process of "varying" which characterizes the investigation of essences. This investigation begins from a particular datum taken as an example. Phantasy *(Phantasie)* transforms this example in whatever way it cares to; it "varies" it freely. Through this free varying, something is revealed which necessarily persists through all possible variations *(Abwandlungen)* of the example from which one has begun. This *invariant* is the universal essence. The universal essence of an object is hence "that without which an object of the kind in question cannot be thought." [27]

26. *FTL*, p. 246.
27. *Erf. u. Urt.*, p. 411.

If some statements in the *Ideen* (cf. § 70) were separated from their context, one could believe that the perceptual datum presents a privileged field of examples suitable for beginning the varying. Actually, Husserl tells us explicitly that originarily giving perception — more specifically, external perception — has an advantage over all species of presentiation such as re-membering, image-consciousness, etc., in that it can furnish us with "clear and firm singularizations for universal eidetic analyses of the phenomenological sort." [28] Actually, "external perception has its perfect clarity with respect to all object-moments that have actually become given it in the originary mode." [29] To be sure, as we have seen, perception gives us the object only in a unilateral fashion; it can occasion only an in-adequate evidence. But what is given us of the object is present *originaliter*. It is a *Selbst da* which is before us. The cor-responding evidence, even though imperfect because in-complete, nevertheless is an evidence of clarity. Moreover, the object of external perception is not dispelled by reflection. One can easily return to it. Hence one can study its universal essence and stay "within the bounds of originariness without particular efforts to produce clarity." [30] And yet Husserl adds that these privileges of the originary datum do not have as great an importance for the phenomenological method as one might think. Actually, "there are reasons why in phenome-nology, as in all other eidetic sciences, presentiations and, to speak more precisely, free phantasies acquire a position superior to that of perceptions and do so even in the phenom-enology of perception itself — excluding, to be sure, the phe-nomenology of *data* of sensation." [31] And *ex abrupto* Husserl refers to the attitude of the geometer: "In his investigative thinking the geometer operates upon the figure or the model incomparably more in phantasy than in perception; even the 'pure' geometer, the one who dispenses with the algebraic method." [32] Having analyzed the attitude of the geometer, Husserl affirms that "for the phenomenologist, who has to do with reduced mental processes and correlates belonging to

28. *Ideen*, p. 130.
29. *Ibid.*
30. *Ibid.*
31. *Ibid.*
32. *Ibid.*, p. 131.

them essentially, the situation is not otherwise in its most universal features." [33] This parallel between the attitude of the geometer and the attitude of the phenomenologist shows itself as immediately significant. We should in fact show that the method of mathematical idealization has been the very source of the elaboration of the phenomenological method of investigating essences and that the example which served as starting point for the phenomenological variation has the same role as the particular figure about which the geometer reasons.

Every mathematician knows quite well, as Leibniz says, that "the force of the demonstration is independent of the figure drawn, which is there only to facilitate the understanding of what is meant and to fix the attention." [34] This means that the model is only a prop which "releases" the geometer from obligations to "clear intuitions" that establish the progressive steps of his thinking. [35] But to speak in Kantian terms, "intuitive clarity" should be no obstacle to "logical clarity." The geometer should know how to read the relations among essences out of the particular figure. He must not let himself be blocked by the particularity of the example he has chosen. Also, the "phantasied" figure has its own privilege, that of not remaining self-identical in the fullness of its particular characteristics.

> In actually drawing and actually constructing a model he [namely: the geometer] is restricted; in phantasy he has incomparable freedom in the arbitrary transformation of the phantasied figures, in running through continuously modified possible formations, accordingly in the production of innumerable new formations; a freedom that alone opens up for him access to the world of essential possibilities with their infinite horizons of eidetic cognitions. [36]

We shall see below the sense in which this possibility of running through *all* possible forms must be understood. For the moment, let us take note of the emphasis on the consciousness

33. *Ibid.*
34. Leibniz, *Nouveaux essais*, Bk. IV, Chap. 1, § 9, ed. Janet, (1866), pp. 368–69 [our translation].
35. *Ideen*, p. 132, n. 1.
36. *Ibid.*, p. 131.

of *freedom* which accompanies the imaginative constructions which the geometer uses.

We discover this consciousness of freedom specifically in the phenomenological varying. The varying is a free varying. This freedom lets us reach the essence and releases us from all attachment to "factualness," to the singular. "In any case, here too freedom of eidetic research necessarily demands operating in phantasy." [37] This is so much the case that Husserl can rightly say, in full consciousness of the provocative character of this paradoxical formula, "that *'fiction' is the vital element of phenomenology, as it is of every other eidetic science.*" [38]

Just as the geometer must go back to the actual figures from time to time, so, too, the phenomenologist must avail himself of the resources of perception. He does so to such an extent that the "factualness" reappears which we were thinking had been eliminated by our showing that, contrary to appearances, phantasy is the privileged field of operation for the eidetic sciences. It can happen that the phenomenologist starts from actual examples provided by external perception. It seems that this initial insertion of phenomenological varying into actuality brings an irreducible element of factualness into a procedure meant to reach results pertaining to essences. But even in the case where actuality is necessarily taken as starting point, it must be recognized that the necessity of this *starting point* should not affect the development of the process it initiates. The necessity of a starting point is not perforce a necessity in principle. It is often, so to speak, an occasional necessity. There is, for example, a genuine break between the necessity of reference to a figure in geometry and the necessity of the demonstration itself. There is more. Actually, the real datum from which the geometer and the phenomenologist can set out is taken *as an example.* An example as such is never considered for its own sake, in its individuality. Even when the mathematician "reflects on the figure," he has a sort of conscious distraction regarding the figure, which nevertheless serves to "fix" his attention. The consciousness which deals

37. *Ibid.*, p. 132.
38. *Ibid.* In a note here Husserl adds: "A sentence that, as a quotation, should be particularly suitable for a naturalistic ridiculing of the eidetic mode of cognition."

with the example is a consciousness that one is able to *substitute* another example for this example. The "behavior" of the example always implies an immediate consciousness of its being "chosen arbitrarily" *(beliebig)*. As *Formal and Transcendental Logic* says, in place of the example chosen, "any variant of the example could have served equally well." [39] We said that there was a danger that this particular individual upon which one was working would become an obstacle to the grasping of essences in mathematics just as in phenomenology. But to be precise, if we treat it consciously as an example and not as an actual datum considered for its own sake, the individual loses its noxiousness and enables the "exercising" of the phantasy through which perfect clarification is attained. For if, as we recall, the datum presents itself in clarity, then, when we operate on the plane of phantasy, we have to establish the clarity. Hence it is necessary "to fertilize one's phantasy by observations in originary intuition that are as abundant and excellent as possible; but naturally this fertilizing does not signify that experience as such has a function in establishing validity." [40] This is why, fully recognizing that the phenomenological varying begins from "de facto single cases of actuality or possibility" (247), Husserl can say, in *Formal and Transcendental Logic*, that it is "released from all restrictions to facts accepted beforehand." [41] Now we understand the notion of the freedom of variation more completely. The varying is "free" since it is released from every bond *(Bindung)* with factuality in its point of departure as well as in its advance.

Though there is good reason to respect this free character, a tendency remains to interpret the phenomenological varying as an *empirical* varying. Certain of Husserl's metaphors are particularly spatial and invite such an interpretation. The many variants "diverge," but despite their differences they "coincide," they cover each other *(sich decken)*. This "coincidence amidst divergence" *(Deckung in Widerstreit)* comes to light in a continuous synthesis. Hence one is inclined to think of the essence as that which numerous individuals have in common. Then an objection comes to mind. If the invariant

39. *FTL*, p. 248.
40. *Ideen*, p. 132.
41. *FTL*, p. 248.

is "the indissolubly identical in the different and ever-again different" (248), how can one be sure of having reached the essence in a definitive manner, since each new variant perceived or phantasied can reduce the common characters which appear in the synthesis of preceding variants? But, actually, if such an empirical interpretation of variation is possible, this is because one has not fully penetrated what the notion which Husserl terms *Beliebigkeit* [optionalness] implies, i.e., the notion of arbitrary choice. *Erfahrung und Urteil* specifies that the varying made up of processes formative of variants itself has this character of optionalness. That is to say, we can "break off" (*abbrechen*) the varying. There is no need for us to run through all of the possible variants as we would be obliged to do if it were a question of an empirical comparison of factual data. "Each of the particulars has the character of exemplary optionalness, an optionalness always belongs to the variation-manifold as well. . . . This remarkable and extremely important consciousness of 'and so forth according to option' belongs essentially to every variation-manifold." [42] The *Beliebigkeit* in the process of variation hence not only signifies that one can pass freely from one variant to another; it also implies the consciousness of a fundamental potentiality, a consciousness that one can continue without being actually obliged to do so. *Beliebigkeit* in the choice of the example implies a consciousness of possible substitution, for *instead* of this example we can take another. *Beliebigkeit* in the varying itself implies a consciousness of the possible "and so on." As *Erfahrung und Urteil* says, "in such expressions 'optional' should never be just a way of speaking and should not signify some irrelevant activity on our part; on the contrary, it belongs *to the fundamental character of the act of viewing ideas that it be 'optional.' "* [43]

But how are we fully to understand this *Beliebigkeit* in an immediate manner if the examples of the investigation of essences are limited to such things as the essence of red, the essence of sound, etc.? Are we not in such variations *naturally* subject to the empiricist temptation? Are we not tempted to think of the variants as a series of *particular* data, even though phantasied ones, such as this red here, that red there, which

42. *Erf. u. Urt.*, p. 413.
43. *Ibid.*, p. 422.

must actually be run through? As *Erfahrung und Urteil* indicates explicitly,[44] the totally free variation is not enough to enable us to reach the universal as *pure* universal. The universal can still retain a reference to actuality. Every link to particular data as such must be deliberately excluded. To attain the essence red, for example, we can easily perform a free varying, all the while continuing to think, without being explicitly aware of it, that the different reds which we have phantasied are reds which we can see in the world, which other men can have seen or will be able to see. In short, we think of them as reds *"in der Welt."* Hence there is a tacit presupposition which relates all of the variants to the world which exists in fact. And this presupposition remains hidden due to its very universality. On the contrary, with mathematical idealization we are sheltered from such presuppositions. The mathematician has a genuine use of *Beliebigkeit.*[45] He knows how to read the "pure" universal out of the individual. "When we designate the circle a conic section, there is no question of an actual surface such as can be seen in Nature." [46] All geometrical propositions relate to conceivable figures and not to actual figures. One cannot give a geometrical proposition any other sense unless one would be a Berkeley, who among other vain objections would say to the mathematician that he has no right to speak of the superimposition of two triangles, since "the under triangle is no triangle—nothing at all, it not being perceiv'd." [47] On the other hand, Leibniz says: "If in geometry we can accept what we learn from the images . . . we would be deprived of what, relating to contemplation, I most admire in geometry, which is to let the true source of eternal truth be seen." [48] There is what amounts to a transparence about the mathematical example which lets us see the essence through it.

Is it then necessary to say that only mathematics can give us pure essences and that mathematical idealization is the only

44. *Ibid.*, p. 423.
45. Note that the term *beliebig* [optional] is precisely the term currently used by German mathematicians to indicate the arbitrary character of their choice of examples.
46. *Erf. u. Urt.*, p. 425.
47. Berkeley, *Commonplace Book*, No. 532.
48. Leibniz, *Nouveaux essais*, Bk. IV, Chap. 12, § 6, pp. 479–80 [our translation].

genuine "varying"? Husserl is far from thinking any such thing. In *Erfahrung und Urteil,* after noting that all of mathematics works with "pure" essences, he emphasizes that "there are not the slightest grounds for considering the method of apriori thinking . . . as belonging exclusively to the sphere of mathematics." [49] To be sure, we believe that Husserl often drew upon the living thought of the mathematician. We have already shown that one can find inductive analogues in mathematical thinking for the phenomenological notions of reduction, constitution, and transcendental intersubjectivity.[50] But in no case have we claimed to reduce phenomenological thinking to these mathematical "antecedents." If in many respects one can establish a parallel between the intuitions presented to us by the living experience of mathematics and the fundamental intuitions of phenomenology, one cannot forget that, for Husserl, philosophy is "a genus of investigation that in a certain sense gives to them all a new dimension." [51]

On the point with which we are concerned, it can be said that, in operating with his concepts, the mathematician *at the outset* breaks with all empirical considerations. The philosopher, on the contrary, who practices varying in order to obtain the essence of perception — the essence of color, the essence of red, the essence of sound, etc. — must perform a reduction, the phenomenological reduction, in order to abstain from every empirical temptation. In the natural attitude we unconsciously have reference to the finished actual world as an example. Hence every eidos retains a reference to the actual world. "If we now become conscious of this bond, *consciously put it out of play,* . . . we achieve complete purity. Then we stand so to speak in a pure phantasy-world, a *world of absolutely pure* possibility." [52] Only then do we see the "pure" universal. Only then has the investigation of essences reached its goal.

In order to render access to the investigation of essences easier, we have begun this study in a unilateral fashion by directing our attention exclusively toward the data and not toward the corresponding modes of consciousness. But, actu-

---

49. *Erf. u. Urt.,* p. 428.
50. Cf. *supra,* pp. 74 f.
51. "Philosophy as Strict Science," p. 74, n. a.
52. *Erf. u. Urt.,* 424.

ally, the correlation between data and modes of consciousness is such that the investigation of the essence of such and such an intentional object is indissociable from investigation of the essential style *(Wesensstyl)* of the corresponding intentionality. The varying of the datum goes hand in hand with the varying of the modes by which the datum is grasped. There is an eidetic correlation between the constituting and what is constituted that cannot be broken up, and Husserl is able to speak of "an essential form with two correlative sides." [53] The ontic Apriori is the correlate of a constitutive Apriori "that is concretely united with it, concretely inseparable from it." [54]

But then all that we have said about the nonempirical character of the variation that starts from a datum taken as an example is going to have its analogue in the explication of the life of consciousness. If every fact can be conceived as being only an example of a pure possibility, even "the *de facto* transcendental *ego* and particular data given in transcendental experience of the ego have the significance merely of examples of pure possibilities." [55] If we place the empirical self in parentheses with the transcendental reduction, within the transcendental sphere we encounter again the distinction between fact and essence, the distinction between the transcendental *ego* given in fact and the *eidos ego*. In the present chapter of *Formal and Transcendental Logic*, at the moment when Husserl develops the problems of intersubjectivity, he proclaims the "necessity of starting, each from his own subjectivity" (title of § 95). It is to be regretted that here Husserl does not specify the role of eidetic variation as he did in the *Cartesian Meditations*.[56] The explication of myself is precisely what I must perform in order to bring to light the "constitution" of the other. But the transcendental *ego* from whom I begin, my transcendental *ego*, should be considered only as an example of a pure possibility. I am to perform an eidetic variation of myself by transforming myself freely in imagination[57] and thus

53. *FTL*, p. 248.
54. *Ibid.*
55. *CM*, p. 73.
56. It is true that in *Formal and Transcendental Logic*, where remarks on the method are not incorporated into the presentation of the transcendental problem-set, as is the case in the *Cartesian Meditations*, it is difficult for Husserl to be specific on this point.
57. *CM*, pp. 84–85.

arrive at the transcendental *ego* in general. Even when interest in the transcendental explication is applied to the constitution of my own *ego* and no longer to the constitution of the other, I must refer to "the apodictic principles that pertain to this *ego* as exemplifying the *eidos ego*," [58] Thus the transcendental analysis is fundamentally an eidetic analysis which uncovers the universal *eidos* of the transcendental *ego* in general.

Since every eidetic analysis leads ultimately to the *eidos* of the transcendental *ego*, we can begin from any intentional experience in order to reach that *eidos*. This is why Husserl says that every intentional and constitutive analysis must itself be considered as an analysis initially taken as an example.[59] What is more, this remark has equal reference to the exposition Husserl makes of the eidetic method. One cannot explicate this method by following an empirical procedure which would "describe" a factual situation. "Only in eidetic intuition can the essence of eidetic intuition become clarified" (249). To be sure, the validity of the method is shown by starting from intentional "experiences" which one "describes." But these intentional experiences should be considered simply as examples, in place of which other intentional experiences could just as well have been chosen.

We have just insisted upon the eidetic character of the phenomenological method because, while proclaiming that phenomenology is a science of essences, one often tends to misunderstand this character when one follows the Husserlian analyses in a factual manner.[60] But, of course, the emphasis on this eidetic character should not lead us to minimize the intuitive sense of the phenomenological method. The phenomenological explication is not a "theory" which more or less explicitly takes over the "prejudices" of traditional metaphysics. Rather, it excludes all "metaphysical adventure," all "speculative excess." It employs only the data of pure intuition. But if phenomenology follows an intuitive method, there is no reason to lose sight of the fact that the intuitive character of phenomenological explication has a value that goes beyond the methodological framework. This intuitive

58. *Ibid.*, p. 72.
59. *FTL*, pp. 248–49.
60. Later (p. 192) we will come back to what seems to be the reason for this misunderstanding.

character makes it possible to solve the *transcendental solipsism* to which the transcendental problems infallibly lead. The objection of transcendental solipsism is actually imposed on us. As Husserl recognizes, "If everything I can ever accept as existent is constituted in my *ego*, then everything that exists does indeed seem to be a mere moment of my own transcendental being." [61] No existence escapes this universal reference to my transcendental ego, as the following profession of transcendental faith, which is as extreme as can be conceived, reveals: " . . . the subjective Apriori precedes the being of God and the world, the being of everything, individually and collectively, for me, the thinking subject. Even God is for me what he is, in consequence of my own productivity of consciousness; here too I must not look aside lest I commit a supposed blasphemy. . . . " [62] But, actually, the reduction to the transcendental ego has only the *appearance* of a solipsism, since the existence of others, the existence of the world—in a word, the existence of all transcendencies—are *facts* of my own transcendental sphere. I have only to *develop* the analysis of my transcendental experience to dispel the appearance of solipsism. By following the data of pure intuition, I progressively *explicate* the life of my consciousness and, never abandoning the transcendental attitude, I find that other transcendental egos are constituted in me, and so on. So Husserl can say: "Can the transcendental illusion of solipsism withstand this onward march of mere *concrete explication?*" [63] By strictly adhering, as Husserl demands,[64] to the pure data of transcendental reflection and by taking them exactly as they are themselves given in the intuition of direct evidence, the problem of transcendental solipsism, to which the transcendental problem-set led, *before* being explicated on all of its progressive levels, is solved.

Thus, from the fact of its investigation of essences and from the fact of its concrete explication, eidetic analysis gives phenomenology its style by making it *simultaneously* an intuitive and an apriori discipline. It is not a question of *explaining* the world and the human being through theories.

61. *FTL*, p. 241.
62. *Ibid.*, p. 251.
63. *Ibid.*, p. 242.
64. *CM*, p. 36.

Rather it is a question, thanks to a purely intuitive method, of uncovering the profound sense of the world and of the human being. But this uncovering makes essences appear which reveal *apriori* structures. And these apriori structures are revealed not only in the objective world but even in the constituting subjectivity. Until now Husserl has spoken only of the objective Apriori. Yet the problem of an apriori ontology of the actual world continues to be, as is said in the *Cartesian Meditations*, a *one-sided* problem.[65] For this objective Apriori can be a "philosophically intelligible" Apriori only if it is specifically related to the *ultimate* sources of intelligibility, i.e., to the essential necessity which reigns in the transcendental sphere. In order to understand the world, we must bring to light "the necessities that satisfy the essential rootedness of any Objective world in transcendental subjectivity."[66] In short, the *subjective* Apriori must be brought to light. This Apriori dominates the totality of the constitutive functions of the *ego*. The constituting consciousness is a *coherent* unity of structures from which all being derives its sense. Then the whole of phenomenology is under the sign of the Apriori. This is what the Fifth Cartesian Meditation indicates in what we believe to be the most revealing affirmation of Husserl's philosophical project: "That a procedure drawing insight from eidetic intuition is called phenomenological and claims philosophical significance is justified only by the circumstance that every genuine intuition has its place in the constitutional nexus."[67]

This coherent constitutional nexus includes an infinity of actual and potential apriori types pertaining to intentional life. A field of research is then opened up for the phenomenologist who wants to study this infinity of intentional forms. By its very richness this totality is difficult to master, and Husserl admits in the *Cartesian Meditations*[68] that the totality of the constitutive problems started to become clear for him only in the last years preceding the appearance of the meditations. But despite its diversity, this constitutional nexus is open to a systematic study by the fact that it obeys essential

65. *Ibid.*, p. 137.
66. *Ibid.*
67. *Ibid.*, p. 138.
68. *Ibid.*, p. 74.

laws. These essential laws determine the *compossibility* of the various intentional types in the same *ego* at a given moment and over the course of time. The life of the *ego* presents itself as an interconnexion of constituting performances which have relations of conditioning and conditioned among them. It is somewhat repugnant for Husserl to use the "dangerous" term *causality;* he prefers the term *motivation,* which enables him to avoid any confusion between the purely psychic sphere and the sphere of the physical world. The laws of motivation govern the multiplicity of mental processes of the *ego;* thus intentional analysis necessarily becomes *genetic* analysis. "The *ego* constitutes himself for himself in, so to speak, the unity of a 'history.' " [69] This history can be established only by participating in the universal form of all genesis, which is time. Thus, before we envisage the genesis of the *ego* pertaining to the higher levels, a genesis determined by a complex motivational system, we must begin with the study of the temporal form within which the life of the *ego* unfolds.

In the course of the text of *Formal and Transcendental Logic,* Husserl simply mentions the temporal form of intentional genesis. Only in Appendix II, while indicating more specifically the tasks of a genetic intentional explication, does he show the role of the temporality which dominates the entire concrete life of consciousness. *The Phenomenology of Internal Time-Consciousness*[70] brings out numerous analyses of immanent temporality by referring to the intentional character of the consciousness of time (which then was a new theme for phenomenology). But Husserl had not yet arrived at the systematic implementation of the genetic mode of intentional explication at that time. On the other hand, in Appendix II of *Formal and Transcendental Logic,* the results

69. *Ibid.,* p. 75.
70. Published by Indiana University Press in 1964; translated by James S. Churchill from "Edmund Husserls Vorlesungen zur Phänomenologie des inneren Zeitbewusstseins," edited by Martin Heidegger in *Jahrbuch für Philosophie und phänomenologische Forschung,* IX (1928). The first part of this phenomenology of the consciousness of internal time includes the lessons taught by Husserl at Göttingen during the winter semester of 1904–5. The second part includes the additions to these lectures which were written during the years 1905–10.

of the analyses in the time lectures are reinserted into the horizon of the genetic method.

In order to understand more deeply the characteristics of this genetic method, let us contrast it to the purely static method. As we have already seen, static analysis takes the intentional object as a clue, and its task, beginning from the confused manners in which the object is given and tracing the various intentional implications, is to rediscover the *original* manner in which the object is "itself" given with the clarity of presence. Intentional explication is "clarification" in the specifically Husserlian sense: it is a "fulfilling" clarification where one truly has "experience" of the thing itself. It can always rediscover the original manner of givenness by means of the property that every nonoriginal consciousness of an object has of *pointing back* to the original consciousness of the same object. For example, every confused judgment points back to the corresponding clear judgment, the judgment which gives the state-of-affairs itself. On many occasions Husserl repeats that every intentional modification in itself points back to the unmodified. But, to our knowledge, nowhere else but in Appendix II of *Formal and Transcendental Logic* does he say that this essential property has a counterpart. This counterpart

> lies in the fact that, conversely, every manner of original givenness carries with it its possibilities of transition to "corresponding" manners of non-original givenness, which can be united with it synthetically and belong to a fixed set of types. To be sure, we cannot speak of a *counterreference* here, as a reference in the proper sense, such as we find in the "intentional modifications." But, at all events, *every consciousness* has, of essential necessity, its place in a particular *multiplicity of consciousness* that corresponds to it, a synthetic open infinity of possible modes of consciousness of the Same—a multiplicity that has, so to speak, its teleological center in the possible "experience." [71]

This important text stresses the structural character of intentionality. In it there is no question of a structure relating exclusively to clear data. Moreover, there is no question of a reference simply to the coming-to-be of a clear datum that will inevitably be obscured. The various nonoriginal conscious-

71. *FTL*, p. 315.

nesses of an object *make up part* of a *structural* totality which is centered about the original consciousness of the same object, and this in a purely static manner.

But there exists another type of explication which no longer takes as its center of interest the finished unity of the object and the modes of consciousness that relate to it but instead takes the concrete totality of mental processes in which these modes of consciousness are situated. Then inquiry turns to the subjective life itself and its own *history*. From this genetic point of view, experience is still the privileged mode of consciousness. We would willingly say, permitting ourselves a play on words which is foreign to the German language [but works in English as well as French], that, if experience is then the privileged mode of consciousness, this is not so much because it gives us the *presence* of the object but because it gives us the *present* of the object, because it gives us the object present to the consciousness in an original Now. To this original Present is necessarily attached the intentional modifications, the most primitive of which is the "retentional" modification: a modification that changes what is presently given into a datum *which has just been (soeben)* but which is not completely gone *(vergangen)*. "As now present, this modified consciousness functions, in accordance with the same law, as the primitive mode relative to a new modification (a modification of the modification); and so on, continuously." [72] The time lectures insisted upon the *continuousness* of this modification.[73] This character of continuousness is what specifically distinguishes retention from reproduction, for, while there is a break between the impression and the reproduction of this impression, there is continuity between the consciousness of the present datum and the retentional consciousness. "Continuous retentional modification proceeds up to an essentially necessary *limit*." [74] The present gradually fades away until it is lost in what Husserl calls the universal subsoil, i.e., the "unconscious." Then the profound sense of Husserl's metaphor of "sedimentation" is revealed to the reader. That which, as present to consciousness in the original mode of the Now, or even in the retentional mode, was *de-*

72. *Ibid.*, p. 318.
73. *Internal Time Consciousness*, § 19.
74. *FTL*, p. 319.

tached (abgehoben) and was imposing itself on our attention, fades into the background and leaves our attentional field. It becomes sedimented in the unconscious.[75] But there is no reason to believe that it has, for this reason, become inoperant — that it is lost forever. Sedimentation in the unconscious is indeed "forgetting," as is said in the "Ursprung der Geometrie"; [76] this does not prevent Husserl from affirming that the unconscious, "far from being a phenomenological nothing, is itself a limit-mode of consciousness." [77] For this unconscious has an effect on the living present; it has an evoking role. Here we touch upon a characteristic aspect of Husserlian phenomenology. The marginal, the latent, the potential, the sedimented — all of these have an active role in the determination of the sense of the intentional object. And if one takes the term *horizon* in a sense broad enough to include all of these forms of inactuality, one can sum up the problems of a universal phenomenology which integrates genetic tasks into its explicatory tasks by saying that one must not separate the being from its horizon and by recalling that "all wrong interpretations of being come from naïve blindness to the horizons that join in determining the sense of being, and to the corresponding tasks of uncovering implicit intentionality." [78] Moreover, in our opinion, if the *Logische Untersuchungen* is not yet in a position to master the phenomenological problem-set, this is because it did not yet possess this notion of horizon.

Let us consider the function of what is no longer present by taking the example of the judgment. In an original activity we produce judgments. But soon this activity takes on a secondary form which is no longer activity; it changes into the *passive* form of retention. The judgment is not yet gone from our consciousness; it is still in our possession; we still have it in our grip *(nach im Griff)*. And, thanks to a "passive synthesis," we are aware that the judgment which was constituted in original activity "but a moment ago" remains the same in retention. Hence we bestow on the judgment an existence which persists, not only during the active constitution that produced it, but

75. This unconscious has, to be sure, nothing to do with an affective unconscious.

76. "Ursprung der Geometrie," p. 212.

77. *FTL,* p. 319.

78. *CM,* p. 85; cf. also p. 48.

even in the course of retentional variation until it is sedimented. But, even when it has been sedimented, this judgment can emerge again in a recollection which Husserl terms "passive" recollection because the memorial regrasping of a former judgment does not imply a repetition of the activity which originally produced that judgment. An association revives in us the remembering of a past judgment. Then we have to do with a *passive genesis*[79] governed by essential laws, the laws of *association*.[80] These laws of association give rise not only to the reappearance of memories but also to the formation of apperceptions. In a purely passive manner, judgments can come to mind or be evoked *(erweckt)* without our having previously formed such judgments. These judgments can, nevertheless, by the same principle as rememberings, be considered as passive modifications of an original activity in the sense that they too refer back to former judgments, judgments which present an *analogy* to them. We have seen that the constitution of the other rests upon an association of the apperceptive type. In the case of the judgment, this apperceptive association conditions numerous judgments which, to be sure, do not have the privilege of evidence in the present but which permit an inventive anticipation to rational praxis that must finally conclude in true judgments, i.e., judgments that have an evidence in the present. Then the two centers of interest of static and genetic intentional analysis clash. Associative passivity gives rise in us to judgments which, from the very fact of their passivity, remain confused. If these judgments formed by association are to become true judgments, it is necessary that, simultaneously, they be taken up into an active *present* and be thought in an explicit manner—that they be given "themselves" and not in a confused anticipation.[81] Hence, associative passiv-

79. Cf. *ibid.*, "§ 38: Active and Passive Genesis."
80. Cf. *Erf. u. Urt.*, "§ 16: *Das Feld passiver Vorgegebenheiten und seine assoziative Struktur*," pp. 74–79.
81. The situation is complicated by the fact that the judgment is at once expression and signification. Then association functions not between one judgment and another judgment but between the judgment as expression and the judgment as signification. Contrary to all terminological habits, Husserl will here speak even of apperceptive association. In designating by apperception all association by analogy, Husserl takes the term apperception in certainly a special sense but still in a sense then currently employed by certain German

ity has important functions within the framework of reason from the fact that it gives rise in us — in a confused but suggestive fashion, of course — to judgments which have lost their original force and which, later on, are susceptible of being truly reactivated.

In Husserl's own terms,[82] association is a "fundamental concept" *(Grundbegriff)* of transcendental phenomenology, and yet Husserl recognizes at the same time that phenomenology only late found its way to the study of association. How is it that this fundamental concept arose so late for phenomenology as a fundamental concept?[83] Let us use Husserl's words:

> It is phenomenologically evident, but strange to the tradition-bound, that association is not a title merely for a conformity to empirical laws on the part of complexes of data comprised in a "psyche" — according to the old figure, something like an intra-psychic gravitation — but a title (moreover an extremely comprehensive one) for a conformity to eidetic laws on the part of the constitution of the pure *ego*. It designates a *realm of the "innate" Apriori*, without which an *ego* as such is unthinkable.[84]

The late introduction of the *phenomenological* concept of as-

---

authors, Herbart in particular. If it is permissible to use the term apperception in the case of thoughts which the signs of language give rise to in us, this is, he explains, because he does not consider — as is ordinarily done — the sign and what it signifies as a *thematic unity.* On the contrary, Husserl takes the sign and what it signifies as a perceptual element that can be considered separately from what it, by itself, has as an inductive power to stimulate thinking. We rediscover language's indicative functions, pointed out by Husserl in his "Preparatory Considerations" as well as in Part I, Chapter 1. Now that we have seen the important role of association in phenomenology, we can more completely justify the interest of a study of judgment on the level of language by noting that in every case the suggestive forces of the language can lead to a true cognition only if they are controlled by an explicit and clear rational activity.

82. *CM*, p. 80.

83. Nevertheless, Husserl does see the "germ of genetic phenomenology" *(Erf. u. Urt.,* p. 78) already in the *phenomenological* examination of indicative signs *(Anzeige)* undertaken in the *Logische Untersuchungen* (cf. First Investigation, § 2, *Log. Unt.,* Vol. II, Pt. I, pp. 24 ff.). He was already concerned with association, not qua objective induction, but qua purely immanent connexion of two things, one of which "recalls" the other.

84. *CM*, pp. 80 f.

sociation can be understood if one thinks, on the one hand, of the difficulty of dissociating association from the empirical and, on the other hand, of the difficulty of conceiving a passivity which has its role to play in the heart of activity. With Husserl passivity has, in fact, a *constitutive* role. Every active constitution always and necessarily presupposes a passive constitution. Activity applies its constitutive power to objects which it finds "already made" yet which actually can be objects only by means of the synthesis of passive experience. Not only does passivity have a preconstitutive role as the passivity of the temporal stream, but it has a constitutive role, an objectivating role. It is a sort of *passivity in activity,* as *Erfahrung und Urteil* says, continuing: "This expression shows that the distinction between activity and passivity is not rigid. These are terms that cannot be definitely fixed;[85] they are rather means to describing and contrasting." [86] The passive synthesis of experience which enables the object to be constituted in its unity, in its persistent unity, should be adapted to the universal form of time which is itself constituted in a "continuous and absolutely universal" passive genesis. Thus Husserl can speak of universal genesis, of the enigmatic "all-embracing genesis" [87] — enigmatic from the very fact of its universality — that conditions all constitutive activities of the *ego*.

Husserl does not hide the irrationality that can overcome all these constitutive activities, for in these constitutions "the particular fact is irrational." [88] But, inasmuch as it is an "egological fact," it is in the apriori form-system and is *possible* only therein. Then the fact, with its irrationality, "is itself a structural concept within the system of the concrete Apriori." [89] Thus the whole life of the ego presents a universal structural Apriori, an "all-embracing apodictic Apriori," [90] and every explication of the particular egological data participates in this

85. There is no reason to forget that, in order to appreciate the sense of the distinction between activity and passivity in Husserl, it is necessary in each case of intentional analysis to relate to a concrete situation under study and to get beyond the traditional opposition between activity and passivity.

86. *Erf. u. Urt.,* p. 119.

87. *CM,* p. 135.

88. *Ibid.,* p. 81.

89. *Ibid.*

90. *Ibid.,* p. 103.

universal Apriori. As we have already said, it was late when Husserl began to have insight into the systematic nexus of investigations concerning the essential structures of the concrete *ego;* it occurred, he says, once he had found "new ways of access to the *specifically universal* problems of the transcendental *ego's* constitution."[91] The logical way which is followed in *Formal and Transcendental Logic* lets Husserl bring to light the universality of the transcendental problem-set. Actually, after he had separately indicated the ideal objectivity of logical formations, Husserl was led beyond the particular problem of their subjective constitution to the transcendental questions *in general*. A way as indirect as this in appearance can only make the universality of the constitutive Apriori to which it leads re-emerge.

In summation, transcendental subjectivity is not a chaos of intentional mental processes. It is not even a chaos of intentional types each one of which has an organization relating to a species of intentional objects.[92] The intentional types are themselves grouped into an organized structure. These types in their totality form an *ordered* system. The task of transcendental phenomenology then consists in carrying out in a systematic fashion the different constitutive investigations corresponding to these intentional types. The method adapted to this task must of necessity be both eidetic and genetic.

But there is a danger here for the reader of Husserl: that of interpreting the explications of transcendental experience as psychological analyses of internal experience. There are numerous reasons for this "psychologistic falsification," as Husserl calls it. In the first place, it is difficult to eliminate, in a radical and definitive manner, the tenacious and often completely hidden presupposition of the world's existence-in-itself. Moreover, pure psychology already represents an apriori conversion of empirical psychology which seems to detach us in a satisfactory fashion from the natural attitude. On the other hand, even when we are conscious of the transcendental character of the Husserlian analyses, we are from time to time bound to recognize in these analyses empirical descriptions which insidiously lead us to their psychological interpretation. Actually, taking into consideration the difficulty of this type

91. *Ibid.*, p. 74.
92. *Ibid.*, pp. 53 f.

of analysis, Husserl often hesitates to bring us immediately to the level of properly eidetic analyses. Hence he conducts his investigation, even in the heart of the transcendental sphere, in an empirical manner, and only by a second step does he transpose his analyses into eidetic analyses. Husserl has occasion to invite us to perform this transposition.[93] But often, caught up in the movement of his investigation, Husserl does not see

93. For example, at the beginning of the Fourth Cartesian Meditation, Husserl refers back to the analyses of the preceding Meditations, indicating the provisional character of their empirical style: "The excessively great multiplicity of novel discoveries and problems was meant to act at first in the simpler attire of a merely empirical description (though conducted purely within the sphere of transcendental experience). The *method of eidetic description,* however, signifies a transfer of all empirical descriptions into a new and fundamental dimension, which at the beginning would have increased the difficulties of understanding; on the other hand, it is easy to grasp after a considerable number of empirical descriptions. . . . What is involved here will become clear directly in particular examples. Let us pick out no matter what type of intentional process (of perception, retention, recollection, declaration, liking something, striving for it, and so forth) and think of it as explicated and described in respect of its sort of intentional performance – accordingly: in respect of noesis and noema. This can signify (and so we have understood it up to now) that types of de facto occurrences in the de facto transcendental ego are in question and that the transcendental descriptions are therefore meant to have an 'empirical' significance. But involuntarily we confined our description to such a universality that its results remain unaffected, regardless of what the situation may be with respect to the empirical factualness of the transcendental ego.

"Let us make this clear to ourselves, and then fruitful for our method. Starting from this table-perception as an example, we vary the perceptual object, table, with a completely free optionalness, yet in such a manner that we keep perception fixed as perception of something, no matter what. Perhaps we begin by fictively changing the shape or the color of the object quite arbitrarily, keeping identical only its perceptual appearing. In other words: Abstaining from acceptance of its being, we change the fact of this perception into a pure possibility, one among other quite 'optional' pure possibilities – but possibilities that are possible perceptions. . . . Perception, the universal type thus acquired, floats in the air, so to speak – in the atmosphere of pure phantasiableness. Thus removed from all factualness, it has become the pure '*eidos*' perception, whose '*ideal*' extension is made up of all ideally possible perceptions, as purely phantasiable processes. Analyses of perception are then '*essential*' or '*eidetic*' analyses. All that we have set forth concerning syntheses

the need of commenting on the method which he is following and, remaining in the initial empirical orientation along with him, we risk remaining unaware of the "essential" style that transcendental analyses, in the fullest sense, have. Husserl is aware of this ever possible misunderstanding of the ultimate sense of phenomenological work: "Access to the ultimate universalities involved in problems of eidetic phenomenology is, however, very difficult. This is particularly true with respect to an *ultimate genesis*. The beginning phenomenologist is bound involuntarily by the circumstance that he takes himself as his initial example." [94] In reality, what is ultimately to be reached in eidetic phenomenology is the *eidos ego*.[95] Once this essential style is assumed, "the *ego* varies himself so freely that he does not keep even the ideal restrictive presupposition that a world having the ontological structure accepted by us as obvious is essentially constituted for him." [96]

However these things stand, Husserl's concessions to the demands of pedagogy in no way alter the principle of the distinction between transcendental phenomenology and intentional psychology. Psychology, even if it abstracts from all that is physical in man and limits itself to the study of the purely psychic life, remains for all that an "anthropological" and hence a "mundane" *(weltlich)* discipline. Transcendental phenomenological investigation, on the other hand, is connected to the *inviolable* observance of the transcendental reduction,

---

belonging to the type, perception, concerning horizons of potentiality, and so forth, holds good, as can easily be seen, *'essentially'* for everything formable in this free variation, accordingly for all imaginable perceptions without exception—in other words: with absolute *'essential universality,'* and with *'essential necessity'* for every particular case selected, hence for every de facto perception, since every *fact can be thought of merely as exemplifying a pure possibility"* (CM, pp. 69–71).

94. *Ibid.*, p. 76.

95. Previously we indicated the uncertainty in which we are left by *Formal and Transcendental Logic's* exposition concerning the point of departure for the transcendental problems of intersubjectivity. Having shown the necessity of beginning from the subjectivity belonging to each of us, Husserl expressly would have to add that the ego given in fact, who constitutes the starting point, must himself undergo eidetic variation.

96. *CM*, p. 77.

which parenthesizes all that is mundane. Husserl denounces *transcendental psychologism,* which specifically confuses transcendental phenomenology and pure psychology—the transcendental psychologism that, he says in the *Cartesian Meditations,* "has misled and paralysed the whole of modern philosophy." [97]

But transcendental psychologism is more than a philosophical error that one can be satisfied simply to reject. Rather it is necessary to *go beyond* it by *explicating* it—by understanding why, despite everything, it has power. In fact, beyond the already indicated reasons which can lead us to misunderstand phenomenology's proper transcendental sense, there is another reason which, one can say, is grounded in the nature of the things. Transcendental phenomenology and pure psychology are concerned, in an intimate way, with the same things, albeit the same things considered from extremely different points of view. Husserl recognizes that in transcendental analysis and psychological analysis "the contents to be described on the one hand and on the other can correspond," [98] that the content of these analyses is the same. [99] There is, he often says, a *parallelism* between transcendental phenomenology and pure phenomenology which connects the two disciplines. [100] The phenomenologist must keep this parallelism in view, but he must also understand it as it is supposed to be understood. On the other hand, if there is a parallelism between transcendental and psychological analyses, these analyses diverge as to their philosophical orientation. More exactly, phenomenology is philosophy, while pure psychology remains a "positive" science. On the side of pure psychology,

> we have data belonging to the world, which is presupposed as existing—that is to say, data taken as psychic components of a man. In the other case, the parallel data, with their like contents, are not taken in this manner, because the whole world, when one is in the phenomenological attitude, is not accepted as actuality, but only as an actuality-phenomenon. [101]

97. *Ibid.,* p. 144.
98. *Ibid.,* p. 32.
99. Cf. *FTL,* p. 253, and "Nachwort," p. 556.
100. Cf., in particular, *CM,* pp. 32, 131, 142 f.; "Nachwort," p. 556; and *FTL,* p. 255.
101. *CM,* p. 32.

In this there is perhaps only a "nuance," as Husserl says; but this nuance has decisive importance for the philosopher.

> The wholly unique significance of this "nuance" can become evident only through a radical self-understanding of the philosopher with regard to what he is properly aiming at under the name philosophy and the extent to which he must aim at something fundamentally different from "positive" science, therefore at something other than theoretically mastering the world given beforehand by experience.[102]

On the other hand, while separated from pure psychology by this fundamental nuance, transcendental phenomenology serves psychology as its ground. As is said in the *Ideen*,[103] phenomenology is to claim a methodological role with regard to psychology. We have noted that apriori psychological analysis is a way into phenomenology and that we can pass from the former to the latter through a sort of transposition. Once we have understood the transcendental sense of phenomenology, we can perform an inverse transposition which in principle is valid for psychological analyses.[104] Then phenomenology will have a grounding role with regard to the positive discipline which opened the way to it. This is why, in the *Cartesian Meditations*, Husserl says that "it would of course be pointless to treat the positive science of intentional psychology and transcendental phenomenology separately." [105] But such affirmations by Husserl would be no reason for contending that he remained aware of a psychologistic seduction. Even when Husserl says that "intentional psychology already has the transcendental hidden within itself," he does not forget that an "ultimate sense-investigation" is necessary for intentional psychology; this transcendental sense-investigation ⟨is needed⟩ "in order to make the Copernican shift, which does not change the content of psychology's intentional results but only leads back to its 'ultimate sense.' " [106] Psychology, while concurring in the "determining effect on the sense," "must be consciously 'parenthesized,' so that this content, which itself is not modified by this parenthesizing, acquires a transcendental signifi-

102. "Nachwort," p. 557.
103. *Ideen*, pp. 2–3.
104. *CM*, pp. 131 f.
105. *Ibid.*, p. 147.
106. *Ibid.*

cance." [107] To claim, from this fact, that transcendental phenomenology, despite its antipsychologistic declarations, continues to be latently psychologistic is to judge a science uniquely by what it actually brings us as "results" and to minimize a change in attitude which gives a new *significance* to what we already know.

Actually, it happens that Husserl overcomes the problem of transcendental psychology while explicating it. In fact Husserl emphasizes the strict connexions between pure psychology and transcendental phenomenology, but at the same time he shows that one should not make an exception from these connexions in order to require transcendental undertakings from a pure psychology.

Husserl concludes Chapter 6 with historical remarks whose purpose is to show how the forms which transcendental philosophy has taken in the past prepared for the coming of phenomenology—which in Husserl's eyes is the only genuinely transcendental philosophy—and at the same time to show how they retarded its emergence. Even though Husserl applies himself to the philosophies of only Hume and Kant, his historical critique has a very complex expository structure. Actually the relations between Hume and Kant are, as is known, themselves very complex, for on the one hand Hume and Kant are on two evolutionary lines stemming from Descartes—the empiricist and the rationalist lines[108]—while on the other hand there still exists an undeniable influence of Hume on Kant—an influence which renders Kant dependent upon Hume, specifically in his reaction toward him. Moreover, as he says in *Krisis*,[109] Husserl views this historical situation in a teleological fashion, beginning from the present state of phenomenology and, despite their "errors," trying to find the hidden intention of those philosophies which makes them precursory witnesses to transcendental phenomenology. In thinking of all these reasons for complexity, we can understand why Husserl mixes criticisms with approbations and why, in criticizing

107. *FTL*, pp. 254 f.
108. *Krisis*, § 21.
109. *Ibid.*, § 26.

Hume's philosophy, he comes to criticize the Kantian criticism of the philosophy of Hume.[110]

There is no reason to open the historical debate here. We shall limit ourselves to the broad outlines of Husserl's polemical scheme.

Husserl sees the greatness of Hume in the fact that he was "the first to *treat seriously the Cartesian focusing purely on what lies inside.*"[111] Hume grasped what Husserl calls the consitutional problem-set, for he understood that the cognition of the world is a problem and that it is necessary to wonder how subjectivity can find an Objectivity qua transcendent Objectivity in an "experience," an Objectivity which is specifically the one that goes without saying for those who do not philosophize. And he grasped this problem in a *concrete* manner, for, in avoiding metaphysical hypotheses, he examined states of consciousness and the operations of the mind in a genuine "mental geography."[112] Hence Hume destroyed the claims of naïve objectivism, an enterprise that in Husserl's eyes could only be glorious. But Husserl reproaches him for not having seen the essential property of psychic life – intentionality – which was the means for Husserl's discovering the objectivating functions of subjectivity. Because he did not understand the intentionality of consciousness, Hume did not get beyond the sphere of immanence and fell into what Husserl complacently calls an absurd fictionalism. "All categories of Objectivity, scientific as well as prescientific, categories in which everyday life thinks a world that is objective and external to the psyche, all of these are fictions."[113] Also Husserl says that Hume's philosophy leads to a "bankruptcy of Objective cognition."[114] And if Hume remained blind to the intentionality of consciousness, this was because he was dominated by a sensualistic psychology which sees in psychic life no more than a collection of data.

> If the *pure* concrete *ego,* in whom all the objectivities and worlds accepted by him are subjectively constituted, is only a senseless

110. On the relations between the philosophies of Husserl and Hume, cf. Gaston Berger, "Husserl et Hume," *Rev. int. de philosophie*, No. 2 (January, 1939), pp. 342–53.

111. *FTL*, p. 256.

112. Hume, *Enquiry Concerning the Human Understanding*, ed. L. A. Selby-Bigge (Oxford, 1902), p. 13.

113. *Krisis*, p. 89.

114. *Ibid.*, p. 90.

bundle or collection of *Data* — which come and perish, cast together now in this way and now in that, according to a senselessly accidental regularity analogous to that of mechanics (the sort of regularity ascribed to association as it was then interpreted[115]) — then the result is that only surreptitious reasons can explain how even as much as the illusion of a real world could arise.[116]

To be sure, one can maintain, even in the same spirit of *parti pris* that one reproaches in adversaries, that the accusation of sensualism is grounded in a caricature of Hume's philosophy, and one can show, as Jean Laporte does, that gestaltist tendencies can be discerned in some of Hume's texts:

> The very term "composite impression," which Hume uses to characterize spatial and temporal notions, shows clearly that for him the materials of perception present themselves to the mind with "composition" or, if you will, a "configuration," which it is no less important to notice than their "qualities" properly so called. Besides, Hume indicates, much as a gestaltist would, that the "manner" in which successive sounds appear to us in a musical phrase can then be considered "without considering these particular sounds" [117] and without their being joined to others.[118]

But such an argument has no polemical force against Husserl's criticism, for to him,

> here obviously it makes no difference, speaking fundamentally, whether one lets the psychic Data be blown together atomistically like sand piles, though according to empirical laws, or regards them as parts of wholes. . . . In other words, atomistic psychology and *Gestalt*-psychology both remain, in the same fundamental sense (defined by what is said above), a psychological "naturalism" which, in view of the phrase "internal sense," can be called also sensualism." [119]

115. We have seen that, for Husserl, association not only is an empirical law combining psychic data but is also an essential law of intentionality. In phenomenology a specifically new signification is given to the Humean concept of association, which Husserl says (*Cartesian Meditations*, p. 80) is a "naturalistic distortion" of the corresponding intentional concept.

116. *FTL*, p. 255.

117. Cf. Hume, *A Treatise of Human Nature*, ed. L. A. Selby-Bigge (Oxford, 1888), p. 37.

118. J. Laporte, "Le scepticisme de Hume," *Revue philosophique*, January–June, 1933, p. 79 [our translation].

119. "Nachwort," p. 565. We find the same notion expressed in al-

Only the profitable exploitation of the discovery of intentionality can release us from this attachment to the psychic *data*.

Hence, on the one hand, Husserl recognizes in Hume's philosophy an entirely new manner of judging the Objectivity of the world – one that can be brought close to the phenomenological manner of setting up the problems of constitution. On the other hand, he refuses the naturalistic presuppositions which contaminate this healthy insight into the problem of cognition.

On his part, Kant took over the constitutional problem of Hume. But, reacting against Hume's empiricism and not separating concrete and empirical procedures, he did not consider the subjective problems in a concrete manner. "In fact Kant fell into a peculiar sort of mythical locution, whose verbal sense, it is true, refers us to something subjective, but to a mode of the subjective that it is essentially impossible for us to make intuited, either in factual examples or by genuine analogy." [120] Moreover, while struggling against sensualistic psychology, Kant never carried out a radical critique of it and in fact remained dependent on it. In particular, Husserl remarks that only psychological sense can be made of what Kant calls "internal perception." [121] And Husserl claims that Kant builds his system of "mythical" concepts higher and higher in order to avoid a contradiction he was heading toward; for, awakened by Hume to a suspicion of the tradition, he legitimately considered recourse to psychology as a perversion of the genuine problems of knowledge, and yet he understood internal perception in an empirical, psychological, sense. Yet from his encounter with Hume, Kant acquired insight into the problems of intentionality, particularly in his doctrine of synthesis, and explicitly introduced into philosophy the transcendental problem-set, though he never provided it with an ultimate ground.

One of the main criticisms Husserl addresses to Kant is

---

most the same terms in Chapter 7 of *Formal and Transcendental Logic* (p. 286): "It is actually a matter of indifference here, whether one thinks of these Data as separate 'psychic atoms' swept together into more or less cohesive bundles according to unintelligible matter-of-fact laws, like those of mechanics, or talks about wholes and *Gestalt*-qualities. . . . "

120. *Krisis*, p. 116.
121. *Ibid.*, p. 117.

going to lead us to the transcendental problem *particular to logic* and show us once more the important place of the transcendental problem of logic in the set of transcendental problems in general.

It goes without saying that Husserl does not contest the fact that Kant understood logic to be an apriori discipline independent of psychological principles. But he reproaches Kant for accepting this Apriori purely and simply without question. Kant "asked no transcendental questions about [logic], but rather ascribed to it an extraordinary apriority, which exalts it above such questions." [122] Husserl explains this Kantian position toward logic by Kant's attitude regarding Hume, an attitude formed of both reaction and dependence. In fact, on the one hand, contrary to Hume and to all English empiricism, Kant saw the apriori and pure character of logic. On the other hand, in reacting against Hume, who misunderstood the existence of synthetic apriori judgments, Kant focused uniquely on the problems of synthetic apriori judgments. It never occurred to him to question the analytic Apriori itself; in this he was influenced by Hume, who left the analytic judgments free of doubt or at least left undoubted what Kant interpreted as being purely analytic in the eyes of Hume. [123]

Husserl sees the deeper reason for this attitude, which one could qualify somewhat ironically as "dogmatic," in the misunderstanding of the specific ideality of logical formations. In the first place, the problem of the ideality of the judgment could pass for a particular problem which remains within the purely technical framework of logic. But now that we have come to the end of Husserl's reflection, we are in a position to understand that the problem of the ideality of the judgment has been a guiding problem for *Formal and Transcendental Logic*. In fact, the progress of Husserl's reflection could be determined simply by following the deepening of this problem throughout the book. At the level of Part I, [124] Husserl considers the emphasis on the ideality of judgment only as a factor in the conver-

122. *FTL*, p. 258.
123. We know that, according to Kant, Hume took mathematical propositions to be analytic (cf., in particular, the *Critique of Practical Reason*, Bk. I, Chap. 1, No. 11). But the Kantian interpretation has been frequently contested (cf. Laporte, *op. cit.*, pp. 66–71).
124. Cf. Chapter 2, § 26.

gence between formal apophantics and formal mathematics. In Part II, Chapter 1, this problem of the ideality of the judgment appeared as a key problem for the constitution of a genuine theory of the judgment, of an intentional theory of the judgment. At the same time, the general sense of the struggle against psychologism is specified: psychologism does not recognize the objective character of logical formations and, more generally, of ideal objects. It does not understand that the evidence of ideal objects is analogous to that of individual objects. And phenomenological idealism rightly receives its sense from the criticism of this psychologism closed toward ideality. Finally, we are now going to see that beyond this genuine theory of judgment the problem of the ideality of the judgment opens the way for us to the transcendental questions concerning the "constituting" subjectivity. Only when one has grasped that the logical formations are, in their way, *objects* can one ask the transcendental questions of their subject. Beginning at the moment when one considers the concept, the judgment, etc., as objects that exist over and against the contingent multiplicity of our subjective acts, one can wonder how these objects have precisely the sense of objects, even though they originate in our subjective activity. This "even though" *leads* us to reflection. Then logic must necessarily be examined along two lines, the objective line and the subjective line, and the field is open for the constitutional problem-set. Paradoxically, only when one fails to see the logical formations detach themselves from subjectivity with the sense of objects does one fail to raise the truly subjective problems regarding them, the problems of their "consitution" by a transcendental subjectivity.

In Hume there is a clear "substitute" for the transcendental problem of ideal formations, viz., the problem of abstraction. But Hume raises the problem only to dissolve it. "All abstract ideas are really nothing but particular ones, consider'd in a certain light; but being annexed to general terms, they are able to represent a vast variety, and to comprehend objects, which, as they are alike in some particulars, are in others vastly wide of each other." [125] Hence Hume does not consider the abstract ideas as data of a proper "experience," and thus he

125. Hume, *A Treatise of Human Nature*, p. 34.

does not raise the question of abstract ideas as a problem parallel to that of the data of external experience.

Kant, for his part, studies the logical formations from an objective point of view, but, specifically, from a purely objective point of view—from a naïvely objective point of view—which does not imply the necessity of a correlative subjective examination. Undoubtedly referring to the Kantian definition of logic as the "science of the legitimate usage of the understanding and reason in general," [126] Husserl remarks that, if one responds to what Kant says, one could believe that Kant's logic is a science directed toward subjectivity. In truth, having defined logic as the science of the simple form of thinking in general, Kant specifies that it is "not a subjective science, i.e., not carried out according to empirical (psychological) principles, but an objective science, i.e., carried out according to apriori principles determining the manner in which the understanding must think." [127] This simple specification shows us in a decisive fashion that Kant does not conceive of a subjective examination of logic as something other than an examination involving empirical psychology.

Once the ideal objectivity of logical formations is fully recognized, logic still has to overcome the "phenomenological naïveté," as Husserl says,[128] for it must understand the necessity of an intentional investigation which raises transcendental problems analogous to those which were posed by Hume and by Kant where Nature is concerned.

> Even after having learned to recognize that which is ideal, logic must be more than a merely positive science of logico-mathematical idealities. Rather, with a continuously two-sided research (results on either side determining inquiries on the other), logic must go back systematically from the ideal formations to the consciousness that constitutes them phenomenologically; it must make these formations understandable, in respect of their sense and their limits, as essentially products of the correlative structures of productive cognitive life, and it must thereby fit them, like each and every other Objectivity, to the broader, the *concrete*, nexus of transcendental subjectivity.[129]

126. Kant, *Logique*, trans. Tissot (1840), p. 10 [our translation from the French translation].
127. *Ibid.*
128. *FTL*, p. 263.
129. *Ibid.*

In addition, this inclusion is not a secondary requirement. "Intentionality is not something isolated; it can be observed only in the synthetic unity that connects every single pulse of psychic life *teleologically*" (262). And the intentional life has "a universal Objectivating structure"; from this fact "the predicative judgment gains universal significance for psychic life." [130]

Not only does the transcendental problem of logic parallel the transcendental problem of the natural sciences, but in fact there is an internal connexion between these two problems. One cannot legitimately set up the transcendental problem of the natural sciences while according an absolute value to the logic which has a place beyond all transcendental questions, for logic is involved as a presupposition in the problems of Nature, at least in the problems of the Nature studied by the natural sciences. Hence Husserl reproaches Kant for not recognizing that the transcendental problem of logic precedes the transcendental problem of the natural sciences and for not having distinguished between prescientific Nature and scientific Nature. For if a transcendental inquiry can precede that of logic, this can only be a transcendental inquiry into the prescientific Nature grasped in a pure experience, an experience which is prior to any categorial activity.

Actually, if one sets up a transcendental problem in the radical manner, by investigating the truly ultimate constitutive sources, and if one reaches that primitive basis of all transcendental investigation which is phenomenological subjectivity, then, by the same token, Husserl says, "the *totality* of transcendental problems and their uniform sense throughout are already given" (265). Radicalism is inseparable from universality.

130. *Ibid.*

7 / Objective Logic
and the Phenomenology
of Reason

AFTER THIS HISTORICAL DIGRESSION, Husserl returns to his main theme, the problem of the radical grounding of logic. We have seen that this radical grounding involves adopting the transcendental perspective in all its breadth. Hence it seems that, in having reached transcendental radicalism, the "criticism" of objective logic has come to its end. But actually we shall see that the problems which this criticism has "resolved" reappear in a fashion more acute than ever, since these problems now present themselves at the most profound level of the Husserlian reflection. At the beginning of his reflection, Husserl showed that the possibility of science could not be proved by the fact of the existence of the sciences. Logic qua formal theory of science is to furnish the apriori norms for every possible science. But logic, in turn, was placed in question by a grounding "criticism." This criticism led us from logic conceived as objective theory to transcendental logic, "subjective" logic, which is then the theory of logical reason. But, Husserl recognizes, "are we not drawn into a game of endless questions? Does not a new question immediately become urgent:[1] How is a theory of logical reason possible?"

1. [At this point Professor Cairns adds the following translator's note: "Reading *unabweisbar* for *unbeweisbar* (unprovable)." Professor Bachelard translates from the original reading: *"ne peut être prouvée."* – Translator's note.]

[205]

(267). Husserl claims that the preceding chapters (Chapters 5 and 6) answer such a question, for the theory of logical reason

> is radically possible as the phenomenology of logical reason, within the frame of transcendental phenomenology as a whole.[2] If this science is then, as may be expected, the ultimate one, it must show its ultimacy by showing that it can answer the question of its own possibility, therefore by showing that there is such a thing as an essential, endlessly reiterated, reflexive bearing ⟨of transcendental phenomenology⟩ upon itself, in which the essential sense of an ultimate justification by itself is discernibly included, and that precisely this is the fundamental characteristic of an essentially ultimate science.[3]

But even if we accept this reflexive bearing of transcendental phenomenology upon itself, we are not finished with our questions and must ask ourselves whether the insertion of logic into transcendental philosophy does not strip the notion of logic of all its sense. Can Husserl escape from the dilemma which Jean Cavaillès has formulated without recognizing that subsequent phenomenological investigations at least might make it possible to contest "a dilemma so brutally set up": "If transcendental logic truly grounds logic, there is no absolute logic, i.e., no logic governing the absolute subjective activity. If there is an absolute logic, it can only draw its logic from itself; it is not transcendental."[4] At least it seems that one cannot avoid considering such a dilemma. But before bringing the Husserlian concept of a transcendental logic to judgment, we want to trace the argumentation of Chapter 7. Undoubtedly, the general intention in this final chapter is to sum up the results of the preceding chapters. However, new intuitions are also introduced which in a specific manner enable us to form a clearer idea of Husserl's ultimate intentions. So we shall keep this dilemma as a hypothesis concerning the present discussion, without for the moment becoming involved in the debate raised by it.

On the one hand, with transcendental logic we have acquired an absolute basis in which objective logic can be grounded;

2. Phenomenology is the phenomenology of reason insofar as it it concerned with truth and more generally with all doxic positings.
3. *FTL*, p. 268.
4. J. Cavaillès, *Sur la logique et la théorie de la science* (Paris, 1947), p. 65.

but, on the other hand, with the discovery of the transcendental problem-set we are involved in a relativization of the notion of truth — all truth being related to the transcendental subjectivity which is its source. Hence transcendental logic destroys the claims of the sciences and objective logic, which vindicate *truths-in-themselves*. Thus truth becomes entirely "subjective." But then, can one still maintain the idea of logic if there is no absolute truth or, rather, if the only absolute truth is subjective truth? Husserl is aware of this problem: "What about truth and principles of logic there, where true being is 'merely subjective'?" (269). Husserl recognizes that transcendental logic is not a logic in the usual sense — that there is a break between it and objective logic. Husserl draws attention to this break by emphasizing a "surprising" fact: all of the positive sciences are "mundane." "Naïvely natural logic, the logic that could be concerned only with positive sciences, presupposes the world";[5] transcendental logic does not. Actually, the concepts, the judgments, the "truths" with which transcendental logic is occupied are uniquely drawn from the sources of transcendental experience. The notion of truth in the heart of transcendental logic makes for much more difficulty since, as we have seen in Chapter 6, the transcendental theory which is genuine theory and which presents itself on the most fundamental level is a purely "egological" discipline, intersubjective phenomenology being a theory of the second constitutive level.[6] Thus we have a transcendentally solipsistic discipline "with eidetic truths, with theories, that hold good exclusively for me, the *ego* — that is to say: truths and theories that can rightfully claim to hold good 'once for all,' but without relation to actual or possible other egos."[7] To be sure, the truths which one encounters on this level are "essential" truths since, as we have seen, my transcendental ego given in fact and the particularities of my transcendental experience are no more than simple examples of pure possibilities and are subject to eidetic variation. But truth "is no longer 'truth in itself' in any normal sense, not even in a sense that has relation to a transcendental 'everyone'" (269). Then Husserl says: "With that discipline there also arises, then, the question of a subjective logic with an

5. *FTL*, p. 269.
6. Cf., in particular, *CM*, pp. 155–56.
7. *FTL*, p. 270.

Apriori that can hold good only solipsistically" (270). But these inquiries by Husserl into the sense that a transcendental logic can have, solipsistic or intersubjective, are in reality pseudo-inquiries. As we are going to see, Husserl does not seriously question the notion of transcendental logic.

It seems that for Husserl what can appear to us surprising in the conception of transcendental logic is explained suffi-ciently by our attachment to the prejudices of objective logic, which accords an undeniable privilege to the notion of truth-in-itself: "All that we actually wanted was a 'formal logic' that would go just a little further than pure mathematical analytics" (270). But if one does not want to be a mere technician of logi-cal theory, if one wants truly to be a philosopher, one must see, he says, that the questions of evidence lead us to tran-scendental subjectivity. And only by beginning from the transcendental constitutive subjectivity can one understand the sense of the existents of different levels to which judgment is applied. At this price one can reach a philosophical intelligi-bility. But transcendental logic implies more than an investi-gation of the sense of a possible world: "A formal ontology of any possible world, as a world constituted in transcendental subjectivity, is a non-selfsufficient part of another 'formal ontology,' which relates to everything that exists in any sense: to what exists as transcendental subjectivity and to every-thing that becomes constituted in transcendental subjectivity" (271). Then logic becomes the science of the total Apriori – of the subjective Apriori no less than the objective Apriori. In a moment we shall return to the difficulties which this notion of formal ontology implies for the constituting subjectivity. For the moment, let us retain this most general idea of a formal ontology. Husserl wonders how one can satisfy this idea and how it is constituted within the framework of transcendental phenomenology. Before answering these questions, Husserl adds others. Besides formal ontology, as Husserl describes it in Part I of *Formal and Transcendental Logic*, there exists an ontology "in the real sense" (*im realen Sinne*), hence an ontology related to the material theories. What is the relation-ship between these two apriori sciences of the "mundane" existent? This question is all the more pressing because Hus-serl characterizes ontology in the real sense as also being for-mal, but in a sense other than that of "formal ontology." In

contradistinction to the last mentioned, ⟨ontology in the real sense⟩ explicates

> the idea, any possible world whatever, in respect of the structural forms essentially necessary to a world—forms in a new and very different sense: as the "form," allness of realities, with the allness-"forms," space and time; or such as the "formal" articulation of a world as comprising regions of realities; and so forth (271).

What is the relationship of these two ontologies, "each of them 'formal' in a different sense" (273), if both are grounded in the original sources of transcendental subjectivity?

It must be recognized that Chapter 7 raises more problems than it solves. It opens horizons for subsequent investigations, and the questions here are only indications for a plan of work to come. We are given, without explanation, the key answer by which we will be able to accomplish the tasks of a total science, ⟨a science⟩ which would present us with the universe of the sciences and their various correlations. The ultimate justification of every science, whatever it be, requires a return to the only absolute existent which is "in and for itself," i.e., transcendental subjectivity—and, more broadly, transcendental intersubjectivity. To ground cognition absolutely is possible only in the heart of the universal science of transcendental subjectivity. Let us examine this ideal of the grounding of cognition a bit more closely. On the one hand, this return to a unique source gives a unity to the sciences which derives entirely from this source's constitutional production. "There is only one philosophy, one actual and genuine science; and particular genuine sciences are only non-selfsufficient members within it" (272). Self-sufficiency pertains only to the ultimate science; the particular sciences form integral parts of this unique science once they have been made genuine by its grounding action. On the other hand, this ultimate science, precisely from the fact that it is the ultimate science, has an Apriori "resting on itself and justifying itself by itself," as is said in the Fifth Cartesian Meditation.[8] If this is how things stand, it is because the essence of the absolute existent implies the possibility of the investigation of its own sense: "An absolute existent is existent in the form, an intentional life—which, no matter

8. *CM*, p. 156.

what else it may be intrinsically conscious of, is, at the same time, consciousness of itself" (273). Here we arrive at a fundamental concept of Husserlian phenomenology: *constitutional subjectivity can look at itself*. So much is this the case that Husserl can say that the whole of phenomenology is nothing more than transcendental phenomenology's self-examination. "Thus the ultimate grounding of all truth is a branch of the universal self-examination that, when carried through radically, is absolute" (274). Once I have reached the absolute apprehension of my self as *ego*, thanks to the transcendental reduction, I have only to become aware of what I can find in myself by working on the different constitutive levels:

> [A]s indicated earlier,[9] I separate that which is primordially my own (that which is constituted as inseparable from myself) and that which is constituted in me at different levels (on the motivating basis of what is primordially my own) as something "alien": that which is constituted, in me, as real or else as ideal; constituted, in me, as Nature, as psychophysical being, as a human community, as a people or as a state, as reified culture, as science, — also as phenomenology and, in the first place, by the effort of my own thinking (275).

And, as he also indicates a bit later, as phenomenology arrived at through the efforts of the community.[10] This self-examination should not be "transformed" into a naïve positivity; it should instead remain a continued, continually willed, self-examination. And this will to examine the self marks the intended purpose of the philosopher: "for it is still the case that, as a philosopher, I will, and can will, nothing but radical self-examinations, which, of themselves, become self-examinations on the part of the intersubjectivity existing for me" (275). The philosopher as such can only will to explicate himself with himself; and, as it is said in the "Nachwort," [11] beginning there one can understand that there is a motivation which necessarily drives the philosopher to raise himself above the natural attitude and to engage in the phenomenological attitude. This self-examination first functions in an immediate fashion, with a certain naïveté, with what Husserl on several occasions calls

9. Cf. Chapter 6; cf. also *CM,* pp. 153–54.
10. While being practiced, phenomenology has phenomenology qua objectivated science as the theme of its sense-investigation.
11. "Nachwort," p. 557.

transcendental naïveté, but it is next concerned with its own logos in a critical manner. Thus, in the very heart of the transcendental sphere, the *ego* must follow the same epistemological course which runs from naïveté to criticism, even though the transcendental attitude made it possible to transcend the naïveté of the positive sciences and to initiate a genuine criticism of these sciences. And the criticism of the transcendental logos also proceeds, by discovery, from vague opinions to the original self. This is why the first phenomenology, still affected with "apodictic naïveté," needed a self-criticism that could determine the extent, the limits, and the modes of its apodicticity.[12] The *Cartesian Meditations* insists upon the fact that transcendental phenomenology must be carried out in two steps.[13] In the first step it is necessary to work through the still unexplored transcendental experience of the self; the second step would have as its object the criticism of transcendental experience and the bearing of its apodictic principles. The *Cartesian Meditations* remained only at the first step, having already much to do in the tasks of describing the immense domain of transcendental experience. It thus had to trust the methodical procedures of transcendental cognition, without, however, forgetting the necessity of a final criticism of transcendental experience. As for *Formal and Transcendental Logic,* it only outlines the framework within which the ideal of an absolutely grounded cognition is situated. We have shown previously that the criticism of logic leads to the most general set of transcendental problems. Now we see not only that the criticism of logical evidences is possible only in the heart of transcendental phenomenology but that this criticism leads in a definitive manner to a criticism of the phenomenological evidences themselves, to a self-criticism *(Selbstkritik)* of phenomenology. At the time of the *Ideen,* Husserl recognized that "the principles of logic demand a deep phenomenological clarification," [14] but he was still far from thinking that the criticism of cognition is founded on the self-criticism of phenomenological cognition.

It was very late before I recognized, not only that the entire criticism of evidences, and particularly of judicative evidences

12. Cf. the "Conclusion" of the *Cartesian Meditations.*
13. *CM,* p. 29.
14. *Ideen,* p. 301.

(more precisely, the evidences included among categorial activities) should be carried on within the frame of phenomenology – in the present exposition this is a matter of course –, but also that this whole criticism leads back to an ultimate criticism: a criticism of those evidences that phenomenology at the first, and still naïve, level carries on straightforwardly.[15]

Husserl ends Chapter 7 by returning to the transcendental criticism of logic in order to insist on the relative character of all truth. He has already vigorously exposed the main prejudice of logic: belief in a world which exists in an absolute manner and which is the substrate of absolute truths. But in the last pages of *Formal and Transcendental Logic* we are in the presence of something new; we are in the presence of a veritable *revaluing of relativity*. How should one understand this revaluing of relativity deep within an ideal of absolute radicalism? We are far from the psychologistic relativism against which Husserl struggles; in fact, Husserl means to guard himself simultaneously against the two dangers of skeptical relativism and logical absolutism. Absolute truth and relative truth each have their legitimacy. Absolute truth is a guiding idea "situated at infinity." Every truth without exception can be normatively related to this guiding idea. Nevertheless, it remains an *essentially* relative truth. But this relativity is rich; it has infinite perspectives. To take truth-in-itself as the "exact" sciences and traditional logic represent it – as the one sort of truth – is to "overlook . . . the infinitudes of relative and, only in its relativity, rational being"; Husserl also says that it is to "overlook the infinitudes of life and its cognition" (278). In what sense is this reference to the truths of life to be understood? Can one speak of a continuity between scientific life and everyday life? On many occasions we have indicated how phenomenology in each case is concerned with the stratification of its field of study into levels. In particular, where the productions of consciousness are concerned, there are levels which go from pure and simple experience to the most abstract theoretical activities. Yet, even when one considers the highest level, one must remember the fundamental level. And if one must keep this memory of the origin alive, this is not only because the "complete" sense needs its "history" in order to be

15. *FTL*, p. 289.

fully grasped, but it is also because the original intuition teaches us a methodological style that is not to be denied: to see the things "themselves" while resisting the "speculative excesses" of theories which take us away from the things. On *all* levels, as is the case in the practical life of the "informed and forward-looking" man, one must come to discover how the things actually are. "That is the beginning of all wisdom though not its end; and it is a wisdom we can never do without, no matter how deep we go with our theorizings . . . a wisdom that we must therefore practise in the same fashion when at last we are judging in the absolute phenomenological sphere" (279). This simple phrase should preserve us from any one-sided interpretation of phenomenology. The reader who has retained from phenomenology that it is mainly the apriori science of essences and intentional structures will have the tendency—we confess to it willingly!—not to recognize that knowing how to see with a fresh naïveté is the beginning of *all* wisdom. The existentialist reader, on the other hand, will undoubtedly forget that this is not the end. If one wants to remain true to the style of Husserlian phenomenology, it is hence necessary to follow this twofold precept of method: know well how to see and seek to know; unite the memory of original experience and the teleological effort of cognition.

Thus Husserl can speak of the naïveté of phenomenological self-examination, this time not attaching any pejorative accent to the term naïveté. It is not a question, here, of the naïveté, of the insouciance, of everyday life. Nor is it any longer a question of the naïveté of the positivity of scientific life, unaware of its "prejudices." It is rather a question of a paradoxical naïveté, since it is, so to speak, a *deliberate naïveté*. Quite exactly, it is a question of willing purely to adhere to what original intuition actually gives, not letting oneself be imposed upon by the tradition—even the tradition of the exact sciences—and to live continually in the feeling of self-responsibility. This is even more difficult to institute and maintain when it is in the service of questions concerning the essential structures and the laws of the transcendental sphere.

And if one gives oneself over to this *continuing* inquiry into the things, one is led from intentional implication to intentional implication, from relativity to relativity. "We have the *truth* then, not as falsely absolutized, but rather, in each case, as

within its horizons — which do not remain overlooked or veiled from sight, but are systematically explicated." [16] The existent is no longer considered as an existent in itself. Hence one has a cognition of it which is less dogmatically affirmed, but one always knows more and more about it, insofar as the explication of the horizon proceeds. It is not studied in isolation, but, insofar as it is the center of a complex bundle of intentional implications, it is studied *with* its horizon. In our commentary on the preceding chapter, we have emphasized that the horizon contributes to the determination of the sense and that it then prescribes for the phenomenological analysis a method "of a totally new kind," as Husserl says in the *Cartesian Meditations*.[17] Here we see even more profoundly the importance of the notion of horizon, for the systematic explication of the horizon reintroduces a sort of absolute — the absolute of the ever-more in place of the dogmatic absolute of the in-itself. The notion of horizon is thus revealed to be a fundamental concept of phenomenology.

Instead of this, an absolute existent and an evidence which is to be an absolute grasping of this existent are usually admitted in advance, no other guarantee for this evidence being found except a *feeling* of evidence. Actually, however, one should inquire into "experience," i.e., into what gives us the thing itself, and this inquiry should include the ⟨experience's⟩ horizon. Within this horizon other possible experiences are brought to light which can confirm the experience considered, but it can also manifest itself with experiences which are in conflict with it and which correct or even "cancel" *(durchstreicht)* it. The possibility of deceptive evidence can be accounted for in terms of the failure to separate the being from its horizon.

As we have seen, there are various essential *types* of experience — and hence of evidence — and the phenomenologist's task is to bring them to light through his eidetic intentional analyses. Experience in the usual sense is only one type of "experience" among others. But it is very instructive for the theory of evidence, for it shows us in an undeniable way that it gives us the thing itself; and starting from that point, one can understand that the fundamental sense of any type of "experience" precisely qua "experience" is that of being the original giving of the things themselves. Husserl says that Descartes, though he crit-

16. *Ibid.*, p. 279.
17. *CM*, p. 48.

icized the value of sensuous experience by bringing out its possibilities of illusion, did not see this. It is true that sensuous experience is an imperfect evidence. It must definitely be perfected through enlargement by more and more numerous concordant experiences, and it is always marked by relativity. But this relativity conforms to the essence of the type of experience which is sensuous experience and in no way affects its fundamental character, which is the giving of the things themselves. "Therefore [Descartes] does not see that the essential style of experience stamps on the being-sense of the world, and of all realities, an essentially necessary relativity, and that, accordingly, the attempt to remedy this relativity by appealing to the veracity of God is a countersense" (282).

The phenomenological analysis of sensuous experience must explicate the stream of experience in an intentional manner, not only experience relating to particular natural objects but even to "the entire synthetically unified, world-experience, extending throughout the life of the simple *ego* and throughout the life of the transcendental community" (283); and this experience of the world must be examined both eidetically, according to its own universal style, and genetically. This style is *imposed* upon us in its originality. Then we find realist accents from Husserl's pen which contrast with the professions of absolute faith in idealism encountered slightly earlier:

> The being-sense of Nature has the essential form absolutely prescribed for it by the essential style of the experience of Nature; and therefore even an absolute God cannot create a "feeling of evidence" that absolutely guarantees the being of Nature — or, in a better formulation, a self-contained process of ⟨external⟩ experience that, no matter how different it might conceivably be from "our" sensuous experience, would give something-itself apodicticly and adequately.[18]

18. *FTL*, p. 284. Some lines above, Husserl writes: "Few would hesitate to ascribe this absolute evidence to the infinite intellect (even if they had recourse to the infinite intellect only as a limit-idea in epistemology), though that could not be one iota better than wanting to see divine omnipotence express itself in the mathematical sphere by the ability to construct regular decahedrons, or by any other theoretical countersense" (284). We should recall that the regular decahedron is a mathematical impossibility. Thus even God must obey the demands of the style of "experience" — here the experience of the mathematical sphere. In the *Ideen* (p. 157), incidentally, con-

Ordinarily, one therefore denies to sensuous experience the status of evidence by the fact of its imperfection; and the only evidence which one recognizes is internal experience, which, without discussion, one qualifies as absolute evidence. But internal experience, as it is conceived by the theories of cognition — which, according to Husserl, are always tainted with psychologism — is a "mundane" experience. Instead of this "mundane" experience, the internal perception by the *ego* of its *cogito* must be considered. The *immediate* contact with this immanent sphere of pure internal experience does not prevent one from dealing with very complex problems. Immanent objects are constituted in the flux of presentations, retentions, and protentions in a complex intentional synthesis which is that of the consciousness of internal time. This situation is the more confused since "this manner of givenness *of* the temporal mental process is itself, in turn, a mental process, though of a new sort and dimension." [19] As in the case of external experience, one no longer has complete objects pregiven. Without recollection, without the consciousness that I can always come back once more to what I have sensed, etc., I could not speak of *the* immanent object. Moreover, in the immanent sphere a distinction obtains between hyletic data and intentional functions.

---

cerning the necessity of reflection for the cognition of consciousness, Husserl even says that "God himself is bound by this absolute and evident necessity, just as He is by the evidence whereby $2 + 1 = 1 + 2$." In a note on the same page he specifies that he is not carrying the debate to the level of theology but that instead he remains on the epistemological level: "The idea of God is a limiting concept necessary in epistemological discussions or it is an indispensable index in the construction of certain limiting concepts beyond which even the atheist cannot go when he philosophizes." One can even read (p. 81) that "no God can prevent $2 + 1$ from making 3, or prevent any other essential truth from subsisting."

19. *Ideen,* p. 163, a passage that continues: "For example, I can at first have exclusively in my regard the joy that begins and ends and in the meantime endures; I go along with its temporal phases. But I can pay heed also to its manner of givenness: to the current mode 'Now' and to that fact that, to this Now and, of essential necessity, to every other, a new one and perpetually a new one, in a necessary continuity, attach themselves; that, in union therewith, each actually present Now changes into a Just-Passed, the Just-Passed, in turn and continuously, into ever new Just-Pasts of a Just-Passed, and so forth. Thus it is in the case of every newly attached Now."

This distinction was studied in the *Ideen*[20] and was already pre-figured in the *Logische Untersuchungen*.[21] Certain mental processes [*vécus*], such as the data of color, of sound, the sensations of pleasure, of pain, etc., have in them a "sensual" element which is not intentional. These data undergo an intentional forming *(Formung);* they are implicated in the intentional functions which confer a sense on them. These data are given as matter with respect to the intentional forming. This is why Husserl calls them *hyletic data* or materials or, more simply, stuffs *(Stoffe)*. He prefers the expression "hyletic data" to that of "sensuous data" not only because this expression brings out the contrast between matter and form but also because it can just as well be applied to the affective and volitive as to the strictly "sensuous" sphere. "That which forms the stuffs [*Stoffe* (plural)] into intentional mental processes and brings in the specific character, intentionality, is the very thing that gives to the word consciousness its specific sense, according to which consciousness as such points at something of which it is conscious." [22] This "conscious moment" Husserl calls the noetic moment, the noesis. Thus it is necessary to undertake, where the immanent sphere is concerned, hyletic and noetic phenomenological analysis, the latter being by far the more fruitful. Actually, from the functional point of view, the hyletic has signification only insofar as it furnishes a possible material for the intentional formings. And the functional point of view is essential to phenomenology. "The functional point of view is central in phenomenology," [23] Husserl says in the *Ideen*. Instead of studying mental processes taken in an isolated fashion, they are studied in phenomenology from the teleological point of view of their function in the stream of mental life. One of the main tasks is to show how the various intentional functions mingle together. In effect, the stream of mental life is a unity where the mental processes connect with one another, where the evidences are in connexion with one another, cooperating in order to form evidences of the higher level. In a more general fashion, one can

20. *Ideen*, "§ 85. Sensuous *hylé*, intentional *morphé*."
21. Sixth Investigation, § 58, *Log. Unt.*, Vol. II, Pt. II, p. 180, where Husserl does not speak of hyletic *data* but rather of primary contents.
22. *Ideen*, p. 174.
23. *Ibid.*, p. 176.

say that "the manifold object-categories that become constituted are, of essential necessity, combined with one another.
Accordingly it is not only the case that, for each object, there
is a peculiar evidence: the evidence of it and the object itself,
as evident, exercise functions that overlap." [24] There is more:
evidencing productions are connected with "nonevidences"
such as the sedimentation of retentions, empty intentions,
opinions, etc. While the traditional theory of cognition considers evidence as a special datum, phenomenology considers
evidences of every type as "structural forms belonging a priori
to the unity of a life" (290).

In a few concluding pages Husserl outlines the new themes
of investigation which would orient logic toward the material
province of the sciences. Thus logic would become the material
— and no longer only the formal — theory of science. In *Formal
and Transcendental Logic*, in Husserl's own terms, he meant
only to circumscribe the essence of a formal theory of science,
and he has brought only this formal theory to its transcendental
form.[25] Is it, then, only a simple "preface" to tasks of a *higher*
importance? To reproach Husserl for halting at the threshold
of the true logic would be to misunderstand the importance of
the structural character which pertains to all spheres of beings
and objects. It is true that the transcendental science of the
Apriori can be a total science only if it includes the material apriori sciences, and it is true that it must tend toward the accomplishment of this, which will give it its full sense. But before
referring to the regions of existence in their materiality, the
transcendental science of the Apriori already has its novel sense
in relation to traditional formal logic. Besides, the fact that *Formal and Transcendental Logic* was able to develop the transcendental ideal while remaining within the formal perspective
should suffice to convince us of the importance of the formal.

In this conclusion Husserl only indicates different levels of
study for a genuine mundane ontology *(mundane Ontologie,
Welt-Logik)* — "genuine" since this mundane ontology would
not presuppose in a naïve fashion, as traditional logic does, a
world having an absolute existence. The fundamental level of
this ontology would treat of the eidetic problem of a possible
world in general qua world of pure experience prior to the per-

24. *FTL*, p. 288.
25. *Ibid.*, p. 293.

formances of science. There one would describe the Aprioris of simple experience which govern the passive synthesis that constitutes the passive unity of the object and also that of a Nature prior to all categorial activity. In particular one would study the Apriori of space and of time. Husserl designates this fundamental level with the expression "transcendental aesthetic." He takes over this Kantian term because "the space and time arguments of the *Critique of Pure Reason* obviously, though in an extraordinarily restricted and unclarified manner, have in view a noematic Apriori of sensuous intuition." [26] But the Husserlian project extends further than the Kantian transcendental aesthetic does. It means to consider in a material fashion every Apriori of intuitive Nature and to introduce constitutional phenomenological problems. In *Formal and Transcendental Logic* Husserl says: "As a level founded on the logos of the aesthetic world, there rises the logos of Objective worldly being, and of science, in the 'higher' sense." [27] The *Cartesian Meditations* specifies that this level of the analytic logos is not the level immediately superior to that of the aesthetic logos:

> It would not be consistent with the sense of the correlative Kantian title, "transcendental analytics," if we used this as a name for the upper stories of the constitutional Apriori, which pertain to the *Objective* world itself and the multiplicities constituting it (at the highest level, the Apriori pertaining to the "idealizing" and theorizing acts that ultimately constitute scientific Nature and the scientific world). The theory of experiencing someone else, the theory of so-called "empathy," belongs in the first story above our "transcendental aesthetics." [28]

But for logic, the constitution of the other—important as it is, since it makes possible the grounding of the Objectivity of the world—is a theme taken up only in passing. This is why it is not mentioned in this rapid outline of *Formal and Transcendental Logic*. At this level of theoretical activity one finds exact geometry and the exact science of Nature. The contrast between their method and that of the aesthetic level lies in the fact that the latter is an idealizing and "logicizing" method and not a descriptive method. The introduction of a transcendental criti-

26. *CM*, p. 146.
27. *FTL*, p. 292.
28. *CM*, p. 146.

cism of these exact sciences gives rise to considerable problems, which are beyond the limits traced for *Formal and Transcendental Logic.*

Now we should like to return to the questions which we suspended during the course of our commentary on the present chapter. How can a constituting subjectivity in turn be subjected to norms? How can it depend upon a formal ontology?

Without reservation Husserl affirms that phenomenology as the ultimate science has the power to refer to itself, to criticize itself. To such an affirmation the prejudicial objection formulated by Jean Cavaillès must be contrasted:

> . . . if the absolute and ultimate science also includes a theory which regulates it, it cannot include it as part of itself. Perhaps it abuses the singularity of the absolute to reserve it for the coincidence between constituting and constituted moments. Besides, there is not just coincidence but insertion of the latter into the former, since the norms of the constituting constitution are only part of the constituted constitutions. Now it seems that such an identification of planes is particularly difficult for phenomenology to admit, where precisely the driving force of the investigation and the ground of objectivities is the relation to a creative subjectivity. If this is in turn subject to norms, a new transcendental investigation is necessary in order to relate its norms to a higher subjectivity, since no content but, rather, only consciousness has the authority to be posited in itself. If transcendental logic truly grounds logic, there is no absolute logic (i.e., logic subjecting the absolute subjective activity to norms). If there is an absolute logic, it can draw its authority only from itself; it is not transcendental.[29]

In the first place, it must be recognized that every discipline which has to return upon itself from this very fact finds itself before an undeniable difficulty. In the *Ideen,* calling upon what could be an "occasion for scandal" in the phenomenological attitude, which demands a return of phenomenology upon itself, Husserl remarks:

> The situation is exactly the same in psychology and likewise in the noetics of logic. The psychologist's thinking is itself something psychological; the logician's thinking is something logical—that is to say: itself belongs to the sphere of the norms of logic. . . .

29. J. Cavaillès, *Sur la logique et la théorie de la science,* p. 65.

To be sure, in the case of all disciplines that relate reflexively to themselves, a certain difficulty lies in the fact that the first introduction to them, and likewise the first investigative penetration into them, must operate with methodic aids that they cannot form definitively in a scientific manner until afterwards. Without precursory and preparatory considerations of matter and method no projecting of a new science can come into being. The concepts, however, and the other methodic elements with which beginning psychology, phenomenology, and so forth, operate in such preparatory labors are themselves psychological, phenomenological, and so forth and acquire their scientific stamp for the first time within the system of the already established science.

In this direction, obviously, no serious objections lie, which could obstruct the actual carrying-out of such sciences and, in particular, phenomenology.[30]

In our opinion, if one can in good conscience avoid the inherent objections to a psychology which has shown us at once the impossibility and the danger of splitting the *ego,* still one should consider more closely the difficulty of the return upon the self when it is a question just as much of logic as of phenomenology. Logic as it is conceived by a philosophy of the concept, under whose flag one can combat Husserl's "philosophy of consciousness," that is to say, logic as an absolute which governs subjective activity, also finds itself before an essential difficulty, for it must *ground* its own steps. If it can claim to do so, it is because it dissociates naïve and critical performances. To think of the development of logic as occurring on one plane is in fact an absurdity. We often tend to forget that here phenomenology has the same resort, for the first phenomenology is only a "naïve" phenomenology, which itself must undergo a criticism. But it is true that these difficulties — which attach to every grounding science, such as logic or phenomenology — are infinitely more serious for phenomenology, which accords primacy over all Objectivity to the activity of the constituting subjectivity. How can the constituting subjectivity criticize itself without using norms, hence without referring to an "Objectivity" which dominates it and reduces its authority?

What are the ways out of such a situation? If one does not lose sight of the fact that phenomenology is set up on different levels, one can conceive of a new transcendental investigation

30. *Ideen,* pp. 122–23.

which relates the norms of the first phenomenological subjectivity to a higher subjectivity; more specifically, one can conceive of a new transcendental investigation which performs a "criticism of those evidences that phenomenology at the first, and still naïve, level carries on straightforwardly." [31] But then one is presented with the danger of an endless regress. Husserl's good conscience in this regard is surprising:

> All transcendental-philosophical theory of knowledge, as "criticism of knowledge," leads back ultimately to criticism of transcendental-phenomenological knowledge (in the first place, criticism of transcendental experience); and, owing to the essential reflexive relation of phenomenology to itself, this criticism also demands a criticism. In this connexion, however, there exist no endless regresses that are infected with difficulties of any kind (to say nothing of absurdities), despite the evident possibility of reiterable transcendental reflections and criticisms. [32]

The Husserlian conception of transcendental subjectivity in fact falls before the objection of the "third man."

Actually, Husserl is unable to maintain his conception of an absolute transcendental subjectivity. J. Vuillemin, in a very succinct note, seems to us to have clearly seen an evolution hidden in Husserl's philosophy:

> In fact the Husserlian phenomenology and, to a certain extent, the Schelerian phenomenology, are at times unconsciously and incompletely oriented toward a new (i.e., dialectical) conception of the concept and reason, but it is then at the price of the "philosophy of consciousness" which metaphysically sustains the investigations concerning the transcendental *ego*. [33]

To us it does indeed seem that Husserl did not remain in the perspective of absolute transcendental subjectivism and that he was "unconsciously oriented toward a dialectic." For our part, we would not say "toward a dialectic of the concept and reason"; we would say, rather, "toward a dialectic of reason and the structural form." In our commentary on § 103, [34] where Hus-

31. *FTL*, p. 289.
32. *CM*, p. 152.
33. J. Vuillemin, *L'héritage kantien et la révolution copernicienne* (Paris, 1954), p. 228, n. 3.
34. *Supra*, p. 210.

serl indicates the possibility which the absolute existent has of becoming conscious of itself, we omitted an enigmatic expression which, it seems to us, orients us toward a less absolutistic interpretation of transcendental subjectivity than Husserl's declarations would make one believe. After saying that "an absolute existent is existent in the form, an intentional life – which, no matter what else it may be intrinsically conscious of, is, at the same time, consciousness of itself," Husserl adds: "precisely for that reason (as we can see when we consider more profoundly) it has at all times an essential ability to reflect on itself, on all its structures that stand out for it – an essential ability to make itself thematic and produce judgments, and evidences, relating to itself." [35] Then it is not precisely a question of a dialectic between subjectivity and its "objective" products, its "contents"; one should rather speak of a duality between subjectivity and the forms in which it necessarily manifests itself. [36] And these forms can be considered as Objectivity over against the constituting subjectivity by means of a strange *Abhebung*. And one often has the impression that Husserl admits that this Objectivity is, by its *structural necessity*, "separated" from the subjectivity constituting the province. This would explain how a formal ontology taken in the broadest sense can be an ontology which applies also to the constituting subjectivity. But, where all of this is concerned, there is nothing explicit in the accounts Husserl has developed. In ⟨these accounts⟩ we can see only the latent sense of a phenomenology that is uncon-

35. *FTL*, p. 273.

36. In the "Preparatory Considerations" of *Formal and Transcendental Logic*, Husserl has already introduced the concept of the form-principles of rational subjectivity as *compelling* structures: "A subjectivity as such (whether solitary or in communication) is thinkable only as having an essential form, whose highly multifarious constituents we obtain with progressive evidence when we uncover to intuition our own concrete subjectivity and then, with the aid of a free changing of its actuality into other possibilities of any concrete subjectivity as such, direct our regard to the invariable that can be seen throughout – that is to say: the essentially necessary. If we stipulate, from the beginning of this variation, that the subjectivity shall always have the capacity to be and remain a 'rational' and, in particular, a judicatively cognizing subjectivity, we encounter restrictive essential structures that fall under the heading of pure reason and, in particular, pure judicative reason" (*FTL*, p. 30).

sciously embarrassed by untenable absolutes and in this way finds the means of reducing the difficulties in which it has let itself become enmeshed.

However these matters stand, we will admit having become aware of this desire for an absolute, because it is the fact of a consciousness which wants to be fully self-responsible, all the while knowing that it can never sit back in the pride of having definitively completed its work. Without doubt the reader who has meditated upon the philosophies of the past can be misled by the naïveté of a Husserl, who sees in phenomenology the first genuine transcendental philosophy. But he must not forget that the self-instruction which Husserl carried out is to be taken as an eternal beginning and that, for Husserl, "philosophy, science in all its forms, is rational. . . . It is however in all things on the way to a higher rationality, it is rationality which, repeatedly discovering its insufficient relativity, is driven forward in the effort, in the will to acquire the true and full rationality." [37]

37. *Krisis*, p. 274.

Index

Abstract and concrete sciences, 43
Activity, 76, 77, 118, 138, 142n, 191,
  191n. *See also* Passivity
Adequation, 17, 85
Affair or thing *(Sache)*, 4n
"And so forth," 122, 178
Anything Whatever, xiv, 32, 68, 131,
  133
Apodicticity, 104, 106
Apophantics, 3, 4, 13, 25, 33, 38, 65,
  72, 81, 84, 86
Apperception, 169
Apriori, 93, 112n, 125, 128, 137, 145,
  153, 172, 174, 181, 184, 191, 193n,
  207, 218
Aristotle, 3, 29, 36
Association, 189 f.

Baldus, R., 62
Bar Hillel, Y., 62n
Becker, O., 122
Being-sense *(Seinsinn)*, 110, 161
Belief, 138, 140, 212
Berger, G., 198n
Berkeley, 110, 179
Bolyai, J., 62
Bolzano, B., 35, 88, 154
Boole, G., 29
Bourbaki, N., 28n
van Bréda, L., 136
Brouwer, L. E. J., 122

Cairns, D., xvi
Cartesian Meditations, 75, 163
Categorial intuition. *See* Intuition

Categories: of object, 3; of signi-
  fication, 3
Category (= form-concept), 66n
Cavaillès, J., 12, 52, 62, 206, 220
Church, A., 62n
Clarity, 17 f.
Completeness *(Vollständigkeit),*
  59-61
Concrete, xxvii
Confusion, 15
Consequence *(Konsequenz),* 23 ff.
Constitution, 38, 77, 95, 109, 117,
  118, 161, 170, 172, 184, 202
Countersense *(Widersinn),* 7, 149
Criticism, 71, 74, 81, 87, 93, 94 f.,
  111, 119, 145, 153, 155, 211

Datum, xiv
Definite multiplicity, 51
Definiteness *(Definitheit),* 51n, 59
Descartes, 155, 156n, 162, 214
Description, xlv-xlix, 113
Distinctness, 15
Doxa, 144
Dubreil, P., 32n

Ego, xiv, 156, 163-65, 170, 181-83,
  191, 194, 210, 221
Eidetic method or analysis, 173, 177,
  180, 193
Eidos, eidetic. *See* Apriori
Epistemology, 68, 73
Epoché, 75, 155-57, 162, 166 f.,
  180 f.
Erfahrung und Urteil, 141n, 143